A HODDER CHRISTIAN PAPERBACK OMNIBUS

DAVID WATSON

You Are My God
Fear No Evil
Is Anyone There?

You Are My God

An autobiography

Hodder & Stoughton

LONDON SYDNEY AUCKLAND

*This David Watson Omnibus edition first published 1996
by Hodder and Stoughton, a Division of Hodder Headline PLC*
0 340 67101 7

10 9 8 7 6 5 4 3 2 1

British Library in Publication Data
A record for this book is available from the British Library

Printed and bound in Great Britain by
Cox & Wyman Ltd, Reading, Berkshire

Hodder and Stoughton
A division of Hodder Headline PLC
338 Euston Road
London NW1 3BH

You Are My God

*To all our Christian brothers and sisters in York who shared with us,
both in joy and in pain, through the seventeen best years of our life.*

Contents

Acknowledgments

In attempting to write an honest account of my last twenty-eight years since I became a Christian, I have included a number of painful incidents, as well as referring to times of great joy and blessing. I am especially grateful to Anne, my wife, for her wise advice during the writing of this manuscript and for her patient acceptance of me over the years, without which this book could never have been written.

I have valued too the encouragements and suggestions of a number of friends who read the manuscript, in particular Edward England, my literary agent whose shrewd counsel I constantly treasure.

Most of all I want to thank Hilary Saunders, my secretary, both for her helpful comments during the exacting time of writing and for her untiring efforts with the typewriter.

Biblical quotations, unless otherwise stated, are from the Revised Standard Version.

Foreword

I knew David Watson many years before. As Archbishop of York, I encountered him again. He had been a curate in St. Mark's, Gillingham, when I was Warden of Rochester Theological College, and we had met several times. However, nothing in his past had prepared me for what I found at St. Michael-le-Belfrey here in the centre of York. It was a church destined for redundancy (as well it might be in a city which boasted nearly forty parish churches) which, within a few months of David's arrival, was attracting large congregations of young and old, and sending them out as enthusiasts for Christ and witnesses to him in the world. The services were of a kind which we now associate with the renewal movement: swinging music, warm fellowship and manifest signs of the Spirit. But what made St. Michael's so significant was that these now-familiar phenomena were under-girded by a consistent thorough programme of teaching undertaken, in the first instance, by David himself. Membership of the congregation was no easy option. It called for persistent attention to the word of God; it discouraged personal fantasies unrelated to everyday life, and it required from everyone some ministry to others, whether it was by way of personal testimony or extended families or drama or running a shop. It has been a huge enterprise, with ramifications all over the world. The 'renewal weeks' have been attended by priests and lay people from as far afield as the USA and Malta. It transcends the boundaries of race and denomination.

Of course, there have been difficulties and David Watson and his fellow ministers would be the last to gloss over them. But in the main it has been a triumph of grace, striking evidence that the Spirit of God is at work among us, and that the Kingdom is not just part of some unimaginable future, but a present reality in the lives of individuals and of groups. David, to me, is not just a highly successful parish priest, but a personal friend who stands for those things I value above all in the life of the Church and in its mission to the world. It is against this background that you need to read the book you now have in your hand. The title is perhaps typical of the man – you may well learn more of God than of David from this autobiography.

Stuart Ebor
Bishopthorpe, York
14th March 1983

Introduction

For years I have resisted the pressure to write about our experiences in York. The growth of a congregation from almost nothing to 700 or more can be overrated. Many other churches have moving stories to tell, and anyway both at St. Cuthbert's and St. Michael-le-Belfrey in York we had suffered in the past from too much exposure. Added to that, I knew that the apparent triumphalism of Christian 'success' stories could sometimes discourage those who were battling with ordinary problems. I was also acutely aware of the spiritual dangers of the 'cult of personality'. This is acceptable in the secular sphere of superstars, but it is divisive in the Christian Church. It was so at Corinth in New Testament days, and it is sadly the same in some Christian circles today.

The Christian Gospel is not about superstars, 'so let no one boast of men' wrote the apostle Paul (1 Cor. 3:21). It is rather about God's extraordinary grace in spite of very ordinary human faults and failings, and also his blessings in the midst of suffering. It is with these truths in mind that I have tried to write honestly about both the pain and the joy that we have experienced. Some of this relates specifically to my personal spiritual pilgrimage in different places and at different times; much of it refers to our corporate experiences as a congregation in York; but some of it deliberately speaks about our own marriage. Both Anne and I know that Christians have no immunity from the marriage problems that afflict society so widely today. For this reason we agreed that I should be open about the difficulties that we too have experienced, especially now that we have worked through these traumas to a more mature and strong relationship.

The glib message of 'Come to Christ and all will be well!', or 'Be filled with the Spirit and your problems will be solved!', finds no echo in the pages of the New Testament. Certainly God promises us the 'unsearchable riches of Christ', and the epistles are full of superlatives: love which surpasses knowledge, peace which passes all understanding, joy inexpressible . . . but interwoven with these are the darker threads of pain and tears, weakness and sin, suffering and strife. The astonishing Good News of Christ is that he loves us just as we are and can work through us just as we are. No human frailty needs be a hindrance to God's infinite grace.

It is obvious that I have had to be highly selective in choosing material, and this book may be more remarkable for what it does not say than for what it does. Where possible I have tried to avoid painful references to any individuals since these would not help anyone. My ultimate purpose is to give a personal testimony to the reality of God in the varied spectrum of human experience. If through the sunshine and storms something of the light of Christ is seen in greater glory, this book will not be in vain.

1

Experiment of Faith

'I'll see you there at four,' said Sam, reflecting my cynical grin, as we accepted yet another invitation.

Our little plan had been working well. As old school friends, Sam and I had just started at Cambridge University. Like every other first-year student, we had been urged to join every conceivable club, from tennis to tiddly-winks, fencing to philosophy. All were offering free sherry or tea parties to entice us into membership. So Sam and I decided to go to everything and to join nothing. We listened patiently to Marxists waxing eloquent about the struggle of the masses, Tories extolling the virtues of free enterprise, oarsmen talking tantalisingly about steaks for breakfast, and Scotsmen explaining how to breathe some Highland sanity in the midst of mad dogs and Englishmen. We even went to the Christian Union at four o'clock one day. No group was too ridiculous for us.

Like Sam, I was a cynical unbeliever – a humanist, as I called myself. My religious upbringing had been a little complicated. I had been brought up as a Christian Scientist, since my father had become one at the start of the First World War when it was fashionable among the intelligentsia. My father had been a classics scholar at Oxford, and the intriguing concept of the power of mind over matter had captured the imagination of many forceful personalities.

Almost the only thing I remember about Christian Science as a child was my Sunday School teacher telling a group of six-year-olds that if we had enough faith we could throw ourselves over a cliff and we would float down safely as if held by a parachute. This is not typical of Christian Science teaching, but it is all that I can remember to this day. Fortunately I never experimented, since I had no faith in my faith. My other memory was that my father never allowed a doctor near our home, since he believed there was no reality in any sickness: it was all a matter of the mind. When my father, a serving officer with the Royal Artillery, was away for many months at a time, my mother, a nominal Anglican, would surreptitiously ask a doctor to call when I had mumps or measles, but such medical interference would have been strongly disapproved of by my father.

So firm was he in his beliefs that when, in India, he was suffering from acute bronchial pneumonia, he refused all medical assistance – and died. The disease which supposedly had no reality killed him, and the human mind was an insufficient saviour.

I was ten at the time, and it was 1943, in the middle of the Second World War. My gentle, bereaved mother did the wisest thing she knew (for which I am now profoundly grateful) and had me quickly 'done' in the Anglican Church: I was baptized and confirmed, becoming a server in our parish church. Perhaps our local priest had never prepared a Christian Scientist for confirmation before, but I understood not a word of what he said, and found the sung eucharist every Sunday a ghastly dirge, which I assumed must be good for my soul since it was bad for everything else. For me it was all a meaningless religious mumbo-jumbo.

Inevitably, I suppose, I began to look for God, or at least for some kind of spiritual reality, in other directions. I took part in a few séances, curious to know if I could get in touch with my father. The experience left me not only disillusioned but with a cautionary awareness that I was dabbling in something dangerous. I now realise that every involvement with the occult (spiritualism, astrology, tarot cards, witchcraft and all the 'black arts') is like playing with an unexploded bomb. You never know when it may go off, and over the years I have had to counsel numerous people who, in one way or another, have been harmed – some of them seriously so – through occult experiences. It literally is a devilish business.

During my teenage years I tried a labyrinth of religious paths: theosophy, the teachings of Rudolf Steiner (since my uncle was a devotee of his), various forms of Buddhism, and was generally intrigued by the mysticism of Eastern religions. I once argued strenuously in a thesis for reincarnation since I found in this belief the only logical solution to the vexed question of suffering. But God was nowhere to be found – the Great Unreality in my life.

My school days were mostly enjoyable and I was satisfactorily successful, but all religious instruction was a total non-event from my point of view. Just once or twice I thought I glimpsed a fleeting shaft of spiritual light breaking through the dense fog of confusion. I was intrigued by a Franciscan monk giving a series of Lenten addresses. We all said, 'Wasn't his talk tremendous!' to give the impression that of course we understood every word; but like most of my friends, I am sure, I failed to grasp with any clarity anything at all. His brown 'dressing-gown' and open-toed sandals fascinated me, though I wondered how on earth anyone with any intelligence could go around like that for the sake of Christ. In fact, every contact with the Church reinforced my growing conviction, 'Not for me!'

The final straw came during my two years in the army. In other ways they were two marvellous years. Naturally there were a few less positive moments, such as when I sank my troop of self-propelled guns in a stinking German bog on the first day of massive military manoeuvres. I had surveyed the ground fairly quickly, so as to position four guns, giving covering fire for the infantry. The ground seemed somewhat squelchy, but in all other respects it was an excellent gun position. The guns swept it without too much difficulty; but when they 'tracked' to respond to different angles of fire, each gun crew reported in turn that they were beginning to sink. We simply had to pull out and find another position, which, had it been a real battle, would have been unpardonable. So we pulled out, only to discover that the ground on which they had been standing was the firmest in the whole area. As they moved forward they plunged into a thick black bog. The language I received from my superiors almost burnt out our entire radio communication system. I had never before or since seen tanks become submarines within a matter of seconds: it was immensely impressive, and I doubt if any other junior officer has accomplished the same feat with such dramatic effect.

But for most of my time in the army I made a lot of friends, played a great deal of sport, and went to countless parties including some eye-opening shockers in the red-light district of Hamburg, the Reeperbahn, notorious for its night clubs, brothels and strip shows. After one of the worst of these evenings, we were chased through the streets of Hamburg at about four in the morning. The German police cars had a tough time stopping our pepped-up Mercedes, though we eventually capitulated to about twelve of them. It was the nearest to a James Bond car chase that I have ever been in, and it was only our lack of sophisticated 007 equipment that caused us to lose. In one sense it was a breathtaking adventure; in reality it was a sordid, stupid, drunken dare which exposed the emptiness of our hearts. And every vacuum craves to be filled.

Army religion, however, certainly could not fill that inner void in my heart. Still on paper an Anglican, I went dutifully to the Regimental services – every decent officer was expected to do so – but the only active Christian I remember meeting throughout my entire two years was the Regimental Padre, who seemed by far the heaviest drinker in our regiment. Ten years later I discovered, through the then Chaplain General to the Forces, that our poor Padre had at that time been suffering a severe nervous breakdown. However, ignorant of that fact, I considered his behaviour my final proof of the futility of the Christian faith, and I became an atheist. Over the years I had found no spiritual reality, and it was a simple exercise to give myself philosophically satisfying arguments for saying 'There is no God!'

I can remember only one real prayer, if you can call it that, which I prayed during those years. After an especially wild party and while lying on my bed still dressed in my dinner jacket, and with a powerful hangover, I said aloud, 'O God, there must be a better life somewhere!'

Not by any stretch of the imagination did I remotely consider such a drunken heart-cry would be answered through that four o'clock tea-party organised by the Christian Union at Cambridge University. Sam would have said that I made two fatal mistakes that afternoon: I wore my old school tie, and I caught the speaker's eye on my way out.

After a nondescript tea-party, organised (I thought in my sophistication) by undergraduates with bright eyes, perpetual smiles and silly badges in their lapel buttonholes, we all had to sit down to listen to a young Anglican clergyman. I paid little attention to his words, since I did not believe in God anyway, though he stressed that the heart of the Christian faith was a personal relationship with Jesus Christ. I did not recall anyone ever saying that to me before, and I had reluctantly to admit that there was something unusually gracious and attractive about this clergyman. He spoke with simplicity and integrity, and unlike most other religious people I had so far met, seemed to speak from a genuine personal experience. It was not so much what he said, but who he was, that got through to me. In spite of all my prejudices and preconceived ideas, I could not help liking him. My cynicism was disturbed by the apparent reality of his faith. For that reason alone I gave him a polite smile as I made for the door, one of the first to leave.

Recognising my tie, he began to speak to me, and we soon discovered a number of mutual friends, some of whom had particularly impressed me by the quality of their lives, although I did not know for what reason. Gently but suddenly he turned the conversation.

'Forgive me for asking you a personal question. You may remember that a moment ago I talked about Christianity as a friendship with Jesus. Do you think that you know Jesus personally, or are you not quite sure about it?'

I was exceedingly embarrassed. In my own upper middle-class background, one never dreamt of asking such personal questions. Religion, if it existed at all, was purely a private affair. At the most one might discuss the Church, usually in highly arrogant and critical terms. But questions about one's personal faith were like questions about one's private sex life: it just wasn't done.

Neatly sidestepping his crash tackle I replied, 'I've been baptized and confirmed.' A good enough reply by any Anglican, I thought. But John Collins was not so easily diverted.

'If I had asked those mutual friends of ours that same question, they would have said Yes immediately,' he commented, again with that disturbingly disarming smile.

I thought back to those friends whom we had discussed a few moments before: Graeme, Michael, Peter. Although they had never once spoken to me about Christ at school, they had about them the same sort of attractiveness that I was beginning to find in John Collins. I realised that their professed faith in Christ could have been the common denominator. The trap was tightening.

Although I had won an exhibition in mathematics at Cambridge (physics and chemistry being my other major subjects), I was starting a degree course in Moral Sciences, which included philosophy, psychology, logic, ethics and metaphysics. Apart from my natural interest in those subjects, this was the humanist faculty in the university. But it also meant that I had some mental discipline in logical reasoning.

Logically it suddenly became as clear as a bell. I knew that this clergyman could not prove God. But equally, in spite of my professed atheism, I knew that I could not disprove God either. In logic, it might be true, it might not be true. If not true, forget it (as I had been doing for the last two or three years at least). But if it was true, I had to admit that it would be the most important truth in the universe. It simply could not be dismissed as irrelevant or unimportant.

'Would you like me to explain exactly how you can find God through Jesus Christ?' asked John Collins.

With my scientific training I knew that any honest seeker for truth ought at least to look at a hypothesis, especially if it seemed even remotely important. Further, if the hypothesis appeared reasonable, however unlikely, the right action would then be to experiment, to test the hypothesis for oneself. This is the very basis of all scientific research and the road to most forms of knowledge.

We agreed to have breakfast together the next day at the Garden House Hotel where he was staying. It was a sumptuous feast: fruit juice, kippers, eggs and bacon, toast, coffee – the lot, because John wanted as much time as possible to explain to me the way to God; and, although I did not realise it at the time, I was incredibly ignorant and confused about Christ and the Christian faith.

He began by asking if I felt any need of God. I could not honestly think of any need, apart from that impulsive cry when I was suffering from a hangover. But that surely was not enough. Perhaps in my more reflective moments I was not too sure of the purpose of my life. 'Is that what you mean by a need of God?' I asked John. He explained that a sense of purpose is certainly included, but that our primary need of God consists in our need for forgiveness. In countless ways we have broken God's laws, we have gone our own way, we have done our own thing. That is why God is naturally unreal in the experience of us all, until something is done about it. Surprisingly, I did not need much convincing about this. I knew there were some things in my life of which I was ashamed. I would not like the whole of my life to be exposed. I could also see that, logically, this was a possible explanation for the sense of God's remoteness and unreality. If he did exist and if I had turned my back on him, it followed that there would be a breakdown of communication.

'Yes,' I said after further discussion, 'I'm prepared to admit that I have sinned and so need forgiveness.'

John then described the next step as believing that Christ had died for my sins. 'Oh dear,' I thought to myself. 'Here are these religious clichés which don't mean a thing. Anyway, how can the death of Jesus all those years ago possibly have any relevance to me today?' John unexpectedly took a piece of toast and placed it on his upturned left hand.

'Let this hand represent you, and this toast represent your sin.' Looking at the semi-burnt piece of cold toast I thought it was a fair analogy. 'Now, let my right hand represent Jesus, who had no sin on him at all. There is a verse in the Bible which speaks about the cross like this: "All we like sheep have gone astray; we have turned every one to his own way; and the Lord (God in heaven) has laid on him (Jesus) the sin of us all".' (Isa. 53:6). As he said that, John transferred the toast from his left hand to his right hand. 'Now,' he said, once again with that winsome smile, almost like a chess player saying checkmate, 'where is your sin?'

My arrogant self despised the simplicity of it all; but logically it was as plain as could be.

'I suppose my sin is on Jesus,' I replied, going along with his analogy. In my heart I was beginning to see it, even though my mind wanted something much more intellectually profound. Perhaps that was the meaning of the cross. Perhaps Jesus did somehow take upon himself the sin and guilt of us all so that we, sinners though we all are, could be free to know the love and forgiveness of God, without any barrier at all. John referred to several other verses in the Bible which made exactly the same point.

'Next,' he said, 'you have to count the cost.' To put it simply I had to be willing to put right (with Christ's help) everything that I knew was wrong in my life, and be willing to put Christ first in my life. We discussed the implications of this for a time, and I could see that, if these things were true, there could be no half-measures. It must be all or nothing.

So we went to the final step to knowing God. John took me to a promise of Jesus that I had never heard before, from Revelation 3:20: 'Behold, I stand at the door and knock. If anyone hears my voice and opens the door I will come in.' We talked a little more, and I could see that faith simply means taking a person at their word. If, in prayer, I asked Jesus into my life, I had his promise that he would come in, and so make God real in my experience.

It all seemed far too simple, and there were still a host of philosophical questions as yet totally unanswered. But at least I understood the directions that John had given me.

'Let me suggest alternatives,' he said. 'Either we could go to my room and have a prayer together, or I could give you this booklet which sums up what I've been saying, and has a personal prayer at the end which you could make your own.'

I was much too embarrassed to pray with him then and there, and anyway I needed time to think. 'I'll take the booklet,' I said, and rose to make a hasty retreat, muttering something about being late for lectures.

'Just one more thing,' said John. 'If you do decide to pray that prayer, would you write to let me know that you've done it? I should be so grateful. Here's my address.'

Off I went, with my mind racing. I had gone to breakfast as a humanist, and now, just an hour or so later, I had the trembling excitement that I could be on the verge of a totally unexpected discovery. Or again, it could be yet another disillusionment which would only deepen my conviction as an atheist.

That evening, alone in my room, I read the booklet *Becoming a Christian* by John Stott, Rector of All Souls, Langham Place, London, where John Collins was a curate. The booklet was largely a summary of our breakfast conversation, but with all its simplicity it was compellingly clear in its logical reasoning. Steadily I realised that, if these things were true, I wanted them to become real in my own life. Awkwardly I slipped onto my knees beside my bed and prayed the prayer at the end of the booklet:

Lord Jesus Christ, *I humbly acknowledge* that I have sinned in my thinking and speaking and acting, that I am guilty of deliberate wrongdoing, and that my sins have separated me from Thy holy presence, and that I am helpless to commend myself to Thee;
I firmly believe that Thou didst die on the cross for my sins, bearing them in Thine own body and suffering in my place the condemnation they deserved;
I have thoughtfully counted the cost of following Thee. I

sincerely repent, turning from my past sins. I am willing to
surrender to Thee as my Lord and Master. Help me not to
be ashamed of Thee;
So now I come to Thee. I believe that for a long time Thou
hast been patiently standing outside the door knocking. I
now open the door. Come in, Lord Jesus, and be my
Saviour and my Lord for ever. Amen.

Absolutely nothing happened. No visions, no feelings, no
experiences, nothing. Everything seemed just the same as
before. I felt let down; and yet as I climbed into bed I had a
quiet sense of peace that I had done the right thing.

The next morning I again felt no different. And yet, what if
Christ really had come into my life? Would it matter if I
trusted his promise, at least for a day or two, to see if anything
happened? So I wrote a note to John Collins to say that I had
done it, and what next?

Two days later I had a charming reply to encourage me, and
he mentioned that he was asking a friend of his to call on me.
'Oh no!' I thought. 'I really have fallen into a religious trap' –
and I did not want to become religious. But I was astonished,
on my return from lectures that very same morning, to find a
hand-written note on my table.

For years I had been a cricket enthusiast; I was not a very
good performer (Captain of the Second XI at school was
about my standard), but of my various cricketing heroes,
none was greater than David Sheppard. With my studying at
Cambridge, living in Sussex and being English, the one
cricketer who evoked in me an enormous admiration was,
naturally, the person who had recently been Captain of
Cambridge, Sussex and England. On numerous occasions I
had seen him play: a magnificent opening batsman whose
command of the game was, for me, totally exhilarating. I
knew of nothing more exciting than watching David Sheppard
scoring runs with what seemed immense power and consum-
mate ease.

Imagine my astonishment, therefore, when I read this short
note on my table:

John Collins wrote this morning suggesting that I look you up. I will look in after lunch, but do not stay in especially.
                Yours,   David Sheppard

2

A Christian at Cambridge

'I don't think I have ever before met anyone who was so confused!' was David Sheppard's comment about me a few months later. Looking back I see now that my religious ideas were like a ball of wool after a playful kitten had been hard at work: an incredible tangle of various beliefs, interwoven with a few strands of Christianity here and there. Interestingly enough a very good friend of mine had given me, a few weeks before I went up to Cambridge, *The Imitation of Christ* by Thomas à Kempis, and this I had found both moving and stimulating, creating in me a measure of spiritual hunger. But my knowledge of the Gospel was effectively zero. I later discovered that I was not the only spiritually blind person. Jesus once said to a thoroughly religious and intelligent man, Nicodemus, 'Truly, truly I say to you, unless a man is born anew, he *cannot see* the kingdom of God' (John 3:3). The brilliant university scholar, Saul of Tarsus, said much the same thing: 'The unspiritual man does not receive the gifts of the Spirit of God, for they are folly to him, and he is not able to understand them because they are spiritually discerned' (1 Cor. 2:14). In more recent times, the eminent philosopher Bertrand Russell wrote a book called *Why I Am Not A Christian*, but it is clear from this book that he had little or no understanding of the basic truths of the Christian faith.

David Sheppard invited me round to his rooms at Ridley Hall, an Anglican theological college in Cambridge, where he was in his final year prior to ordination. Almost every week throughout the academic year I went round to talk to David, often for as much as three hours at a time, and he began to lay a foundation for my faith – or at least helped me to know the only foundation that will stand firm against every wind of doctrine and storm of life, the foundation of Jesus Christ. Normally we read a passage of the Bible together, David choosing a passage carefully each week to meet my particular need at that stage: Psalm 103 on assurance; Psalms 32 and 51 on repentance; Isaiah 53 on the cross; Luke 24 and I Corinthians 15 on the resurrection; James 1 on temptation; John 17 on prayer; Romans 12 on service; and so forth.

It is impossible to stress how vital these sessions were for me. Without them, humanly speaking, I should never have survived as a Christian. My first question, after asking Christ into my life, was, 'How on earth will I be able to keep this up? Won't it be like those useless New Year's resolutions all over again?' It had all faded after confirmation and after various other attempts to turn over a new religious leaf. What I had not realised was that, through the Spirit of God, I had started a new life. The first faint inklings of the reality of this were twofold: first, my army habit of swearing at about every fifth word ceased immediately; and second (much more important), a new love for people slowly began to dawn in my heart.

It was just as well! I had been an appalling snob, and must have been even more unpleasant in the eyes of other people than I am now! To begin with, I was proud of my family background. I had a long Scottish pedigree, my 'family tree' having been carefully researched back to the eleventh century. The Watsons lived for many centuries in Saughton, Edinburgh, and several of my ancestors are buried in Princes Street. One branch of the family, however, moved to the Lake District in 1537; and our family home was Calgarth Park, one mile north of Windermere, until it was handed over as a military hospital in the First World War. It was at one time a 3,000 acre estate, developed by Richard Watson, my great-great-great-grandfather. He married Dorothy le Fleming of Rydal Hall (now the Carlisle Diocesan Retreat Centre), so the family links with the Lake District were strong.

Richard Watson was an able and colourful character. He was born in 1737 and went to Trinity College, Cambridge in 1754. Within ten years, at the age of twenty-seven, he became Professor of Chemistry in the University although he admitted later in his own *Anecdotes*, 'At the time this honour was conferred on me I knew nothing at all of Chemistry and had never read a syllable on the subject, nor seen a single experiment in it.' After fourteen months of study in Paris, however, during which time he once destroyed his laboratory with an explosion, he returned to Cambridge to deliver 'a course of chemical lectures to a very full audience'. He wrote numerous scientific papers within the next two years and was promptly elected a Fellow of the Royal Society.

Only three years later, in 1771, the chair of Divinity became vacant, which Richard Watson considered 'the foremost post of learning in Europe'. He studied Divinity for one year, after which he was unanimously elected to the chair of Divinity although once again he admitted that he only 'knew as much of Divinity as could reasonably be expected of a man whose course of studies had been directed . . . to other pursuits'. Watson's writings as Regius Professor of Divinity were prolific, and probably his most important apologetic work was his *Apology for the Bible* published in 1796 in answer to 'the scurrilous abuse of the Scripture' contained in Thomas Paine's *Age of Reason*. *Apology for the Bible* was particularly well received, although when he handed it to King George III it is reputed that the King retorted, 'I never knew that the Bible needed an apology!' Nevertheless the King made Watson Bishop of Llandaff in 1782 – a bishopric that was the poorest in the country, but was considered by many of his contemporaries as a short stepping-stone for Watson to Canterbury. On a point of conscience, however, Watson clashed with both William Pitt and George III, who subsequently kept him at that safe distance in Wales, where he remained for thirty-four years. It was asked, 'If Watson, Bishop of Llandaff was factious and insolent, what might Watson, Archbishop of Canterbury or even Bishop of Durham, have become?'

It was from that background that I went to school at

Wellington College, where my father, uncles and cousins had all been educated, and then on to the 3rd Regiment of the Royal Horse Artillery, which was rightly proud of its traditions and outstanding military achievements. Understandably, perhaps, I had thoroughly imbibed what the Bible critically calls 'the pride of life', a human vanity based on privilege of birth or personal achievement, and which can prove a considerable stumbling-block to a true knowledge of God. The apostle Paul acknowledged that 'not many of noble birth' had been called by God, (1 Cor. 1:26). In fact God 'opposes the proud, but gives grace to the humble' (Jas. 4:6). These were painful and humbling lessons I had still to learn.

This new life that I had received, therefore, needed much nurturing. In his goodness, God gave me in David Sheppard someone I respected enormously, and it was mostly through his influence that I began to overcome some of my entrenched prejudices. Gently he encouraged me to get involved with the Christian Union in my college, St. John's. This I found extraordinarily difficult. Not only was the whole experience of Bible studies and prayer meetings totally foreign to me – I had not the slightest idea that such things existed and was initially shocked by their religious intensity – but on the surface I had nothing whatever in common with the other Christians in my college. Many of them came from very different backgrounds, and their interests were widely different as well. I read philosophy, and played hockey or squash seven days a week; most of them seemed to read chemistry, and played no sport at all. Today I find such differences quite irrelevant. What Christians have in common in Christ gloriously transcends all these worldly distinctions. But at the time I had almost to be pushed into fellowship with my Christian brothers, since I was afraid of becoming a religious fanatic by associating with them at all. I vividly remember one young man, when he prayed, gripping his chair in such agony that I genuinely thought he was suffering from serious constipation. 'What if my fellow officers from 3rd RHA could see me now!' I used to think to myself.

I was not the only one who was worried. I am not sure what

I wrote about all this to my mother, but she was clearly a little anxious that I had become religious, especially after my father's tragic death. Later I was requested to meet various family friends and relations to assure them that I wasn't rushing off to become a monk! My old school and army friends were frankly puzzled. They could not quite imagine the young officer who had drunk in night clubs in Hamburg now sitting in prayer meetings in Cambridge. 'It will soon pass,' they said charitably. 'Everyone goes through these phases at university. He'll probably be a Communist next term!'

Well, it didn't pass. Certainly I went through some agonies of doubt. A little time after my conversion I wrote in my diary, 'Is it all true, or am I making it up?' David Sheppard obviously saw that I was going through a difficult time, and we read that evening, as a devotional study, Psalm 103:

Bless the Lord, O my soul;
    and all that is within me, bless his holy name!
Bless the Lord, O my soul,
    and forget not all his benefits,
who forgives all your iniquity,
    who heals all your diseases,
who redeems your life from the Pit,
    who crowns you with steadfast love and mercy,
who satisfies you with good as long as you live
    so that your youth is renewed like the eagle's.

My intellectual questions remained unanswered, but the Spirit of God used this psalm to reassure me of God's love, and I was quietly conscious of his never-failing presence. The whole thing seemed so right and true. Here, surely, was something of the 'unsearchable riches of Christ' that countless millions of men and women had discovered all through the centuries. I worshipped God, my Father, through Jesus Christ, my Lord and Saviour.

I knew, of course, that a purely devotional faith would not be enough. If my philosophy lecturers mentioned God at all, they did so cynically, treating the whole subject as a curious historical debate that philosophers used to take seriously, but not, of course, in this age of logical positivism and linguistic analysis. The issues of today had long by-passed any medieval fantasies about God. I was fortunate, however, in having as my psychology supervisor Malcolm Jeeves (at present Professor of Psychology at St. Andrews University), who was and is a deeply committed Christian and who helped me to integrate my faith and intellect. I began to see, for example, the basic difference between the meaning and the mechanism of something. Even if a 'conversion experience' could be described in psychological terms, this in no way invalidated the meaning or significance of it. The significance of an item of news on the television is not at all affected by a detailed scientific description of how a television set works.

I also came to see that there are different forms of knowledge, all of which depend, at least in part, on faith. There is logical or mathematical knowledge; and providing I accept by faith the fundamental principles of mathematics, I gain further knowledge by sheer logical reasoning. Then there is scientific or experimental knowledge; and providing I accept by faith the laws of science, I gain further knowledge by testing hypotheses with empirical investigation. There is also personal knowledge, or the knowledge of persons, which is quite different from either mathematical or scientific knowledge. You can never 'prove' a person. You can only know a person; and you can know a person only if you commit yourself to that person. I realised that the same was true of God. I saw that no scientific world-view, however complete it might one day become, could affect our knowledge of God one way or another. These were some of the issues I was trying to come to terms with in the process of deepening my own relationship with Christ.

An important milestone came when I helped my best friend to find Christ for himself. Tom was a delightful person, amusing, generous, a gifted sportsman, and in every way charming. David Sheppard had carefully taught me within a week or two of my own conversion how to lead someone to

Christ, and so I shared what I could with Tom, who was obviously interested. I am sure that I put it rather badly, but through the help of a visiting preacher to Cambridge, Maurice Wood (now Bishop of Norwich), Tom accepted Christ into his life. I was so overjoyed I literally could not sleep a wink all night, and I have never lost the sense of deep joy and immense privilege in helping someone find God. Tom joined me in my weekly sessions with David Sheppard, and I found all this a huge encouragement to my own struggling faith.

I could see, however, that Tom was still weighing up the cost of true Christian discipleship very cautiously. For him, the account in the Gospels of the meeting between the rich young ruler and Jesus was all-important. Tom was disturbed by the clear instruction Jesus gave to that man to sell everything he had before he could follow him. I told Tom that I was sure that this instruction did not apply to everyone (I felt much too threatened to imagine that it did, anyway), but that riches were the special idol in that young ruler's life, and therefore he needed an unusual and particular challenge before Jesus could be his Lord as well as his Saviour. Tom, however, took the command of Christ both literally and seriously. In order to follow Christ with integrity, he thought, he would have to give up everything. Perhaps in Tom's life there were particular issues that he had to face – there are in most of our lives. But over the first Christmas vacation Tom found the continuous round of social engagements too appealing, and he seemed to surrender his faith.

I have no doubt that Tom was being thoroughly honest with himself. He rightly hated hypocrisy. However, after his conversion we had agreed to share rooms together, only to find that we were now disagreed on what was fast becoming the most important element in my life. Although we still remained very good friends, I personally found this an extremely testing time, although it increased my resolve to put Christ first, whether others came with me or not.

Partly for these reasons I developed a fairly disciplined faith from the start. Having overcome some of my initial culture shock at the 'fanaticism' of those who took the

Christian faith seriously, I began to order my life according to rules that I set myself. Every morning, without fail, I would read my Bible and pray for forty-five minutes at least. I had a rapidly growing list of people and needs that I felt I ought to pray for. Every week I learnt six verses from the Bible, together with their references, and revised the ones I had previously learnt. I began to devour Christian books, reading concurrently a doctrinal, a biographical and a devotional book, in order to feed on a balanced diet. I was committed in terms of Christian fellowship (though I found prayer meetings difficult for a long time), and active in evangelism, taking many friends to evangelistic services and seeing some of them come to Christ. On the negative side I was equally strong. Having experienced the bitterness of some of the forbidden fruits in the world, I decided not to smoke (not that I did anyway), not to drink, not to dance and not to go to cinemas or theatres. Having tasted the new wine of the Spirit, the old wine of the flesh seemed like luke-warm water, and I spat it out of my mouth. Some of my new way of life was certainly too legalistic, but to this day I am grateful for that early note of discipline in an age when such words are no longer fashionable. It provided a rock-like foundation, on which the super-structure could later afford to be more flexible.

Not that everything was quite so pious and simple as it may have seemed. For all my new-found fervour, the one event that I dreaded was an open-air service at the end of the summer term organised by the Christian Union, at The Mill. The Mill was a popular pub by the river where most of my pagan friends spent their Sunday lunch-times drinking beer. On a sunny day there was always a crowd there, hence it was a good target for the Christian Union's open-air service. But however real my ardour for Christ had become, it unquestionably did not stretch to soap-box oratory to my beer-drinking friends.

'Will you be there with us?' pressed my Christian brethren.

'I'm not sure yet,' had been my evasive reply. Imagine my relief when another friend invited me to lunch in his rooms for that very same Sunday. His sister would be there, and I had a sneaking suspicion that this friend hoped I might fall in love with her. She was a delightful girl anyway, so I readily accepted the invitation. What a perfect excuse for missing the service! However, when I arrived at my friend's rooms he said, 'It's such a glorious day, let's get a punt at The Mill and go for a picnic.'

The inevitable happened. I arrived at The Mill, which was now thronged with students, including many from the Christian Union who were immediately conspicuous in their Sunday best. When some of them saw me they were thrilled. They were clearly not so thrilled when I climbed into a punt with my friend and his sister, and pushed off for a picnic. Even worse, when we were some way down the river towards Granchester, my friend (always a tactician) made some excuse about having to do some work, and jumped off the punt to run back to his college. That left me alone with his sister, wondering how on earth I was to get back to the pub without entirely losing face with my Christian friends. There was no way out of it; so back we came, like any other romantic couple on the river that day, arriving at The Mill when the evangelistic thrust of the Christian Union was at its climax. I suspect that I became the object of some fervent prayer for the next few weeks, and my promising friendship with this charming girl came abruptly to an end. I fear that, in my embarrassment, I was ungracious and rude. Many readjustments to my new life in Christ had yet to be made.

Churchgoing had always been a terrible chore for me: something of a penance which I had assumed Christians thought necessary to atone for all their many sins. Escorted by David Sheppard, I began to go to various services where the form was usually familiar, but the Spirit altogether different. I had never before seen so many young people singing hymns and praying prayers as though they really meant them! And the sermons, although some were in biblical jargon which I found incomprehensible, were mostly informative, personal and helpful. I was however horrified by the first evangelistic sermon I heard, only a few days after my conversion: there was far too much hell-fire and judgment for my liking, and I was astonished by queues of undergraduates going up to the preacher afterwards to say that they had accepted Christ. I was so glad I had done it quietly on my own earlier in the week. Never in a thousand years, I thought, would I have joined such a queue of converts. Later I found the constant proclamation of the Gospel, by visiting preachers every Sunday evening in Holy Trinity Church, utterly enthralling, and totally failed to see why some of the many friends I took with me could not embrace Christ there and then. Altogether, it was an exhilarating time of rapid growth.

My first Christmas vacation proved another important milestone, for two main reasons. First, I had the tremendous joy of leading my mother to Christ. We had never talked together about personal matters with ease; but her second marriage, after my father's death, had been difficult, and she was aware of the need of God's help for several reasons. Very simply I outlined the steps I had taken to find Christ, and prayed with her, phrase by phrase, as I helped her to ask Christ into her life. It was wonderful to see her begin to read her Bible and to pray, and I could soon see the difference that Christ was making in her life.

Then, after Christmas, David Sheppard had persuaded me to go as a helper to a boys' camp (or houseparty as it really was), run by the Rev. E. J. H. Nash, affectionately known as Bash. David had to apply some pressure on me, as I had planned to go on a skiing holiday with Tom, two other male friends of ours and four stunningly beautiful girls, one being Britain's top model at that time. I suspect that David saw this as a real and obvious temptation for me, the flesh fighting hard against the Spirit. The Spirit won – but not without a struggle.

After my leadership experience at school and in the army I felt sure that I was just the kind of leader these boys' camps were needing, so I looked forward to organising some activities for them. In fact, I spent almost the entire time peeling potatoes, sweeping floors and scrubbing pots and pans. Imagine doing that instead of skiing with four beautiful girls! I must be crazy! However, that camp, and the next one at

Easter, were a vital lesson, teaching me that humble service is the essential basis of all Christian work and ministry; see the example of Jesus, washing the dirty, smelly feet of his disciples. I also experienced there a quality of warm, accepting Christian fellowship (with sane, intelligent and vivacious contemporaries) that I had never before imagined possible. That, together with the brilliance of the short talks each morning and evening, quite convinced me of the reality and richness of the Christian faith. I had stumbled on a priceless hidden treasure, as Jesus once described it, and I realised that no sacrifice was too great to obtain it.

3

Theology

With David Sheppard as my spiritual mentor, it was perhaps a little too obvious that I should think in terms of ordination. I had arrived at Cambridge with no clear plans about my future. I had vaguely thought of the Foreign Office, but it had all been a distant dream. What about the ordained ministry in the Anglican Church? David asked me if I had considered it.

There were a few immediate objections. Some relatives and friends of my family were not enthusiastic. For them, ordination was only for those who could not think of anything better to do. 'I suppose if you became a bishop it might just be all right,' commented one. Better wisdom came from some older Christians who were beginning to know me. Fearing that I might simply be copying the example of David Sheppard, they strongly suggested a teaching profession instead: 'There is a lot of excellent work you can do as a Christian master in a school,' they said; and indeed I had thoroughly enjoyed a term teaching at Wellington College just before going to Cambridge.

The primary obstacle to ordination, however, was a personal one. I was terrified at the thought of having to speak in public. Shouting orders to a troop of soldiers on parade was one thing; the thought of having to preach a sermon almost paralysed me with fear. The first talk on the Christian faith I ever gave lasted for a nightmarish five minutes. My mouth was dry, my knees knocking, my hands shaking. I thought I would never make it.

'The trouble is,' I protested to David Sheppard, 'I wouldn't know what to preach about.'

'More likely,' David countered, 'when you really begin to know your Bible, you won't know what *not* to preach about!' I was far from convinced.

It was not until Trinity Sunday 1955 that I first attended a service in King's College Chapel. I am not sure why I went, except that most undergraduates go at some time or other because of the beauty of the building and the excellence of the choir. But apart from enjoying the aesthetic magic of the whole occasion, I was completely riveted by an unemotional but powerful sermon on the need of men for the ordained ministry. I had no idea who the preacher was, but later discovered that he had been the Rev. Cyril Bowles, then the Principal of Ridley Hall and now Bishop of Derby. Through him God spoke so directly to me that the call to the ministry, which had been growing slowly stronger over the months, was now abundantly clear. I applied to the selection board of the Church of England, and was duly accepted as a candidate for ordination.

After two years studying philosophy, psychology, logics, ethics and metaphysics, when I did reasonably well in the exams in spite of my increasing preoccupation with Christian work (and still a lot of sport), I changed to theology. As still a very young Christian I found most of the lectures difficult and disturbing. I discovered that it was theology, and not philosophy as Keats had suggested, that could 'clip an angel's wings, unweave a rainbow'. Much of the dry, dusty stuff that we were studying seemed thoroughly destructive. What on earth did it have to do with the knowledge of God? Not that the theological scene was entirely bleak. There was always the saintliness of Professor Charlie Moule that shone radiantly through his lectures, and significantly he began each series with humble prayer, submitting himself to the authority of God and his word. I admired Professor Owen Chadwick for his immense scholarship, combined with a gentle and dry sense of humour. And Professor Henry Chadwick made the theological controversies of the early Church live in an astonishing way, impersonating the fathers and heretics as though he had known each one of them.

However, apart from these, few lecturers spoke with any conviction. One man, who was insufferably boring, used to begin most of his sentences like this: 'It is not unreasonable to suppose that it might not be the case that these two events were not unconnected.' I used to sit there counting the negatives in each sentence on my fingers, to find out whether the final statement was positive or negative. Matthew's comment about Jesus, at the end of the Sermon on the Mount, came home with fresh force: 'When Jesus had finished his discourse the people were astonished at his teaching; unlike their own teachers he taught with a note of authority.'

In sweeping contrast to the dithering caution of most academic theologians, who were efficiently undermining the faith of some of my friends, Billy Graham led a mission to the university in November 1955. Interestingly, when he tried, somewhat unsuccessfully, to be academic, his preaching lacked power. But when he accepted the apparent foolishness of the message of 'Christ crucified' and preached it with simplicity and integrity, the power of God's Spirit was manifestly at work, changing the lives of many undergraduates. It was a lesson I have never forgotten. I had first to work through the vital question of the authority of the Scriptures as the word of God; since then it has been my constant desire over the years to build faith. I could well understand the complaint of Goethe, a self-confessed agnostic, who once said to a preacher: 'You tell me of your certainties; I've enough doubts of my own.'

Any preacher or theologian may of course go through times of agonising doubt, even over the most basic issues of the Gospel; if so, he should share these with a few friends, not preach them from a pulpit or publish them in paperback. I was a curate in Cambridge when John Robinson's book *Honest to God* came out. It seems that it was written during a 'dark night of the soul' in John Robinson's life, and most Christians experience such deep questionings. Perhaps there were no friends close enough to him to help at the time. But such

doubts published in popular book form did untold damage.
When the psalmist was totally baffled by God's seeming
inactivity in the face of suffering, he wisely kept silent: 'If I
had said, "I will speak thus," I would have been untrue to the
generation of thy children.' (Ps. 73:15). Declaring his doubts
publicly would not have helped anyone.

G. K. Chesterton's words are still very much to the point, in
an age when it is fashionable for some preachers to express
their humility by saying how much they do not know: 'What
we suffer from today is humility in the wrong place. Modesty
has settled upon the organ of conviction, where it was never
meant to be. A man was meant to be doubtful about himself,
but undoubting about the truth; this has been exactly re-
versed.'

It would be wrong to conclude that I thought my theological
studies a waste of time. Apart from the enormous gain I
received from Professors Moule, Chadwick and Chadwick, it
was invaluable being made to think through carefully most of
the basic issues of the Christian faith. How far could the Bible
be trusted as the word of God? What was the nature of its
inspiration and authority? Why was the cross so central to the
faith? What was the atoning work of Christ? How convincing
was the evidence for the resurrection? Indeed, how sure could
we be about anything, concerning matters of faith?

When preparing for an essay I would be given a long list of
books to read, and I knew that some of them might be hefty
intellectual attacks on, say, the authority of Scripture. I then
asked one or two academic theologians whose personal beliefs were similar to my own for another list of books on the
same subject written by scholars taking a much more conservative and orthodox view. I would then read at least a few
books from 'both sides' and try to balance my essays with
arguments and counter-arguments. It was hard work, but in
this way I tried to tackle the critical questions seriously
without being 'tossed to and fro by every wind of doctrine' or
theological fashion. Through this process I became intellectually even more convinced of the great themes of the Christian Gospel, and this was important for a healthy growth in

Christ. We are to love God with all our *mind* as well as with all our heart and soul and strength. During this time I also remembered a shrewd principle that someone once gave me: 'Never let what you don't know shake your confidence in what you do know.' I certainly did not have all the answers to various intellectual questions, and yet all the time I was clearly growing in my knowledge of Christ.

Undoubtedly the most formative influence on my faith during the five years at Cambridge was my involvement with the boys' houseparties, or 'Bash camps' as they were generally known. Over the five years I went to no less than thirty-five of these camps: two at Christmas, two at Easter and three in the summer of each year. They were tremendous opportunities for learning the very basics of Christian ministry. Through patient and detailed discipling (although that word was never used) I learned, until it became second nature, how to lead a person to Christ, how to answer common questions, how to follow up a young convert, how to lead a group Bible study, how to give a Bible study to others, how to prepare and give a talk, how to pray, how to teach others to pray, how to write encouraging letters, how to know God's guidance, how to overcome temptation, and also, most important, how to laugh and have fun as a Christian – how not to become too intense, if you like. I also gained excellent grounding in basic Christian doctrines, with strong emphasis being placed on clarity and simplicity. All this was being constantly modelled by those who were much more mature in the faith, and I may never fully realise how much I owe to the amazing, detailed, personal help that I received over those five years. No Christian organisation is perfect, of course; and it would be easy to find fault with a group as powerful and as effective as this one. But if God has given me a useful ministry in any area today, the roots of it were almost certainly planted during those remarkable five years in the camps. It was the best possible training I could have received.

Sadly, I was not so receptive during my two years at theological college, Ridley Hall, which largely through my own fault was such a difficult and negative time. With the combined influence of the Christian Union at Cambridge and these boys' camps, I had developed strong evangelical convictions, and was thus deeply suspicious about everything else within the Christian Church. In my spiritual immaturity, my faculties had not yet been 'trained by practice to distinguish good from evil' (Heb. 5:14). I disliked the formality of Ridley chapel services every day; I rejected any teaching that I considered remotely 'liberal'; I found the staff giving theoretical answers to questions I was not yet asking; and my foremost priority was still my evangelistic work in the university, often at the expense of activities at Ridley Hall, most of which I regarded as interfering with the real work I felt called to do. The staff were patient with my spiritual arrogance and critical attitudes, and I am sure now that I would have grown in my knowledge of God far more had I been a little more humble and positive in my approach. I have since met many students at theological colleges and seminaries of all traditions who are as critical and defensive as I was, digging in behind their own convictions for safety and not being open to other ways in which God may be at work within his world-wide church. Much of this is the inevitable mark of immaturity.

At the same time, serious questions are today being asked (and rightly so) about the most helpful methods of training men and women for the ministry of the Church. More emphasis is being placed (and in my opinion still needs to be placed) on first-hand experience of church work as part of the training. This was the method of Jesus who lived and worked with his disciples. They watched him on the job, listened to him, were sent out by him, reported back to him, learnt from their mistakes, and so on. It was not 'first theory, then practice'. The learning and doing were closely interwoven. They were called primarily to be 'with him', and in this way he prepared them for the most effective leadership that the Church has ever known. There are surely lessons here for every theological college and seminary.

My real training for ministry, therefore, developed during my first curacy in a thoroughly different environment. John

Collins, then Vicar of St. Mark's Church, Gillingham in Kent,
invited me to be his curate. So, from the cultured atmosphere
of Cambridge I moved, almost five years to the day after my
conversion, to the tough dockyard parish in Gillingham.
What would be the effect of the Gospel I had discovered in
Cambridge in a different culture altogether?

4

St. Mark's, Gillingham

'You'll especially enjoy the Youth Club,' John Collins told me, encouragingly. 'David MacInnes has done amazing work there.'

David MacInnes, whom I had come to know at Cambridge and liked very much, was the other bachelor curate who joined John and Diana Collins when they started at Gillingham two years before. For financial reasons we all lived in the Victorian vicarage, together with the Collins's two young children, a Swiss *au pair* girl and Graham Scott-Brown, a brilliant young doctor who was preparing to go to Nepal as a missionary. It was quite a party! We had a marvellous time praying, planning, studying and working together. Many things were beginning to happen in the parish, and so almost every day there were developments to encourage us, or battles to be fought.

It was a privilege to enjoy such close fellowship. We avoided the snare common to many Christians working in tough situations, namely loneliness, and we certainly had lots of fun together. For instance, with various meetings almost every evening until quite late, John, David, Graham (for a few months) and I used to cook a light supper after Diana had wisely retired to bed. I became an expert at omelettes (and nothing else), and calculated that I must have cooked at least 1,000 omelettes during my three years there. For one week we tried to vary the menu with cauliflower cheese made in a pressure cooker; but Diana protested that the smell wafting upstairs was like the Russian army taking its boots off, so back we went to omelettes!

I quickly discovered that the bed-sitting rooms which David and I occupied, just inside the front door, were also the main meeting rooms for the parish: Confirmation Candidates, Young Wives, Pathfinders, Sunday School, Mothers' Union, Youth Fellowship, Christian Night School, and so on; and because of the complexity of various meetings and the shortage of stackable chairs, my first six months in the parish seemed largely taken up with moving forty chairs, several times a week, from the hall five hundred yards down the road to our respective rooms, and then back to the hall again. I felt just like a furniture remover! Was I really ordained for this, I wondered? It was much like scrubbing those pots and pans at the boys' camps; and ever since then I have looked for willingness to serve in simple, menial tasks, as an important qualification for spiritual leadership.

David MacInnes had indeed done magnificent work in the Youth Club, although I felt that John was exaggerating considerably when he said that I would enjoy it. At times I was simply terrified, although I tried hard not to show it. Always it was challenging, and afterwards we could have a good laugh; but David had attracted some lively gangs of teddy-boys (as they were then called), who thought nothing of having a good punch-up or carving one another up with razors, broken glass, flick-knives, or any other weapons available. This was not what I was used to at St. John's College, Cambridge. David had a terrific sense of humour which these tough lads – and lasses – obviously enjoyed, and was thus able to exercise effective control without antagonising potential trouble-makers to the point of violence. He won the respect of virtually everyone who came to that club (we usually had about 140 there each Friday evening) and his fifteen-minute talks during the club epilogues at the end of each evening were quite brilliant. David and I became very close friends, and have continued such ever since, so I was only too glad when he was there running the club, with me playing a minor role, and I always felt distinctly inferior whenever he was away. Every Friday, before going down to the club, I would go on my knees and pray over the relevant verses from Jeremiah 1: 'Be not afraid of their faces, for I am with you to deliver you, says the Lord.'

During my three years at Gillingham we never actually had a fight in the club, but several times came very near to one. One night, when David was speaking elsewhere, I noticed two rival gangs present, each with about twelve members. I kept a close watch on them; but when I was in another room talking to someone else, the two gangs slipped out of the club. 'There's a fight brewing outside!' I was told. So I rushed out of the door only to find, in the small courtyard at the bottom of the steps, the two gangs lined up on either side ready to charge at each other and equipped with a variety of ugly weapons. Without thinking I raced down the steps into the middle of them, and with an authority which surprised even me I told them that on no account could they fight on these premises, since this was a Christian club. I was obviously in a highly vulnerable position, but they accepted my word, and after a few tense minutes walked away. Later I heard, with much sadness, that they had gone to a nearby common and there fought a pitched battle, several of them ending up in hospital.

I am not sure that I ever 'enjoyed' the Youth Club, although we had some hilarious moments, often at the expense of visiting speakers. Through David's undoubted skill I gradually learned a few tricks of the trade, but any speaker had to keep his wits about him. We had a few battered sofas and armchairs which were pulled up for the front row of an audience for the epilogue, and some of the lads would pull out long chunks of stuffing from these chairs, and push them into their ears as soon as the speaker started his talk. Also, if we failed to get all cigarettes extinguished in time for the talk, someone would blow huge smoke-rings across the speaker's face. These rings were always fascinating to watch as they floated in front of us all, and guaranteed to upset all but the most gifted speaker. Others would stuff their pockets with snooker balls immediately prior to the epilogue, and roll them noisily across the bumpy wooden floor. Occasionally a small coin or piece of silver paper would be pushed in at the bottom of a light bulb, so that when the lights were turned on everything fused.

Every summer we would take between seventy and eighty young people for a week's houseparty; and although the majority of those who came had already been won for Christ through the club, life could still be difficult. God never eliminates our personalities, and our Christian members were just as lively as the others. Unfortunately for David and myself endless practical jokes were played – many of them neither practical nor funny, at least not for us! Our cars regularly disappeared, or the wheels were removed from them. I had everything put into my bed from black coal and damp sand to live frogs. And yet these weeks were always magnificent times. Whatever else could be said about the Youth Club, it was never, never dull. Most of the families in Gillingham had moved originally from the East End of London, and so there was a sharp cockney wit which kept us on our toes all the time. I also developed an enormous affection for numerous individuals and families, and it was wonderful seeing the power of Christ changing the lives of so many.

Of course there were casualties, in more ways than one. When one dockyard apprentice found Christ, he was beaten up by his mates in the dockyard the next day, and was in hospital for four days. Thankfully he stood his ground well, and is today a fine Christian leader. Others had too close an identity with the group from which they were converted; and although we spent many hours with them, the pressure of the group proved too much for some, and they fell away from Christ. We also made the mistake of allowing quite young Christians to give their testimonies of conversion too often. They had committed almost every crime in the book before their conversion, and therefore their stories were both dramatic and popular. But those who gave their testimonies invariably went through spiritual attacks later, and some tragically gave up their faith. There were many disappointments, but Christ became real for a growing number, and we often took small teams to other clubs for effective evangelistic evenings. On the whole we were the toughest and liveliest club in the area, so our visits were always popular, and David and I found that the time we spent with these young people, doing all sorts of things together, was always profitable.

In countless other ways I had much to learn. Giving short talks at a camp for public schoolboys was quite different from preaching in a large Victorian church in a dockyard area. Here, both John and Diana Collins were superb 'tutors'. Diana, having been trained as an actress at the Royal Academy of Dramatic Art, worked hard on my voice, trying to change it from the sound of an army officer on parade to something more fitting for a pulpit. She had me first relaxing on the floor and then making all sorts of extraordinary noises which reverberated round the vicarage, much to the amusement (or annoyance) of others who lived there. I found her exercises an enormous help, and it is sad that so few preachers have any guidance concerning the use of the one 'instrument' they are playing all the time.

John too gave me invaluable training, and his curates have always been known as some of the best-trained clergy in the Church of England. After every sermon I preached, John would take the time and trouble to comment thoughtfully on both the points that were good and those that were not so good. He never made more than about three critical comments on any one sermon (even if he could think of thirty-three), so that I was never discouraged. Indeed he was a great encourager all the time; and with his and David's preaching setting me an extremely high standard, I found these years the best training that I could have found in any parish. Over and over again I was astonished to hear from my friends who were curates in other parishes that very few received any practical training at all, and all too often very little encouragement. The work of training others is perhaps the most important work that any Christian leader can do. Both John and Diana have always been marvellous enablers, spotting the potential in others and working hard to develop that potential to its full. It is doubtless for that reason, among others, that the churches they have served have always been unusually blessed by God.

Life in Gillingham was frequently rewarding and we had lots of fun together; but it was never easy. At times it could even be dangerous. One particular night we were attacked in the vicarage by a wild and drunken Irishman. He was well known in the area, as it was alleged that he had shot at his wife with a double-barrelled shot-gun, but fortunately missed. We had given shelter to his wife and children in the past and the man had often been belligerent. On this occasion he was for some reason convinced that we were sheltering his wife again. Although we assured him that we were not, he broke two windows in the vicarage, smashed down a door or two, and by the time the police arrived (we had dialled 999 several times!), the man had in his hands a huge boulder. Inside the vicarage we were pretty scared and had armed ourselves as best we could. I had a broom, John a baseball bat, and Paul Russell (David MacInnes's successor) the ebony statue of an African girl. Diana, the most resourceful of us all, was in the bathroom upstairs pouring jugs of cold water from the window onto the man's head as he tried to smash his way through the front door. In court later on the man said, 'Your Honour, I remember it was raining at the time!'

Among other outstanding memories of that first curacy, a week's visit from that remarkable and courageous Dutchwoman, Corrie ten Boom, was a definite highlight. Knowing that she would be staying with us in the vicarage, we were all a little nervous because of the reputation of her amazing ministry, not only in Ravensbrück Concentration Camp, but throughout Germany after the war. God had particularly used her to release people from satanic powers, and the Nazi reign of terror had been literally a devilish inspiration, partly through heavy involvement with the occult. Hitler often spoke of being guided by voices within him, and was surely devil-inspired, if not devil-possessed. So with Corrie's record of helping those who had been troubled by evil spirits, we just wondered what she might find in an English vicarage! As it transpired, Corrie was the most wonderful, gracious and normal guest you could possibly have imagined. It was hard to think of her suffering all the brutalities of a Nazi concentration camp. She seemed so gentle, so good, and with a delightful sense of humour. Her talks, illustrated by simple and unforgettable visual aids, made a lasting impression on us all. Most of all, she was someone who walked daily with her Heavenly Father; and sometimes in conversation, while we were expressing some anxiety about something, she would turn so naturally to prayer that it took us a few moments to realise that she was talking no longer to us, but to God.

When John, David and I were seeing her off by train, from a crowded Gillingham platform, Corrie wanted to say something to us that we would remember. As the train moved slowly out of the station, she put her head through the carriage window and shouted at us, 'Don't wrestle, just nestle!' All eyes turned towards us, three clergymen, formally dressed in our clerical collars with our faces turning a delicate shade of pink. But I have never forgotten that simple slogan, even if, in practice, I have not always found it easy to rest quietly in the love and peace of the Lord. But God wants all of us to develop a simple trust in the Father's loving care, a trust that Corrie learnt through appalling suffering and grief.

After three years at St. Mark's, Gillingham, I went back to Cambridge for my second curacy, deliberately accepting an invitation to a totally different parish, the Round Church, for the purpose of widening my experience. I had no idea that the next three years would contain some of the most thrilling, confusing, traumatic and painful experiences of my life.

5

Spiritual Renewal

From the very start in Cambridge I became unexpectedly depressed. It was not a severe depression; but even though I had exchanged the relative ugliness of a dockyard town for the outstanding beauty of Cambridge, as I lived and worked in the heart of the finest university in the world (I may be a little prejudiced), I missed the vitality of Gillingham more than I had imagined possible.

Mark Ruston, my vicar, whom I had known well from my previous five years in Cambridge, could not have been more thoughtful and caring, and his steady and faithful ministry for Christ has been one of the outstanding features in Cambridge for over twenty-seven years. However, in sharp contrast to the lively wit of Gillingham, Cambridge as a town seemed remarkably dull. Even the church services, compared with Gillingham, seemed dull. They had little spark about them. Parish prayer meetings felt the same: heavy and depressing. I have never been very patient, and I was aching for some spark of life, just a little enthusiasm, something, whatever it might be, to make God seem more real in our midst. There was nothing wrong with the teaching: it was simple and biblical, and obviously helpful to scores of people. But oh, for some fire of the Spirit!

Looking back, I believe that God used my youthful impatience to spur me into a series of personal studies that proved a major turning-point in my life and ministry. I started to read the great histories of revival, fascinated by the outpouring of God's Spirit on groups of men and women at different times and in different places. Many of the manifestations of revival were totally strange to me, with people weeping before God, prostrate before him, crying out for mercy, sometimes for hours on end. It was hard to discern the sovereign work of the Spirit of God from human hysteria or infectious enthusiasm. But clearly something remarkable had happened in the times of Jonathan Edwards, Wesley and Whitefield, in the eighteenth century, the Revival of 1800, the Awakening of 1858, the Welsh Revival of 1904, and the Hebrides Revival of 1949, not to mention numerous others. I wished that God could send us another revival, not least here in Cambridge; and I began to pray seriously about this, sometimes joining forces with the Rev. Herbert Carson, Vicar of St. Paul's, and Dr. Basil Atkinson, Senior Librarian at the University.

Next, I studied again the Acts of the Apostles, and the conviction was steadily dawning on me that there was a normal spiritual dynamic about the early Church that was almost entirely missing within the Church of today. Even in Gillingham we seemed to have been on a different spiritual wavelength altogether. I remember there studying in our staff meetings 1 Corinthians 12 and 14, where the apostle Paul writes fully about the gifts of the Holy Spirit, especially prophecy and tongues, and we simply had no idea at all what he was talking about.

We took the usual evangelical line that all such gifts were purely for the apostolic period and were not even meant for today. But then why were such specific instructions given for their use within the pages of the New Testament? And what about those strange Pentecostals, whose growth in South America, in particular, had been one of the most remarkable Christian movements of this century? Had they experienced the power and gifts of the Spirit that we were somehow missing? These became insistent, urgent questions that I could not escape.

At the same time I was doing a detailed Bible study on the nature of faith. I could see, in example after example, that God's unusual demonstrations of power came when men and

women dared to take him at his word, whether they understood it all or not. For example, in the Christmas story, the
Virgin Mary is promised a gift of a son who will be 'the Son of
the Most High . . .' She is puzzled: 'How can this be, since I
have no husband?' Once again the promise is given: 'The
Holy Spirit will come upon you, and the power of the Most
High will overshadow you . . .' So she accepts the promise of
God at its face value, and responds in two very important
ways. First, she surrenders her life completely to God: 'Behold, I am the handmaid of the Lord; let it be to me according
to your word.' And then, amazingly, she begins to praise God
that it is *already true*, even though the reality of the actual
experience is still to come. In the *Magnificat* or the *Song of
Mary*, she bursts out in praise:

> My soul magnifies the Lord,
> and my spirit rejoices in God my Saviour,
> for he has regarded the low estate of his handmaiden.
> For behold, henceforth all generations will call me blessed;
> for he who is mighty *has done* great things for me . . .

As far as Mary is concerned, it is already true as soon as the
promise has been given.

Now that is faith, and I began to realise how often we limit
God to our own narrow human understanding, or else to a
specifically scientific world-view. Why should we not take him
more seriously at his word, whether we understand it or not,
whether we immediately experience it or not?

Most significant of all, I began a series of meditations in the
Beatitudes, from the Sermon on the Mount. I had been
inspired to do this after reading two volumes of expository
sermons on Matthew 5–7 by Dr. Martyn Lloyd-Jones. I found
that over a period of three or four months God was taking me
through the first four Beatitudes in terms of my spiritual
experience. It was a painful and humbling business.

Blessed are the poor in spirit. The word for 'poor' in the
Greek is a strong word, meaning poverty-stricken or bank-
rupt. It comes from a word meaning 'to cringe'. In other

words, a man is so overwhelmed by a sense of poverty that he is beaten to his knees and has to throw himself on the mercy of God. To begin with, this was a far cry from my own opinions about myself. After a fairly 'successful' first curacy, I was coming to the conclusion that I had more or less 'arrived'. I was well taught in Christian doctrine and practice, and thought it was my task for the rest of my life to go on preaching the truth and to correct those who disagreed with me! I had also made some sweeping judgments about the dullness and heaviness of the services at the Round Church. So God began to rebuke me for my spiritual pride, my arrogance, my self-righteousness and my critical spirit. Painfully, as he took away those masks, I began to see myself as I really was, as he saw me – and I did not like it. Instead of looking at the speck in my brother's eye, I started to look at the log in my own eye; and I realised that, if I was really in earnest about revival, it had to begin in me. On my knees, alone before God, there was nothing I could boast about, and much of which I was frankly ashamed, although I had become skilled at hiding it from others and even from myself. I found that I was the one who was poverty-stricken, and I found this a most uncomfortable disclosure.

Blessed are those who mourn. Again, the word in the Greek is a strong word, meaning 'lament'. If I dropped a glass and it broke into many pieces, the word I would use in the Greek to describe the scene is the root word of 'mourn'. In other words, blessed are those who are shattered – why? Because of their poverty of spirit. There is natural logic in these Beatitudes: the first leads directly to the second, and so on. As I meditated on this statement by Jesus, I began literally to weep for my spiritual poverty. I saw my low level of faith, my lack of love for Jesus, the poverty of my love towards others, and it deeply concerned me. I saw that it was precisely for such sins that Jesus had been crucified on the cross, and that by my sinful attitudes I was grieving the Spirit of God. Grief is a love-word. I knew that God still loved me more than I could possibly imagine, but there was much in my life that hurt him; and the knowledge of that broke me. More deeply than I can

ever remember, I began to repent of everything that I knew
was wrong in my life.

Blessed are the meek. The meek person is someone who is
so mourning for his spiritual poverty that he is willing for God
to do what he likes in his life. That man will not protest or
complain; he will not dictate his terms of reference; like the
Virgin Mary he will say, 'Let it be to me according to your
word.' Now that I felt broken at the foot of the cross, I was
willing for God to have his own way in my life, whatever that
meant, and however painful it might be. When Mary surrendered her body to become the mother of Jesus, she did not
know what this would mean in later years. Simeon warned her
that 'a sword will pierce through your own soul also'; and her
agony when Jesus was crucified must have cut through to the
innermost part of her being. There is always a price to pay for
spiritual life. Many Christians want to see new life in their
churches; not so many are willing to bear the cost. God
brought me to that point where I was genuinely willing to say,
as far as I understood it, 'Not my will, but yours be done.'

Blessed are those who hunger and thirst for righteousness.
Now that I was broken at the cross, mourning for my spiritual
poverty, I had a consuming desire to be right with God, to be
filled with his Spirit, to glorify him in every area of my life. I
spent much time in prayer, asking God to do something new
in my life. Never before had I known such hunger for God. As
with Jacob, I said in my heart, 'I will not let you go, unless you
bless me.' Time and again I asked God specifically to fill me
with his Spirit, knowing from my study of revival that the
Spirit of God often revealed himself in tremendous power,
falling on men and women in such a way that they were either
struck to the ground or filled with 'inexpressible joy'. But as
much as I was willing for anything to happen, nothing did. I
was disappointed, perhaps a little disillusioned; but the hunger never abated. It may be worth adding that all this took
place during the winter months of 1962–3, some time before
anything was popularly known about 'charismatic renewal'.
However, around that time prayer groups for revival were
springing up all over the place, which I took as a mark of the

Spirit's activity. Often these would be half nights or whole nights of prayer, such was the increasing hunger for God among many Christians. Parallel with my own spiritual search, I heard that my previous parish, St. Mark's, Gillingham, had been holding nights of prayer for revival; and at one of these (I think in February 1963) those who were present were gently aware of being filled with the Spirit. They entered into a new experience of the love of God. Some of the toughest of these men (and women) had fallen in love – with Jesus. There was no doubt that God had done something new and wonderful within the congregation; significantly, it seemed to me, shortly after I had left the parish! My expectation that God would meet with me also began to rise.

Suddenly I realised the missing link. I had been praying and praying to be filled with the Spirit; but when nothing seemed to happen I assumed that my prayer had not been answered. As I shared this with a friend, I remembered the example of the Virgin Mary. Once she accepted God's remarkable promise to her, she began to praise God that it was now already true, before the promise was confirmed in her experience. I had been waiting for the experience *before* I believed that the promise had been fulfilled. It was entirely the wrong way round. I had to claim the promise of the Spirit, believe it to be true, start praising God that it was true, and let the reality or experience of the promise follow in God's own way and in God's own time.

Once again, I confessed every sin I could think of, and asked for God's forgiveness, even the sphere of my unbelief. I told him that I was willing to obey him, whatever the cost. I then asked him to fill me with his Spirit, *and began to praise him that he had now done it*. As I went on praising for perhaps ten or fifteen minutes, I had a quiet but overwhelming sense of being embraced by the love of God. There were no startling manifestations. I did not speak in tongues, and anyway I still believed that these had died with the apostles. But it seemed that the presence of God filled the room in which I was praying. I *knew* I had been filled with the Spirit, and I was bubbling over with new joy.

I went straight round to my dear friend, Dr. Basil Atkinson. 'Basil,' I said, like someone bursting with good news, 'I've been filled with the Spirit!' 'Praise the Lord!' replied Basil spontaneously, and we had a wonderful time of praise and thanksgiving together. The next day I went to a clergy meeting in Cambridge, and I said to one of them: 'Peter, I've been filled with the Spirit!' with the same exuberance I shared with Basil. Poor Peter did not know what to say. Nervously he looked out of the window. 'I think it may rain today,' was his only comment; and he moved to talk to someone else about funeral fees, or whatever was the vital business of that clergy meeting. I began to comprehend that I had to choose my moment, to speak to the right person in the right way at the right time. But God had met with me in a fresh way: of that I was certain. It was hard being silent about it.

6

Baptism or Fullness

No doubt I made many mistakes. Everyone in love tends to say and do stupid things at times. And I was in love with Jesus in a way I had never known before. I devoured the Song of Solomon, that exquisite love poem in the Old Testament, which is a beautiful analogy of a love relationship between the believer and his or her Lord. It expressed what I felt in the depths of my heart. I spent even more time in prayer, mostly praise and worship; and at times the presence of God was so real to me that I would open my eyes expecting to see him transfigured there in front of me. I read the Bible as never before, and certain passages leapt out at me as though they were alive. They all seemed like love-letters from God. In terms of personal evangelism I had never known such fruitfulness, often having the joy of leading four or five people to the Lord every week, and this lasted for months! I loved people with a new quality of love, and found many opportunities of sharing what God had done in my life, especially with those who were hungry for him.

But what exactly *had* God done in my life? The reality of it all was unmistakable and undeniable, but how could I understand it in biblical and theological terms? That was the difficulty. So began six months or more of furious study to try to grasp from the Scriptures what it was all about. With three friends I went to see a man whose ministry we immensely respected and whose concern for revival was well known, Dr. Martyn Lloyd-Jones. As we spent the day with him at Westminster Chapel, he began by asking us to share our testimonies with him, since we had all known a fresh working of the Spirit of God in our lives over the last few months. The testimonies had obvious personal variations, but were significantly the same. To our surprise, Dr. Lloyd-Jones then shared a very similar testimony of his own, when the Spirit had come upon him shortly after the Hebrides Revival in 1949, through the ministry of Duncan Campbell. He said that it had given him a new authority in his preaching ministry. As we talked a little further he said, 'Gentlemen, I believe that you have been baptized with the Holy Spirit.'

To be honest I was not happy with that expression, and to some extent have never been, if it refers to something subsequent to conversion. But the Doctor (as he was often called) was quite adamant in his preaching on this theme. Less than two years before, on May 25th, 1961, the Doctor had said this in a sermon:

> There are some who are guilty of quenching the Spirit by limiting in their very thinking the possibilities of life in the Spirit . . . I am convinced that there are large numbers of Christian people who are quenching the Spirit unconsciously by denying these possibilities in their very understanding of the doctrine of the Spirit. There is nothing, I am convinced, that so quenches the Spirit as the teaching that identifies the baptism in the Holy Ghost with regeneration. But it is a very commonly held teaching today. Indeed it has been the popular view for many years. They say that the baptism in the Spirit is 'non-experimental', that it happens to everybody at regeneration. So we say 'Ah, well, I am already baptized with the Spirit, it happened when I was born again, it happened at my conversion; I've got it all.' Got it all? I simply ask, in the name of God, why then are you as you are? If you have got it all, why are you so unlike the New Testament Christians? Got it all? Got it at your conversion! Well, where is it, I ask?

A fair question! It was one that perfectly summed up my own feelings about a shallow doctrine of assurance that all too easily can lead to complacency. It is true that we are justified in the sight of God the moment that we put our trust in Jesus. But what about the 'fullness of life' that Jesus promised? Where is the evidence of the spiritual wealth that should be ours, as individuals and as a Church, once we are in Christ? The renewing work of the Spirit, whatever it should be called, seemed to be waking us up to the normal New Testament Christian life.

For me, it was essentially an enhancement of the reality of my spiritual life. The Doctor, while rejoicing in what God had done, warned us of certain dangers, notably lest any doctrine of sinless perfection should creep in. In the past, when men and women had been blessed by the Spirit (whatever they called it), they sometimes claimed that they were so dead to sin and so full of love that it was no longer possible for them to sin. When the great Baptist preacher Charles Spurgeon heard a man teaching such nonsense at a conference one evening, he poured a jug of milk over the man's head at breakfast the next morning. By the man's unholy reaction, the doctrine of sinless perfection was speedily disproved!

In my own case, the filling of the Spirit had nothing to do with any claims to sinless perfection, but the whole spiritual dimension had become more real. Instead of going up and down at a fairly low level of reality, God was more real, Jesus more real, prayer more real, the devil more real. However I was still going up and down, albeit on this new level of reality. I had definitely not yet arrived. I was anything but perfect. Indeed one or two unexpected lapses into sin brought me back with a jolt. If I had been renewed in the Spirit, I needed a constant, daily, fresh renewal. I could take nothing for granted.

This was a period of much heart searching, diligent study and many meetings. Because of the growing number of people in the country claiming to be filled or baptized with the Spirit, John Stott was asked to produce a clear paper setting out the biblical doctrines. This he did with his usual clarity, authority and graciousness, but taking a view diametrically opposed to that of Dr. Martyn Lloyd-Jones. In what became his booklet *The Baptism and Fullness of the Holy Spirit*, John Stott said: 'According to Scripture we have been baptized with the Spirit because we have repented and believed . . . I would appeal to you not to urge upon people a baptism with the Spirit as a second and subsequent experience entirely distinct from conversion, for this cannot be proved from Scripture.' What was I to make of this 'clash of the Titans', as a friend of mine once described it? Which view was right? Had I (and others) been 'baptized in the Spirit'? If not, what had happened in our experience?

The expression 'to baptize in the Holy Spirit' comes only seven times in the New Testament, six of them linked with the baptism that John the Baptist said the Coming One would bring.[1] John had come to baptize with water as a sign of repentance, but Jesus would baptize with the Holy Spirit to introduce people into the blessings of the New Covenant. At Pentecost this promise was fulfilled, and this was repeated only in the house of Cornelius, at the Gentile equivalent of Pentecost. As Peter explained, 'And I remembered the word of the Lord, how he said, "John baptized with water, but you shall be baptized with the Holy Spirit."' Peter went on, 'God gave the same gift to them as he gave to us *when we believed in the Lord Jesus Christ*' (Acts 11:16f). Repentance (Acts 11:18; cf 2:38) and faith are thus the only necessary conditions for a person to be baptized in the Holy Spirit.

From those six references it seems clear that the baptism in the Holy Spirit refers to Christian initiation. It is the spiritual event by which all people are brought into Christ, whether Jew or Gentile. This is even more clear in the seventh reference: 'For by one Spirit we were all baptized into one body – Jews or Greeks, slaves or free – and all were made to drink of one Spirit.' (1 Cor. 12:13) Nowhere is it suggested that Christians were, or could be, baptized in the Spirit after their conversion to Christ. Indeed, 'anyone who does not have the Spirit of Christ does not belong to him' (Romans 8:9). Nor is it suggested that Christians should pray or wait for

1. Matt. 3:11; Mark 1:8; Luke 3:16; John 1:33; Acts 1:5; 11:16; 1 Cor. 12:13.

the baptism of the Spirit. The first disciples had to wait for the initial outpouring of the Spirit at Pentecost; but after that, the 'promise of the Spirit' was for all those who repented and believed.

The trouble about speaking of the baptism of the Holy Spirit as a second-stage experience for some Christians (as the Pentecostals and many charismatics do) is not only that it cannot be proved in the New Testament, but it also becomes divisive. The Christian Church is thus split into the haves and have-nots, leading to inevitable dangers of spiritual arrogance on the one hand and resistance to the Holy Spirit on the other. The truth is that we have 'every spiritual blessing in Christ' (Ephesians 1:3), and there is nothing further that we have to seek beyond Christ. This is what John Stott taught so clearly.

The challenge that Dr. Martyn Lloyd-Jones made, however, was a valid and important one, even though I believe that he was wrong to describe it as a baptism in the Spirit. Theologically we may have everything in Christ, but where is it in our lives? Where is the vitality and joy, the faith and love of those first disciples? The fact is that the actual experience of what we already have in Christ may come to different people at different times and in different ways. It is like unwrapping a multiple parcel, and Paul significantly talks about the 'unsearchable riches of Christ'. The truth of what we are and have in Christ may become real in our experience at various stages. When a person is overwhelmed by the love of Christ, filled with new praise, and finds fresh joy in prayer, in the study of the Scriptures and in personal witness, it is understandable if he speaks of this experience as the 'baptism of the Spirit', even if that is not the scriptural meaning of that phrase as we have seen.

The tragedy is that, through the unscriptural use of language, many Christians have held back from those riches in Christ that the Holy Spirit is today renewing in the Church. We cannot settle for a dull orthodoxy or for a low level of spirituality. We need to be open to all that the Spirit is doing in our midst since none of us has yet arrived. We have not yet entered into the 'glorious liberty of the children of God'.

There is much more for all of us to experience of our inheritance in Christ, and we should always remain hungry and thirsty for him.

Most Christians would agree that we all need to be continuously filled with the Spirit, since that is the plain injunction in Scripture (Eph. 5:18). But not all Christians expect anything much to happen. Many believe and teach that it is purely a matter of 'imperceptible growth into Christ'. That is not, however, the constant testimony of countless Christians all over the world who have experienced some form of spiritual renewal, whatever it should be called. A Diocesan Youth Chaplain wrote to me,

> I was aware of the need of something more from God . . . One day I received the Spirit through prayer and the laying on of hands . . . I felt the Spirit pour in until it seemed I must burst . . . For how many years I had been longing for joy! And now it came, joy that welled up within and issued in praise and thanks and adoration to a glorious God. Love also began to appear . . . Christ was more real and more loved. The Scriptures came alive in a new way . . .

That man has developed a powerful and gracious ministry since then; and such stories could be multiplied many hundreds of thousands of times.

Something happens, therefore, when men and women are filled with the Spirit, and that 'something' can often transform a person's life and ministry. Whole churches come alive in a way not known before. If the expression 'to baptize with the Spirit' should be kept for the initiation into Christ, this must not exclude the serious possibility of further significant steps forward that are variously termed 'being filled with the Spirit', 'receiving the Spirit', or 'experiencing the release of the Spirit'. In our Western Christianity we have become so cautious about subjective experiences because of their obvious dangers that we tend to rule them out altogether. However, no one can read the New Testament without seeing that it is shot through with specific and often dramatic experiences of the Spirit. It is because of the comparative absence of these that the Church today stands in such desperate need of renewal. Although it is important to get our terminology right, it is tragic if we allow our debates about terminology to stifle our hunger for God and our openness to the Spirit.

At the same time as Dr. Martyn Lloyd-Jones and John Stott were expounding their different viewpoints, news was coming through from North America of Episcopal and Lutheran churches that were in a similar way being renewed in the Spirit, although most of them testified to speaking in tongues (a love-language of praise in the Spirit) which had not been my experience at all. Several interested Christian leaders met in London with those who came over from North America to share their stories with us. Some of them, to be honest, impressed us very little. We sensed that they had simply been 'born again', and their abundance of stories and absence of theology left us far from satisfied. Others were more impressive, and certainly something seemed to be happening; but whether it was genuinely a work of the Spirit or some Satanic diversion from the true heart of the Gospel was not always easy to discern. One man, at an extravagant luncheon for Christian leaders at the Hilton Hotel, was introduced as 'the greatest Spirit-filled Christian in the world today' (applause for the platform party). This did not go down too well with us conservative English clergy. It was a puzzling period in our lives.

In particular, there was this new emphasis on tongues, together with some reference to prophecy and healing. During my theological studies I had become a 'dispensationalist', following the teaching of such men as B. B. Warfield, believing that all such gifts, whatever they were, were purely for the New Testament period, to establish the truth of the Gospel with 'many wonders and signs', but definitely not for today. However, at a conference for evangelical clergy some months before, I had heard Dr. Edwin Orr speak on his specialised subject of revival. It was a fascinating day, and he made one statement in particular that I remembered. Tracing quickly through history, he pointed out that each significant revival within the Church had brought back something lost since the days of the early Church. He also predicted that the next revival would bring back certain gifts of the Spirit that had largely disappeared since the first few centuries of church history. Was this what God had been doing through the Pentecostal movement since the turn of the century? Was this what he was beginning to do again, attempting once more to break into the historic denominations which had unitedly rejected those gifts earlier, thus forcing the Pentecostal Church to come into being? What was the scriptural teaching about those gifts? Were they really for today after all?

The more I studied the New Testament the more I became convinced: the teaching that these gifts were only for the apostolic age was no more than a rationalisation of their absence for so long. The arguments against them were thin and questionable; I could see that all the gifts could be just as edifying for the Church today as in the first century, and many of them just as effective for the evangelistic thrust of the Church today as in the Acts of the Apostles. Granted that there was a 'foundational' level of prophecy for the completion of Scripture (and therefore not to be looked for today), even in the New Testament Church there were many other levels of prophecy for the building up of believers; so why not today? I could not readily understand the value of tongues, except that, especially with my new longing to worship and praise the Lord, I often felt frustrated by the limitations of language. My spirit often wished to transcend my ability to express myself in grammatical sentences. This was equally true for intercession when I did not know exactly what to pray for, but felt a strong burden to pray for someone.

Such thoughts developed in my mind over a period of about six months, by which time I had started 'earnestly to desire spiritual gifts', according to the command in Scripture. At one time a dear couple laid hands on me and prayed for me for a whole hour, asking that I would be given the gift of tongues. For the first five minutes I prayed with them. For the next five I could only think, 'What *would* some of my colleagues say if they could see me now?' And then for the next fifty minutes I

prayed that they would stop praying. Eventually I won, and
the whole experience was not particularly helpful for me. I
suppose I was expecting God to waggle my tongue so that the
words would rush out. But it never happened to me like that.
Later I was impressed by Luke's statement in Acts 2:4 that
'*they* . . . began to speak in other tongues, as the Spirit gave
them utterance.' They had to do the speaking. The Spirit does
not normally take us over in the way in which an evil spirit
may do.

So eventually I asked God to give me a language in the
Spirit through which I could worship and praise him. I began
to praise him in English, and then let my mind relax while my
spirit went on praising with the first syllables that came to my
tongue. They could be any syllables; there was nothing special
or mystical about them. After some thirty seconds I stopped:
'David, you're just making this up!' I said to myself. Then I
thought, what if God had answered my prayer? What if I had
been speaking in tongues? At the very least I should go on for
a little longer. I was sure that God would not be angry with me
if I were doing the wrong thing. He knew that I genuinely
wanted to praise him as much as I could. So I went on making
these noises for about thirty minutes or more. Every time I
listened carefully to the sounds, I found them most unedify-
ing. But every time I used the sounds to concentrate on the
Lord in worship, I found myself unusually refreshed. Is this
what Paul meant when he wrote, 'He who speaks in a tongue
edifies himself'? I cannot pretend that all my problems about
tongues were solved from that moment onwards. I was deeply
concerned about the integrity of what I was doing, and I
wanted to be *sure*. But increasingly I found the gift to be a
natural and helpful part of my daily devotional prayer life – a
marvellous way of abiding and resting in the Lord.

All language is simply the use of various sounds or syllables
as vehicles of communication. When my spirit is praying to
God, who is Spirit, I need not be confined to those sounds that
happen to form my native language. Any sounds or syllables
will do, providing that they are genuinely vehicles of communication between my spirit and God's Spirit. Of course in

public I must use sounds that everyone understands. But in private that need not be the case. Every Christian acknowledges the importance of silent prayer, or 'sighs too deep for words'. Why not a spiritual language which the mind may not understand? Tongues are not irrational, but 'trans-rational' or supra-rational. God is so much bigger than our own rational thinking. Therefore, Paul concludes, 'I will pray with the spirit (i.e. in tongues) and I will pray with the mind also (i.e. in a known language); I will sing with the spirit and I will sing with the mind also' (1 Cor. 14:15).

Because of the novelty of all this, I kept very quiet about it and told only a tiny handful of friends in strict confidence, that I thought I was beginning to speak in tongues in private prayer. I was living at a Biblical Research Centre at the time, and such news could easily be misunderstood. Imagine my concern, therefore, when I was suddenly asked to leave the Centre and find other accommodation. When I made a direct enquiry about the reason for this, I was told that the committee responsible for the Centre had heard that I was speaking in tongues. This threw me into a dilemma. Was I becoming heretical? Was all this a deception of the devil? Was I in danger of leading others astray if I spoke openly about this? To whom could I turn for wise counsel? It was not an easy period in my life, to say the least; and once more I had to go back to the New Testament to gain a better understanding of the nature and value of spiritual gifts. However, the gift of tongues was constantly refreshing whenever I used it as a genuine prayer language for the Lord.

As I found myself unexpectedly homeless, Mark Ruston graciously took me in, and I tried to continue working in the church much as before. I was anxious to be utterly loyal to Mark and to the ministry of that church, and yet I naturally longed to share something about the renewing work of the Spirit that I had experienced. Obviously I would say nothing about tongues or any of the other controversial gifts. So I continued running the Children's Church, which had been my special and enjoyable responsibility, I continued preaching at the normal services, and I began to become more involved in the work among students. Whatever private misgivings Mark may have had, I have always respected him for his patient and steady acceptance of me as a person, and our relationship over the years is something I have always treasured.

Nevertheless, in the country as a whole during the sixties there was growing opposition by a number of evangelical leaders towards this renewal movement. Various well-known leaders wrote to me, urging me to 'renounce tongues'. One man even offered me a 'plum living' in the south of England if I would make a simple but clean break from all these things. But if I had received a genuine gift from the Holy Spirit of God, how could I possibly renounce it? Would I not be opposing God and quenching his Spirit? Risking the accusation of arrogance, I knew that I must obey God rather than men, although I went over the biblical ground for my new convictions again and again. A number of letters that I received hurt me deeply.

The heart-searching continued. I did not *know* I was right. Perhaps I was all wrong and my critics were right after all. But I knew it could never be right to go against one's own conscience. All I could do was to commit the whole matter to God and ask him to lead me in his way, whatever the cost might be.

I also found that another form of heart-searching was beginning to develop which took me equally by surprise.

7

Marriage

It was Christmas Day 1963. The Christmas morning service had just finished, and I was standing with Mark Ruston at the Norman porch of the Round Church saying 'Happy Christmas' to all the members of the congregation. A very attractive girl suddenly caught my eye. 'Have we met before?' I asked. 'I don't think so,' she replied with a trace of a Scottish accent. 'My name is Anne MacEwan Smith, and I'm nursing at the Maternity Hospital in Mill Lane.'

I had always mistrusted the romantic sentiment of 'love at first sight', but the 'vibes' were undoubtedly there. A little later, driving from Cambridge to my mother's home in Eastbourne, I could think of little else all the way except Anne MacEwan Smith. That brief encounter had made a deep impression on me.

Since my conversion I had considered carefully the advantages of the celibate life. The apostle Paul was strong on this theme: 'I want you to be free from anxieties. The unmarried man is anxious about the affairs of the Lord, how to please the Lord; but the married man is anxious about worldly affairs, how to please his wife' (1 Cor. 7:32). I was now thirty, and since my conversion over nine years ago I had devoted most of my time and energy to the work of Christ. David MacInnes and I had often discussed the matter, and we could think of very few advantages in getting married. We were confirmed bachelors, so I thought. And I believed that a bachelor was a man who never made the same mistake once.

Two facts weakened my resolve, however. The first was

that David himself became engaged! I felt almost betrayed, and yet secretly happy for him, and gladly accepted his invitation to be his Best Man. The second fact was that, to my surprise, I now wanted to get married myself. The time seemed right.

I tried not to think too much of Anne MacEwan Smith in the next few weeks, and in fact I forgot her name (but not her face!) when we next met at a church meeting. I did not plan to rush into things, and I gather that she had the same idea. Brought up as a good Scottish Presbyterian, but living now in England and going mostly to Anglican churches, she felt that she ought to be confirmed in the Church of England. Dutifully and discreetly she approached my vicar, Mark Ruston, and asked if he could prepare her for confirmation. 'You must see my curate,' was his reply. 'I am shortly going on a three-month sabbatical.' She obeyed his instructions and came over to see me.

I had in fact already started the confirmation classes, and since we were covering a carefully planned syllabus, it was necessary for Anne to catch up on the classes she had missed. Whether it was appropriate or not, I arranged to give her one or two private classes before she could join the rest. At our first session I handed her an Anglican Prayer Book and asked her to turn to the Confirmation Service. Following my usual practice, I commented, 'You will find it just before the marriage service!' A word of prophecy indeed!

Correctly we covered the ground that she had missed, but gently I also asked her a few questions about her own relationship with Christ. She had always been God-fearing, but had personally accepted Christ as her Saviour only two or three years before while training at Guy's Hospital. I asked her if she knew what it meant to be filled with the Holy Spirit, and when her reply was a little evasive I gave her a booklet on the subject which I had found helpful.

The next week she explained that the booklet had clarified a remarkable spiritual experience that she had recently known. Apparently she had been reading an article from a missionary magazine which challenged her about her own lack of faith. On her knees, alone before God, she asked him to give her a gift of faith. In answer to her prayer it seemed that the Spirit had fallen on her and she was caught up into God's presence, losing all sense of time. When she became more aware of everything around her, she heard a strange sound and found that she was praising God in a tongue that was foreign to her. She had never heard of speaking in tongues, and feared that she might be going out of her mind. But she continued secretly to use this language because through it she experienced the presence and love of Jesus more than ever before. However, having read the booklet that I gave her, she shared her story with me. I marvelled that, despite the difference of our two stories, the end result was the same. With me, it had been a long, tortuous struggle, filled with intellectual questionings and many doubts. With Anne, it had been a sovereign work of the Spirit of God, without her knowing anything about spiritual renewal or spiritual gifts. As far as I could see, her experience was wholly authentic, and she evidently had a deep love for Jesus. It was probably at this point that my instinctive interest in Anne began to deepen. That increased when I first heard her pray in a prayer meeting. It was a heartfelt prayer which flowed with amazing spiritual authority, vision and understanding. I had already been physically attracted to her, but I felt even more at one with her when we were both on our knees before God; and this, for me, was enormously important. If God were to bless my future relationship, I knew that Christ must unquestionably be first. Indeed, the quality of our individual relationships with Christ would determine the quality of our relationship together. If we were not first and foremost 'one in Christ', I could see no future for us as a couple. It was therefore marvellous to feel so close to Anne in prayer.

We soon became aware of our mutual affection, but recognised the extreme difficulty of pursuing this when I was the curate of the Round Church. A bachelor curate has no privacy when it comes to personal friendships with the opposite sex, especially if the girl is a member of his own congregation. A period of essential subterfuge followed. We knew that we could not be seen together in Cambridge – the news would travel everywhere within minutes – so we planned our free time very carefully. Sometimes I would sit in my car outside the Maternity Hospital, complete with slouched hat and dark glasses, hiding carefully behind a copy of *The Times*. I could well be tracking down the Pink Panther! On other days, Anne would take a bus to some prearranged place several miles out of Cambridge, and I would follow the bus in my car at a discreet distance. I am not sure what the bus driver thought when I stopped every time the bus stopped, but the plan always worked. With this skilful cloak-and-dagger courtship we arrived at the point of announcing our engagement without anyone knowing about it, except for a very small circle whom we had told in confidence. The announcement stunned many in the congregation, but they shared in our joy. We planned to get married in the Round Church on September 19th.

I was as happy as could be! God had blessed me spiritually, and now had given me a beautiful fiancée who had also experienced spiritual renewal.

As the wedding drew near, however, totally unexpected and serious problems arose. During the month before our wedding I was involved in some Christian activity, and an incident occurred which, although slight in itself, seemed to oppose all the new-found joy and freedom in worship that had become so important to me. I felt a deep grief within my own spirit, and sensed that this was only a pale reflection of the much more serious grief of the Spirit of God. Whether or not I was right about this, I suddenly felt in a spiritual strait-jacket. At that moment I experienced something like a steel band tightening round my chest, and I began coughing. That night I continued coughing, and it steadily grew worse so that sleep became more and more difficult. I went to a local doctor who was puzzled. But by this time I was clearly so breathless and ill that Anne was sent for to take me to her parents' home. As the shortness of breath grew more acute I became quite fearful at night and was obviously far from well. The wedding was only three weeks away.

When I returned to Cambridge I was so short of breath that I could not perform the simplest task requiring any effort. Even walking down a street was a major achievement. My doctor diagnosed some form of bronchial asthma, but the treatment in those days was rather a hit-and-miss affair compared with the efficient treatment that asthma sufferers can receive today. On the eve of our wedding I was so ill that Anne seriously suggested that we should postpone the whole affair until I was better. Perhaps we should have done so, but with 250 guests arriving from all over the country the next morning the suggestion seemed impossible. So, supported by drugs, I struggled through the service and endured the reception. At one level I was blissfully happy to have Anne as my bride. But physically I was distressed and mentally anxious. Doubtless Anne was exceedingly worried too.

Our honeymoon was really a disaster. We went to a beautiful spot in North Cornwall, Trebarwith Strand, which we had carefully selected some months before. When we arrived there, we were almost the only ones in a delightful hotel, and the weather for two weeks was absolutely perfect: blue skies, glorious sunshine, fantastic waves for surfing – it could not have been better. Except that I could not breathe! Each night was constantly interrupted by coughing; each day saw a brief struggle to a spot within fifty yards of the hotel, where we had to stay all day, reading, talking, coughing and attempting to sleep. We never went as far as the beach. We never went for one walk.

The nightmare continued on our return to Cambridge. We had rented a small flat, but climbing even one flight of stairs proved an impossible task for me on some days. Anne had planned to go back to nursing to help out financially, but through an amazingly generous gift from a friend (who did not know our situation intimately), no job was necessary and Anne did her 'nursing' instead at home.

We tried to enter into the work together, but this too was fraught with problems. Without realising at all what I was doing, I made a series of disastrous mistakes. To begin with I attempted to make Anne into a mini-evangelist overnight, giving her a crash-course in personal evangelism, and I could not understand why she rebelled so strongly against this. It seemed to me that she was not interested in trying to bring people to Christ, and, since that was my primary calling, how could our marriage possibly work out? I failed to appreciate the importance of Paul's comment that only '*some* are evangelists'. I was; but Anne wasn't. In fact God has given her many spiritual gifts which have blessed countless people over the years, but it took me a long time to recognise the fact that God had planned that our gifts and ministries should be complementary and not identical.

The next mistake came when I tried to mould Anne into the conventional clergyman's wife: a sort of unpaid curate whose job was to support *me* in *my* ministry. This meant, in part, constant hospitality in our flat, which for Anne was far from easy. In our own living room, which was also my study, half the furniture had to be moved every time we entertained anyone for a meal; and anyway nearly all those who came were *my* friends and *my* contacts, not Anne's. 'Supporting me' also meant that I took her with me to meetings and conferences at which I was the speaker, so that everyone knew at once who she was, 'David's wife'. Anne, on her part, knew very few of those present and even began to lose her own identity. Who was she? Was she no more than 'David's wife'? What was her role now that she was married? Was she just an addition to me, like another suitcase that I was carrying around? Who was Anne Watson? In marriage we are called to lose our independence but not our individuality.

None of this did I understand. Even if Anne had articulated the problem to me clearly, I doubt if I would have grasped what she was talking about. As it was, her defence was to withdraw into herself, often curling up on the bed in depressed silence. When I asked what was the matter, she did not answer. When I mentioned that it was time for us to go to this meeting or to that house, often she did not come. Many times during those first few months I had to make the same apology: 'I'm sorry that Anne isn't with me, but she's not too well.' Outwardly I made light of it, but inwardly I was extremely worried. With the hectic pace we were trying to keep up (far from successfully) it was not surprising that Anne had a miscarriage. Mentally and physically we were exhausted, and that in itself is a reason why some marriages flounder from the start. Space needs to be given for mutual adjustment, but these were lessons that we learnt only when it was too late.

We never forgot, however, an incredible sky that we saw on our way to Cornwall for our honeymoon. It was a striking mixture of black, grey and a violent orangey-yellow – an astonishing blend of storm and sunset. And boldly sweeping across the whole scene, in the most vivid colours imaginable, was a *double rainbow*. Had a painter depicted the scene accurately on canvas I would have said it was far too lurid to be true. But it was there before our startled eyes. God, many years before, had set a rainbow in the sky as a sign of his covenant promises. It seemed to us, in that double rainbow before us, that God was giving us a double assurance of his love, whatever storms there might be in the future. Even after such a desperate start to our marriage, we did not realise how much we would need that assurance in the years that lay ahead.

8

St. Cuthbert's, York – Early Days

'What are we going to do with you when we close you down?'
This was the discouraging and unnerving question that I was
asked on my second full day in St. Cuthbert's Church, York.
The questioner was the Chairman of the Church Redundancy
Commission who had come with the rest of the Commission
to consider the future use of the church building. I had only
just arrived, believing that it had a future as a living church;
the Commission were already planning its future as a possible
museum for York University. What a marvellous welcome to
receive, I thought to myself! And what a parable of the
popular image of the Church in the mid-sixties: a museum, an
ancient relic of some bygone days, of occasional interest to
historians and architects but of absolutely no relevance for the
mass of ordinary people. I gave the Chairman what may have
seemed a typically pious remark from a young clergyman: 'If
anyone comes to this church and preaches the simple Gospel
of Christ, believes in the power of prayer and trusts in the
Holy Spirit, this building will be full in no time.' Uncon-
vinced, they gave me one year's grace before, regretfully,
they would have to close St. Cuthbert's down.

Although it was purely a matter of faith, Anne and I were
convinced that God had called us to York. When we knew
that our time in Cambridge was coming to an end, we were
offered four livings, each of which presented a reasonable
salary and a good vicarage. After my happy experience in
Gillingham we were particularly interested in a church in the
East End of London, but I felt that a new pastoral scheme,

attempting to unite two parishes that were totally divided by a huge railway cutting, would never work, so we turned the offer down.

Then someone mentioned this little church in York. Having seen the valuable supporting ministry to students that the Round Church played in Cambridge, I was concerned for the new universities that were springing up throughout the country, most of them thoroughly secular in their foundation. I could see that they needed, far more than Oxford and Cambridge, local churches that were relevant to students. York University had only recently started, with 600 students, and no church in York had obvious potential to play this supportive role. As a few Christians in York were praying about this, the idea of St. Cuthbert's Church came to their minds.

St. Cuthbert's had been increasingly run down for many years. Much of the parish had disappeared through a slum-clearance programme, and in the place of the rabbit warrens of tiny houses, light industry was beginning to emerge. The previous rector of St. Cuthbert's, the Rev. R. V. Bainton, had been at the church for twenty-four years, but had suffered from poor eyesight and was totally blind for the last years of his ministry, which ended in a tragic death early in 1964. The tiny congregation nobly soldiered on, and the parish was annexed to Heworth Parish Church, a mile away, to maintain the necessary services. The total Sunday offerings each week averaged about £2, and the majority of the year's income came through jumble sales, garden parties, whist drives and raffles. In this way the church itself was just solvent, but the fourteen-roomed Victorian rectory was cold, damp, dirty and in urgent need of complete redecoration. The congregation had dwindled to about four or five for the eight o'clock Communion Service, the same for Mattins, and ten or twelve for Evensong. That they stayed there at all was perhaps remarkable, but the future of the church was undoubtedly bleak.

Added to that, when Anne and I first visited York to consider the situation, we arrived on an exceptionally foggy day; and any sufferer will know that fog is not the best

weather for asthma. I noticed that not only was the rectory
cold and damp, with no form of heating apart from open coal
fires in every room right up to the 'servants' quarters' on the
third floor, but the church was heated by two coke stoves
whose fumes, I was told, could be lethal when the wind was in
the wrong direction. With the fog alone (we were given warm
hospitality in someone's home), my asthma was so bad that I
had to spend the whole night upright in an armchair, as I
coughed ceaselessly whenever I tried to lie down. It was one
of many similar nights that I was to experience in the coming
months.

Other prospects also were bleak. With the expected closure
of the church within the year, the Church Commissioners
understandably decided that they would not spend any money
on the rectory at all, apart from any essential repairs. The
house was re-wired, admittedly, but we found only one socket
in each of the huge rooms, and hard lumps of dried plaster all
over the dirty floorboards. Also, with the church annexed to
Holy Trinity, Heworth, I would not be appointed as rector of
St. Cuthbert's, but licensed as curate to Holy Trinity, with
responsibility for St. Cuthbert's. My salary in Cambridge,
when Anne and I were living in a small furnished flat, had
been £900 a year, and that had been inadequate until the
generous gift from my friend arrived which effectively raised
it to over £1200. Now we were to move to a filthy, cold,
unfurnished fourteen-roomed house, and my salary dropped
to £600 a year – a figure, I suspect, well below the poverty-
line. One or two clerical friends expressed concern about this,
but nothing, apparently, could be done. Indeed, out of that
£600 we had to buy two night-storage heaters to try to warm a
part of the rectory, pay for all removal expenses from Cambridge, purchase a duplicator for the parish, and scavenge as
much second-hand furniture as we could. My parents-in-law
advanced their 'will' to us, enabling us to buy some carpets
and curtains; my mother moved from a house to a flat, giving
us what she no longer needed; Mark Ruston's mother did
something similar; old family portraits, trunks and packing
cases were released from storage by my uncle; and when

families living near us in York were buying new pieces of furniture (sofas and armchairs for example) we would gratefully take their throw-outs from them. In this way, the fourteen rooms were gradually furnished, if not exactly to our taste!

Why did we ever go to such an unpromising parish? We were warned that York would be something of a backwater for us. We had already heard about the 'spiritual barrenness' of the north-east, where few churches of any denomination showed signs of spiritual life, but we had no idea how desperately barren it was until we moved there. We were told by several Christians in York that the city was such a tough place as far as the Gospel was concerned that we would lose our spiritual cutting-edge within three years, if we did not watch out. We had no personal links in York; and all that we knew about the city was its Minster, its railways and two famous chocolate factories. So why did we go?

We went because we believed, deeply within our hearts, that God had called us there. I am not a great one for visions and revelations, and have always been impatient with those who say, perhaps a little glibly at times, that the Lord has told them to do this or that. Anne and I prayed carefully about the five parishes that were tentatively being offered to us, and although every human consideration about York seemed totally negative, nevertheless on our knees before God the strong conviction was gaining on us that the Lord wanted us there. In fact he gave us a promise (and I'm not a great one for being given promises, either): 'I will fill this house with glory' (Hag. 2:7, A.V.). Clinging to that promise, at times by our fingernails, we moved to York on July 1st, 1965.

Our first task was to make at least one or two rooms in the rectory habitable. I had never decorated a room in my life; but fortunately Anne had some experience, and with the skilled help of a friend we decorated my study and an upstairs sitting-room within two weeks. After that, the pace slowed down considerably, and it was literally years before we got around to some parts of the house.

Nevertheless, we found the tiny congregation very welcoming, and we began to form deep friendships which have continued and grown ever since. Most of them were Linfoots: Dan Linfoot (the church-warden), Florrie Linfoot, Barbara Linfoot, Harry Linfoot, Ethel Linfoot, Doreen Linfoot, Michael Linfoot, Ethel Linfoot – when in doubt I said 'Linfoot'! Then there was Mrs. Lunn, Mr. and Mrs. Eddie Barrett, Mr. and Mrs. Brown, Mr. and Mrs. Lancaster – they were all the salt of the earth. But there were not many of them. Naturally we visited in the parish as we tried to establish relationships and tell people about the love of Jesus. Yorkshire people are blunt but friendly, although virtually no one understood why we were visiting. Some assumed it must be for money ('The Church is always asking for money'), and a few gave us £1 which they hoped would encourage us. But we wanted them to hear about God's free gift to them of his own Son, Jesus Christ. None seemed interested, and as far as I know no one came to our services as a result of our visiting.

Preaching also was initially a great strain. I prepared my sermons as thoroughly as I could and tried to deliver them with spirit – whether mine or God's, I am not sure. However, the moment I stepped into the pulpit I could see that the congregation mostly switched off; they had just done their bit, with the hymns and psalms, and it was now the clergyman's turn to do his. It was obvious that, with rare exceptions, they simply were not listening. I thought of that jingle:

> The colour of our curate's eyes
> I cannot well define;
> For when he prays, he closes his;
> And when he preaches, I close mine.

One of my first series of sermons was 'Abraham, a Man of Faith'. If anyone at St. Cuthbert's needed the faith of Abraham, I certainly did. So I could not wait to hear my next week's sermon! I believe, however, that God's word is always powerful; and it was a joy, over the months, to see the hearts of some within the congregation opening up to God as a flower opens to the sun. A few, I discovered later, had probably found a living faith in Christ many years before, largely through the ministry of the York City Missioner, but had been in deep-freeze for a long time. They had to be brought out of that deep-freeze and given time to thaw before their faith came to life again. Others had never understood the Gospel of Christ. One or two, inevitably, did not want it or could not accept it, and eventually left; but others slowly – very slowly – found the light of Christ penetrating the darkness within them, and they became fine Christians, a vital core of the congregation for many years to come. As in Gillingham and Cambridge, we saw the power of the Gospel of Christ to change the hearts of individuals, even if we had to learn the New Testament truth, that faith and patience go hand in hand.

Anne and I knew, of course, that if God were to do anything among us, time must be given to serious prayer. On my first Sunday I announced that there would be a short meeting for Bible study and prayer at the rectory on Thursday. It was to be held in my study, the one room we had so far decorated. About four or five turned up, one woman with her dog, and to begin with there was no great promise of revival. After giving a short and simple Bible study, I encouraged everyone to pray a few short prayers, and mentioned some needs. I prayed, and there was a long pause; Anne prayed, and there was another long pause. I prayed again, and Anne prayed again. So we all said the Grace and went home. Yet, from those slender beginnings, our Thursday Fellowship became quite the most important event in our church life, without which the Sunday services and everything else would have lacked the vitality of the Holy Spirit. Repeatedly I emphasised to the congregation the absolute importance of those corporate times of study and prayer, and the response eventually was tremendous.

To begin with, however, nothing much seemed to be happening in the parish, and Anne and I felt that God was calling us to a more sustained time of prayer. We had no children at that time, and there were very few meetings, so it was easy for us to do something about it. Every Wednesday we spent most of the day in prayer and fasting as we worshipped God, reading the Scriptures together, praying about everything in the parish, and asking for God's guidance. We knew that in any church there are always 101 good things one can do. But what was God wanting us to do in our church at that time? We kept up those days of prayer for the best part of a year; and during that year, most of the significant developments in the church came from those days. Through them we gained a sense of God's direction for his work.

One immediate concern, of course, was the matter of giving. At my first Church Council Meeting, someone asked if we could hold a Gift Day, to which I responded warmly, saying that I would be in church all day and would ask people to spend a few moments praying as well as giving. Some of the Church Council members, however, thought quite differently. They said that people would be too busy on a Saturday to come into church to pray, with all the weekend shopping to be done; but if I were to stand in my cassock outside the bus-stop near our church shaking a tin in my hand, a few coins might be given. As another suggestion, we could even string a big sheet between two trees, and passers-by could toss a coin or two into it. We might get several pounds that way.

It was, I think, the only time that I resolutely refused to do what the Church Council proposed. I insisted on being in church, inviting people to pray as well as give, and if they were too busy to say even a short prayer I was not very interested in their gifts. God looks first and foremost for the love of our hearts, not the offer of money. If the gift of money, or anything else for that matter, is a genuine expression of our love and thanksgiving to the Lord, it becomes a part of the worship that glorifies him. But nothing can be a substitute for that love-relationship that God wants us to enjoy with him in Jesus Christ.

The Council eventually acquiesced to my ideas after a brief struggle. I do not think that any previous Gift Day had yielded more than about £13. This one yielded £81 which, for that tiny and dispirited congregation, was astronomical! Over the years we never had appeals, and the jumble sales and whist drives soon died a natural death. Each year, on the Sunday before Harvest Thanksgiving, I would preach from the Bible about the principles of giving. The following Friday we would have a special time of prayer, often a half-night of prayer (as well as the Thursday Fellowship), and on both the Saturday and the Sunday people would come with their thank-offerings to the Lord. The following year the total was £214, then £300; £411; £925; £1,037; £1,120; £1,590; £2,115; £3,701; £4,154; £5,109, and so forth. All these were specifically for missionary support, not for the work in York. Throughout the years the weekly offerings steadily rose too, and there were occasional extra Gift Days to meet special expenses caused by the expanding work. The offerings were never what they could or should have been, but the giving of any church is a fair barometer of the spiritual state of that church, a clear evidence of the grace of God flowing among his people. We had much to encourage us, although nothing to leave us complacent.

The first visible breakthrough in the Sunday services came after six months when we held a monthly Family Service in the place of traditional Mattins, and three months later this became our weekly morning service. I had been impressed by the value of family services both in Gillingham and Cambridge, and felt that St. Cuthbert's could benefit from a similar approach. The Family Service is not just a children's service. It is for the whole family, although children play an active part by reading the lesson, helping with the offering, and (a few years later) playing in the orchestra, praying the prayers with the rest of their family, or taking part in a dance, mime or piece of drama. The talks likewise are simple and always with visual aids of one form or another, which hold the attention of all but the youngest children and usually get through to the parents, often with much greater clarity and force than most conventional sermons! The philosophy behind the Family Service is also important. Whereas with the Sunday School one part of the aim is to reach the parents through the children (in practice this very seldom happens, with a huge fall-away of children from the church during the teenage years) with the Family Service the aim is to reach the children through the parents. Thus although many parts of the service are designed with the children in mind, we have always found this service one of the best ways of winning parents for Christ; and once they become Christians there is much more chance of helping the children through that rebellious and questioning teenage phase. We were unashamedly out to see whole families brought to Christ, not just individual boys and girls. With the Family Service, too, in contrast to the Sunday School, children begin to feel a part of the wider family of God's people from a very early age. Children are as much a vital part of the family of God as anyone else, though still young and immature, and need to be welcomed as such.

As soon as the Family Service started we saw many encouragements. At one level, when the first new family joined us, the congregation immediately doubled! With each new family, the growth was excitingly visible. Seventeen years later, the Family Service has naturally developed in various ways, but all through the years it has been a marvellous family occasion which appeals to almost all ages and backgrounds. Countless visitors to the church, especially those from overseas, used to comment that they had never seen anything like it, and were clearly deeply moved by the whole service. Occasionally it could be noisy, but we always had a crèche where little children could be taken at any time, so that others could more easily concentrate on this family act of worship.

The development of any church, however, is far from easy. Traditionally, at least within the Anglican circles, most church-goers regard the church as a club: it is there for the convenience of its members whenever they want to go, but few expect to take a very active part. Most clergy have sadly perpetuated this distortion of the nature of the church. But in the New Testament Church every person, as a member of the Body of Christ, played an indispensable part. With our traditional Anglican heritage, Anne and I began by doing almost everything ourselves. We did have two marvellous weeks in the spring of 1966 decorating the whole church, when many people joined in, and it was like a mission to the congregation: it brought us much closer together. But, apart from that, Anne and I gave all our time and energy to try to build a firm foundation for the future.

The congregation started to grow. After about eight months the local press cautiously commented that 'there was a reasonable chance that St. Cuthbert's would continue, according to a member of the Archbishop of York's Commission on Redundant Churches.' Replying to this I said in my newsletter, 'We praise God that if the Redundancy Commission came to our church on some Sunday nights, they would be hard pressed to find a seat.' We were once picketed by some York University students, protesting about the waste of these empty, redundant church buildings. I noticed that the students engaged in the protest were a little surprised to see streams of families coming into St. Cuthbert's, and when we invited the pickets to join us for the service we had to find extra chairs for them since all the others were occupied!

In January 1966 another major sphere of work for me began to open up: I led my first university mission, at Reading. For twenty-five years successive student committees at Reading had discussed the possibility of a mission, and eventually they decided to hold one. I assumed that by the time they had made their initial plans all the well-known speakers were booked up, so they stumbled on me. The team working with me were equally inexperienced and nervous, and I could see at the pre-mission houseparty that something had to happen if the mission were to make any impact at all. At that houseparty I spoke on the nature of faith and the vital importance of being filled with the Holy Spirit if we were to be effective as witnesses to Christ. I then asked everyone to go back to their rooms and for the next half-hour to seek the power of the Spirit in their own lives. During that half-hour God met with many of the students in a gentle but unmistakable way, and from that moment onwards they went into the mission full of boldness and faith. There were only fifty members in the Christian Union, but with daring faith they put out 120 chairs for the first evening's meeting. Over 300 turned up, and twelve gave their lives to Christ that night. For six nights the mission continued like this, and by the end of the time at least sixty students had found Christ, most of them standing firm as Christians in the months and years ahead. Proportionately it was probably the most fruitful of the eighty or so university missions that I have had the privilege of leading since then.

The cost of these developments in personal terms, however, proved considerable. In our first few months in York Anne suffered a long and deep depression, once again withdrawing into herself and often sleeping for twelve hours or more each night. Whatever were the basic reasons for this depression (exhaustion doubtless being one of them), it was only through a time of prayer and ministry by Michael and Jeanne Harper and others, that the depression was lifted and she was again free.

I, too, had my own problems. Wonderfully I had received a temporary healing from asthma shortly before moving to York. Anne and I had been at a gathering of friends at Gillingham where a remarkable person called Edgar Trout had been ministering. Although some of his work was unorthodox, the power of God was manifestly with him. This gathering of friends unexpectedly turned into a whole night of prayer. During it I was coughing away as usual, and so Edgar decided to anoint me with oil and asked everyone to pray for me. This they all did, and then started to praise God that he had answered their prayer for healing. It was all very fine for them, I thought to myself. They were having a great time of praise, but I was still coughing miserably. It is easy to thank God for healing when you do not have the affliction yourself! At about eight in the morning Anne and I tumbled into bed for a couple of hours, feeling a little discouraged by the night's work, but when I woke up and got dressed I realised that I was no longer coughing. I could walk down the street, even run up the stairs, and still not cough. Thus healed, I was able to enter into all the strenuous work at York without the affliction of asthma.

After the first nine months of demanding physical, mental

and spiritual work, however, the asthma started to return with some severity. It was an extraordinarily worrying time for us both. With the strain of getting the work going in York our relationship had often been tense. We did not really understand each other, since we thought and reacted in such different ways.

It was into that stressful atmosphere that our first child, Fiona, was born, on August 10th, 1966. My attitude then towards family life, and its relation to church work, was typified by my first visit to hospital after Fiona's birth. It was a brief visit, when I hope I said and did all the right things, prayed a short prayer of thanksgiving, patted Fiona gently on the head, gave Anne a little kiss, and then rushed off to lead our Parish Fellowship. 'First things first' had always been my unspoken motto; and for me, at that time and for many years to come, the work of the church came unquestionably before my responsibilities to my family. Since I hardly knew my father before he died, I understood little about fatherhood, and I fear that I have frequently been a poor husband and a worse father. Although Fiona at once brought us a tremendous amount of joy, her arrival caused endless broken nights for nine months or more, which brought Anne to exhaustion once again. This in turn increased my asthma, and (as I saw it) the rapidly growing work of the church was hindered. I had much to learn about God's priorities in life. The apostle Paul wrote that the quality of a man's relationship at home is a major factor in his qualification for Christian ministry.

A major crisis came in January 1967 when I was in Switzerland, without Anne and Fiona, speaking at the winter sports party organised by the Officers' Christian Union. In many ways it was a wonderful time when we saw God powerfully at work in people's lives; but the asthma became increasingly severe, possibly aggravated by the high altitude, and after two or three hopeless nights of total sleeplessness, a decision was made to fly me home a few days before the party was over. When I saw Anne at the railway station, I noticed her look of anxiety, gave her a weak smile but scarcely had the breath to say 'Hallo'. Anne had to push me along the platform as I sat, wheezing and coughing, on a porter's trolley.

Like a madman, as I see it now, I was off the next month to lead another university mission, this time in Trinity College, Dublin; but once again had to leave two days early due to severe asthma. By this time something had to be done. Reluctantly I cancelled another university mission, in Durham, which I had been booked to lead ten days later, as my condition was becoming serious.

Once I was so ill that Anne sent for our doctor in the early hours of the morning. I had been struggling for breath, and was so disorientated through lack of oxygen that I apparently asked Anne, at 3 a.m., if she was my optician! What I thought I was doing in bed with my optician at three in the morning I cannot begin to imagine! Our doctor duly arrived and gave me an injection, but it had no effect whatsoever. I was still gasping for breath. He gave me another injection which eased the situation a little, and he came back first thing in the morning with a consultant to ask for his professional advice. The consultant explained that normally he would send me to hospital straight away, but since Anne was a nurse he was prepared to take the risk of sending the two of us, plus Fiona of course, away from York for three months' convalescence.

As I think about it now, I suppose it was a partial breakdown. Although it was a relief to be away from all responsibilities for a time – I could not think straight about anything – I felt utterly crushed by the apparent implications of it all. The work in York was beginning to be really exciting. St. Cuthbert's Church had been packed out for several Sundays, and we were having to apply for an extension to seating in the church. The Thursday Fellowship had also grown fast, and we were now relaying the Bible study to several rooms in the rectory because so many people wanted to come. The universities, too, had unexpectedly opened up, and God was apparently using me for effective evangelism among students. My first book, on youth work, called *Towards Tomorrow's Church*, had been published and was well received. Everything seemed on the point of blossoming.

As I went away from it all for those three months, depression initially set in. I genuinely thought I would never preach again, never return to the work in York, never lead another mission, never write another book, and never really cope as a husband and father. I felt a complete and total failure in virtually every area of my life. I had come to an end of myself. My natural strength had failed, and I had to release to the Lord all that had become very dear in my heart. It may be that I had come to love the Lord's work more than the Lord himself. Whatever were the spiritual reasons for that painful period, I had to hand back everything I knew to the Lord, and humbly, with empty hands, ask for his mercy, healing and grace. The future was totally uncertain, and all I could hope for was the Lord himself. The one thing I could do during those three months was to spend the time with Anne and Fiona. And that was the best thing possible.

9

St. Cuthbert's – Growth

'Your absence has been such a blessing to us!' was the greeting we received on our return to York. It was good to know that we were not indispensable, and we took that delightfully ambiguous remark as a sign that God had by now established his work in York, at least at a foundational level. Others had taken on the responsibilities and had grown spiritually as a result.

The three months away from York had also been of considerable blessing to us as a family. In spite of all the traumas and tensions Anne and I had known, we still loved each other very much – which is probably why the tensions had been so traumatic. The time we had together, doing nothing except enjoying each other's company and taking constant delight in Fiona, reinforced our love, and in the peacefulness of those weeks my asthma subsided. By the end of our convalescence I was able to think about the work without always provoking another spasm, and I realised, after this period of humbling and chastening, that my work for the Lord had not yet come to an end. In York, in fact, things had only just started.

During 1966 I had preached often about the Person and work of the Holy Spirit, and spoke simply about the spiritual renewal that God was now bringing all over the world. From that time onwards, a growing number within our congregation were not only finding a personal relationship with Christ, but were also consciously being filled with the Spirit. Some were speaking in tongues, mostly in private in their own personal prayer life, but occasionally in public during prayer meetings, providing an 'interpretation' followed.

Some were also beginning to prophesy as they shared what they felt God was saying to us, and we saw immediately how immensely edifying this gift could be in the life of a congregation. It was never a substitute for the regular teaching from the Scriptures, but God could use a simple message to touch the hearts of his people in a remarkably personal way. We could see why the apostle Paul wrote so positively about this gift in 1 Corinthians 14.

We discovered the value of prophecy in evangelism too. A student came to our church one evening, brought by her Christian friend. The student was not a Christian herself, and she was embarrassed to discover that it was a Communion service. Feeling increasingly out of place within that atmosphere of joyful corporate worship, she walked out of the service half-way through. Later, however, she realised that she had left her scarf behind, so she returned when she thought that the service would be over. Since we had come to the end of the administration of the bread and the wine, the girl went up to the front pew to collect her scarf. At that moment there was silence, following a flow of continuous praise, and then two members of the congregation brought words of prophecy that they thought they had received from God. The student wrote to me the next day: 'I heard my actual thoughts in the second prophecy – something I have never heard before. I heard God actually telling me, in a church with hundreds of other people present, not to run as I had done so often before . . . I felt and experienced God's presence – something terrifying yet wonderful.' There and then she surrendered her life to Christ. The apostle Paul once wrote: 'If all prophesy, and an unbeliever or outsider enters, . . . the secrets of his heart are disclosed; and so, falling on his face, he will worship God and declare that God is really among you' (1 Cor. 14:24f). This is exactly what happened with the girl. We had hundreds of instances when God spoke directly to both Christians and non-Christians alike, all with positive results affecting people's lives and drawing them closer to Christ.

We also prayed much for gifts of healing: some were healed, and some were not. The whole ministry of healing left us often puzzled and confused, having to bow before the sovereign purposes of God; and yet when prayer for healing was sensitively handled, there was always a blessing in one form or another. We discovered also the values of the gifts of 'knowledge' and 'wisdom'. Sometimes God gave us by his Spirit an insight into the real and hidden needs of a person who obviously needed God's help, and we were able to get to the heart of the problem quite quickly. During all the years that followed there was never once a split in the congregation over this issue of spiritual gifts.

Many other gifts were developing, too. I was particularly encouraged to see spontaneous gifts of evangelism emerging. People who had found the reality of God in their lives talked naturally to their friends about Christ. Some were brought to the regular 'Guest Services' which we held about six times a year, when we would try to explain, as simply as we could, how anyone could find Christ. Many did. At the first service, only one young schoolgirl responded. She courageously pushed her way through the stream of the congregation as they were leaving the church. She was Pauline Hornby, a York girl, who became a faithful and much-loved member of our congregation for years, later joining my full-time travelling team for four years, before marrying our assistant organist, Andrew Shepherd. At each subsequent Guest Service we saw any number, from three at the least to eighty at the most, outwardly profess faith in Christ, although there were doubtless many more we did not know about at the time. Consequently these Guest Services became well known and popular, and soon they had to be relayed to a nearby hall because St. Cuthbert's, now packed to the doors, could hold no more. Later, a regular closed-circuit television system had to be installed for all the evening services, as the numbers steadily increased. The Family Services, too, had a 'repeat performance' each Sunday morning.

With good New Testament precedent, we had numerous house meetings also. We were aware that a new Christian has many friends, neighbours and colleagues who are not true believers, so that he is in an ideal situation for sharing his faith with them. We found, too, that these friends were interested in hearing more about all this, and were quite willing to come into the informal atmosphere of a home where a speaker would give a short talk, followed often by a lively discussion. It was a marvellous and natural sphere for evangelism, and at most of the many house meetings that were held for this purpose we saw at least one person become a Christian as a result. We felt much the same as St. Luke when he wrote about Samaria 2,000 years ago, 'There was much joy in that city.' It was a time of spontaneous and joyful expansion.

The vision of our church as a resource centre for students was also being fulfilled. Large numbers of students came to us from York University, St. John's College of Education, and other colleges nearby; and over the years a great many students came to Christ as a result, or were strengthened in their faith. We also had a simple hospitality scheme, linking students with families in our congregation wherever possible. Many deep friendships were formed in this way, and students loved getting away from campus life every now and then to spend time, often a Sunday, in ordinary family life. As the work grew we were often able to make one or more of our full-time staff available for counselling students, and naturally we worked closely whenever we could with the chaplains concerned.

In this way we saw ourselves in a serving, supportive role. We did not mean to offer a substitute for Christian fellowship and witness on the campus itself (if students are not committed to the evangelism of students, however tough that might be at times, no one else will be), but it seemed obvious that one or more churches in the city could help student Christians to feel a part of the wider church. Indeed, we specifically sought to help students prepare for the transition from their rather specialised activities at college or university to membership of local churches after they left. It was also possible,

through our ordinary Sunday services, to give students a taste
of worship and of the body of Christ which they could never
have known in the enclosed community on the campus itself.
Many of them were also able to benefit from the regular
preaching they heard, and significantly there were comparatively few tensions in York University, for example, over
some 'charismatic' issues compared with some problems in
other universities. Today it is a constant joy meeting active
Christians in many walks of life – not a few on the mission field
or in the ordained ministry – who first became Christians
during their student days in York, partly at least as a result of
what they had experienced at our church.

The heart of the congregation was also growing in depth
and maturity, although we were still a very young church. The
number at the Parish Fellowship each Thursday was regularly
about 140, filling six rooms to capacity in the rectory. The
Bible study was relayed to the rooms and followed by a time
of prayer within each room. As every mid-week meeting in
the church had to take place in the rectory (there was nowhere
else available), it was not easy for Anne, especially when
Fiona was woken by the constant coming and going, with bells
ringing and doors slamming; but somehow we managed it –
often at the cost of depression for Anne, asthma for me, and
tensions between us.

It would obviously be wrong for me to suggest that, during
those early years, we knew nothing but pain and tears. Our
love for one another was always there, in spite of many stormy
scenes, and we had some hilarious moments as well. With so
many people coming to the rectory each week, we found it
difficult having only one lavatory, and that was up a flight of
stairs. A friend of mine, who was an officer in the army
stationed at Catterick, said that his soldiers were doing
nothing much, and so volunteered a work-party to build us
another lavatory in a downstairs passage. After considerable
difficulty they found the necessary plans showing the position
of the water pipes and drains, and the council's permission
was obtained. The soldiers then dug, through thick clay soil, a
huge trench which wound its way gradually round our home.

By now winter had set in, and with the back door frequently left open as soldiers went to and fro for cups of tea and visits to the one lavatory, the rectory became an ice-box. When the trench was at its largest, all the troops were suddenly posted overseas, and we were left with an impressive moat round our house, which rapidly filled with water and ice. One night an unfortunate tramp actually fell in, becoming covered with wet clay which he then brought into the house. With all the pressures of work, asthma and general inefficiency, I am afraid it was months before I filled the trench in. Few tramps visited us after that, and we waited for almost ten years before our second 'loo' was installed.

My outside speaking engagements were now increasing rapidly, especially in universities; and during the ensuing years I led missions at Cambridge, Oxford, Durham, Southampton, Keele, Sussex, Manchester, Birmingham, Aston, Bangor, Bristol, Leicester, Liverpool, Nottingham, Sheffield, and at various other places, including several universities overseas. Most of these missions proved extraordinarily fruitful, with many hundreds of students finding Christ as a result. Letters kept pouring in. 'I have never known such utter joy and quietness of mind,' said one research student. 'It is like living in a world which suddenly has an extra dimension.' Another wrote, 'I shall never be able to express my gratitude to Christ for the way in which he has become so real and living.' Today it is a constant joy meeting some of those who professed conversion years ago and who are now actively serving Christ in different parts of the world.

Such frequent travelling, however, was an undoubted trial for Anne. Although she knew that it was God's will, which she accepted, each time I went away she experienced a deep sense of rejection and abandonment. This produced tension between us, often for two or three days prior to my departure, so much so that I would often cry in desperation to God on my way to some university, 'O Lord, I'm not sure how much more either Anne or I can take. If you really want me to do this work you will have to give us more grace.'

For Anne, especially, it was a lonely time. With me leading

all the church services and meetings, and often away on other engagements, she was left alone in the rectory with Fiona, missing the fellowship that others were enjoying. I too became anxious because, mainly due to the domestic upheaval which follows the birth of any child, Anne was no longer reading her Bible and praying as she used to – at least not in the regular, disciplined way which had been her pattern in the past, and which was still very much my own. Nevertheless, it was during this period of considerable loneliness and pain that Anne learnt to listen to the Lord, to hear him speak to her. She discovered how to meditate on a word, a phrase, a verse or an aspect of God's character. She found a new way of communicating with the Lord which was not dependent on the regular 'quiet time' of her evangelical heritage. At times she would read her Bible for hours, but at others the Bible was closed for days or even weeks. It was during this period, however, that she began to develop the prophetic ministry that God has especially used to touch the lives of so many people. The irritating thing for me was that despite Anne's haphazard devotional life and my dogged discipline, Anne often seemed much more in touch with Christ than I was! Reluctantly I had to admit (and later to rejoice) that most of the best developments in York over the years came through Anne's prophetic vision, which I had then to work out in my own terms, giving the congregation the necessary biblical teaching for each fresh idea and then leading them in that direction. Invariably, though, it was a direction that Anne had already seen several months, if not years before.

The birth of our second child, Guy, happened in April 1969 in unusual circumstances. We probably got our dates wrong, but according to my diary the child should have been born by about April 8th. Therefore I readily accepted the invitation from a good friend of mine, Dick Lucas, to preach at three of his Tuesday lunch-hour services, on April 15th, 22nd, and 29th. By then Anne and the new baby should have been safely back at home. I was particularly keen to visit again St. Helen's Church in Bishopsgate, London, where Dick Lucas was rector, because of the amazing work among city businessmen that God had developed through him. Although I have now visited a good many cities in many parts of the world I have never seen any comparable work amongst businessmen which has been so thorough and effective. It is truly a remarkable demonstration of the power of God through the straightforward proclamation of his word in the Bible.

I became increasingly apprehensive, however, as April 15th and 22nd came and went, and still no baby had been born. Early in the morning of the 29th it all started to happen. I rang for the midwife, and then dashed for the station to catch the London train since I had to preach my third sermon at St. Helen's that lunch-hour (my priorities still needed a drastic overhaul!). When I arrived at St. Helen's I rang the Maternity Hospital. 'Put the phone down at once,' snapped the nurse at the other end. 'It's all happening right now!' Five minutes before the service was due to start I nervously rang again. 'You have a son, and both are doing fine!' The subject of that sermon had been advertised some weeks before: it was 'The New Birth'! Nonchalantly I said from the pulpit, almost as an aside, 'Ten minutes ago a son was born to me in York.' I was told that the few women present (the church is always packed out with men) ceased to listen to another word, their minds captivated by the thought of that new-born baby. But I could not resist the evangelistic challenge that this provided. 'My wife was three weeks overdue,' I said, not entirely sure of my medical knowledge. 'Had it gone on much longer, it would have been dangerous for her. Some of you, spiritually speaking, are not three weeks overdue. You are thirty to forty years overdue. If you go on much longer it may be dangerous for you. Jesus said that you *must* be born again.' The effect was quite dramatic.

We were obviously overjoyed with Guy's birth and praised God for the gift of a son as well as a daughter. But once again we experienced broken nights for at least nine months, with few exceptions, leading to more exhaustion, more asthma, more tension and further 'interruptions' to the work. Yet through it all God was continuing to bless the church in York and the missions in the universities.

There is always a mysterious and inescapable link between
suffering and blessing. The apostle Paul knew much about
this, and he learnt to be 'content with weaknesses, insults,
hardships, persecutions and calamities; for' he said, 'when I
am weak, then am I strong'. It was when he was weak that the
power of Christ especially rested upon him (2 Cor. 12:7-10).
Indeed he realised that God had actually given him 'a thorn in
the flesh'. No one knows what this was, but most commen-
tators believe that it was some physical handicap. God used it
to keep him weak enough to receive grace for usefulness. He
was promised sufficient grace, 'for my strength is made
perfect in weakness'. I came to view my asthma as a 'thorn in
the flesh'. Like Paul, I asked for it to be removed; but
constantly I have found that God's grace is sufficient in all my
weakness, and his presence has always been evident in any
suffering we have known. Human weakness makes room for
divine grace. Our story is not one of human achievement,
human wisdom, or human greatness, and our church in York
bears testimony to divine grace given during a continuing
experience of weakness, physical and spiritual, out of which
came the joy of new life.

It is sometimes said that whereas God loves us just as we
are, he loves us too much to leave us as we are. J. B. Phillips
once wrote a book called *Your God Is Too Small*. It is a good
title, since most of us have a much too narrow vision of God. I
soon discovered that God was now wanting to expand my own
vision of him in ways that brought me a 'sunshine of surprises'.

10

Widening Vision

A significant milestone in my life came through an international conference for spiritual renewal organised by the Fountain Trust at Guildford in 1971. Michael and Jeanne Harper had courageously sought to encourage renewal within the Church, in spite of considerable misunderstanding and opposition, and Anne and I had already benefited from a number of Fountain Trust conferences they had promoted, as we tried to gain a clearer grasp of what God was doing by his Spirit. The conference at Guildford, based at Surrey University, proved particularly challenging as it was the first time that I found myself, as a speaker, on the same platform as Roman Catholic speakers. Since my conversion, I had come to think that the Roman Catholic Church was an apostate Church: it effectively denied the great Reformation doctrine of 'justification by faith' through its insistence on many religious observances as necessary to salvation; it exalted the Virgin Mary to a position that seemed at times even greater than that of Christ himself; it taught that the bread and wine at the Mass became mystically the body and blood of Christ; it gave Papal infallibility and Roman Catholic dogma an authority equal to that of the New Testament; it undermined the truths of salvation by its teaching about purgatory and by its prayers for the dead. In other words, it preached 'another gospel'; and the apostle Paul once wrote that anyone doing such a thing would be cursed by God! For me, the Roman Catholic Church was virtually synonymous with the anti-Christ: a massive and powerful organisation that had all the form of the Christian religion but was in fact a Satanic conterfeit of the real thing. My 'anti-Rome' attitude was almost akin to that of the most extreme Protestants in Northern Ireland, although I was less vocal about it. Nevertheless I was totally convinced of the truth of my own convictions, although I confess that very rarely did I actually talk to Roman Catholics, and still less did I attempt to listen to what they were saying.

Once or twice in Cambridge I discussed the matter with Dr. Basil Atkinson, whose own attitude towards Catholics was even more colourful than my own. There was always a delightful eccentricity about Basil which could shock those who did not know him at all; but anyone who knew him realised how much he loved the Lord and how much he loved all those who knew Jesus personally, as he manifestly did. Therefore, in spite of his strongly anti-Roman background, I remember Basil once asking me if I thought it were possible for Roman Catholic nuns to be saved. 'Why do you ask?' I replied. 'Because I have just met two nuns who seemed to be radiant for Jesus. It seemed impossible, and yet it was true!' After that day I too met quite a number of Catholic nuns, priests and laity who also gave me the same impression, and I had to do some theological gymnastics to cope with it. However, these were still my own private thoughts, and I had not yet made any public comment about them.

The conference at Guildford was quite another matter. How could I share the same platform with leaders from an apostate Church? And, by so doing, was I not compromising the truths for which many of the Reformers had died? I took the risk, and cautiously engaged in conversation with some of the Catholics present who were theologically articulate. Two facts came home to me. First, they showed me much more love and acceptance than I was able to show them. Second, when we got down to the basic issues – justification by faith, the finished work of Christ on the cross, the place of the Virgin Mary, the doctrine of the Mass, and supreme authority of Scripture – I was quite astonished to find that some of the problems had been purely a question of 'semantics' (using

words in different ways). The more I listened the more I was
impressed by the biblical position that they held. We did not
agree totally about everything; but concerning many essential
elements of the Gospel there seemed little if any difference. I
also realised that some of this had been directly the result of
the renewing work of the Spirit in their own minds and hearts
(the Holy Spirit is always the Spirit of truth), and I felt that
some of the views of those present at this conference were
not typical of official Catholic teaching, at least not before
Vatican II (1963–5). How then could they remain in the
Roman Catholic Church and not demonstrate their new life
in Christ by coming out of it?

As I thought and prayed about this, I felt that God was
saying something to me: 'David, I'm not first and foremost
concerned about your convictions, but I am concerned about
your attitudes. And your attitudes towards those with whom
you do not agree are all wrong. First get your attitudes right,
and then we can talk about your convictions.' I wanted to
protest, because on various important issues I was so sure that
I was right and that others (not only Roman Catholics) were
wrong. But Paul once wrote, 'And if . . . I understand . . . all
knowledge . . . but have not love, I am nothing.' Those words
hit me very powerfully. I began to repent deeply of my
negative, critical attitudes. I confessed my spiritual arrogance. I acknowledged my lack of love towards others,
especially towards professing Christians with whom I did not
agree. The battle was not won overnight – far from it, in fact.
But as I continued to ask the Spirit of God to change my
negative attitudes I found that God was giving me an
altogether new love towards many non-evangelicals, even
Roman Catholics.

What is more, as my attitudes changed, so I began to listen
to people – some of them for the first time. I began to hear
what they really believed, not what I thought they believed. I
discovered vast numbers of true brothers and sisters in Christ
whom I never knew existed. I tried to believe the best about
people instead of always fearing the worst. I learnt that God
had many things to teach me, often through those from

different traditions than my own. I began to see how rich and varied is the world-wide Body of Christ, and I praised God for releasing me from the spiritual blinkers that I had worn for so long. The sovereignty of God, working in different ways amongst different people, was more wonderful than I had ever previously understood. Even passages of Scripture spoke to me in new ways as I tried to fathom a little more the 'depth of the riches and wisdom and knowledge of God'.

All these new impressions were confirmed many times over in the ensuing years, and often I had remarkable times of fellowship with all sorts of people I would never have associated with previously. One unforgettable experience was the Third National Conference on Charismatic Renewal in Ireland, at the Royal Dublin Society Showground, in September 1976. I had gone as the opening speaker, and was amazed to find 6,000 present, of whom 5,000 were Roman Catholic including many hundreds of nuns and priests, and the rest were Protestants of all denominations. It was an incredible conference. I was especially impressed by the God-centred, Christ-centred nature of it all. Every meeting began with a prolonged time of worship; it seemed that the people were not willing to listen to any speaker until they had first fixed their minds and hearts on God himself. It was the Lord whom they wanted to hear, not just some ordinary speaker! Equally obvious was their hunger for God's word: they loved to hear the Scriptures expounded. They were also profoundly aware of the difference between religion and the 'real thing'. It was astonishing for me to hear Roman Catholic priests from the platform saying to this vast crowd: 'It is not enough being born as a Catholic; you need to be born again by the Spirit of God. It is not enough to come to Mass each week; you need to know Jesus Christ as your personal Lord and Saviour.' It was almost like a Billy Graham evangelistic crusade!

Most moving of all was the Service of Reconciliation on the Saturday night. Led by a small group of Protestant and Catholic leaders, we saw, from a good exposition of Ephesians 2, that the cause of our divisions in home, Church and society is always sin in the heart of man. Through simple drama enacted in front of a huge empty cross, we saw that the only place for reconciliation is at the foot of the cross. When we come to the cross, we come not as Protestants or Roman Catholics, but as sinners; and when we put our trust in the one Saviour who died for our sins once for all, God accepts each one of us as 'My son, my daughter', and this means that we should now say to one another, 'My brother, my sister'. We were then all invited to go to anyone within that huge hall, to ask for forgiveness for anything we had said or done in the past that grieved the Spirit of God. I was at once surrounded by a large crowd of nuns and priests asking for forgiveness from me, as a representative Protestant, for things that they had said and done that were not right; and of course I reciprocated. Then we embraced one another as brothers and sisters, experiencing at a deeper level than I had ever known before what it means to be 'one body through the cross'. If we belonged to Christ, we belonged also to one another; and what God has joined together through the death of his own Son, let not man put asunder.

The next day, in obedience to our respective traditions, we separated for the Catholic Mass and the Protestant Eucharist. Most of us were in tears for much of the service because we felt deep within our hearts (I had never experienced this before) the grief that Christ must feel over his torn, lacerated and divided body here on earth. There are over 20,000 registered Christian denominations alone, quite apart from the tensions and divisions within any given denomination or local church. Ever since that conference I have sensed a little of the pain that Christ must always feel when we separate from one another, when in effect we say to him, 'You died to make us one, and we don't care!' Jesus surely weeps for the state of his Body, the Church, on earth today.

I began to speak more openly about the importance of our oneness in Christ, and the urgent need for reconciliation in the Church if we were to have any credible ministry of reconciliation in the world. At the Nottingham Evangelical Anglican Conference (NEAC) in 1977 I gave one of the Bible Readings, speaking on the Mission of the Church from Luke

10. One of my points was the vital importance of unity, and *in that context* I went on to say that 'in many ways the Reformation was one of the greatest tragedies that ever happened to the Church. Martin Luther,' I explained, 'never wanted to split the Church, simply to reform it. We no doubt glory in the biblical truths that were rediscovered at the Reformation (as I certainly do), but from the Reformation onwards the Body of Christ in the world has been torn from limb to limb into hundreds of separate pieces.' When I called the Reformation one of the 'greatest tragedies' in the Church, there was an audible gasp in the conference hall. In the context in which it was said, it was a perfectly fair statement. If only the Church of 1517 had been willing for the reformation that Martin Luther, himself a Roman Catholic monk, had tried to effect, we might never have divided into these thousands of little fragments.

That sentence was inevitably a gift-horse for any journalist: 'David Watson says that the Reformation was the greatest tragedy in the history of the Church!' Taken out of its context it sounded worse than heresy to any warm-blooded Protestant. I had many stinging and condemning letters sent to me from some of my Reformed brethren, and I still receive the occasional one. Some will never forgive me for that remark, and would like to see it inscribed on my tombstone, no doubt! Yet, having repented of my own critical attitudes (and I keep on having to do so), I longed that a new spirit of repentance should come upon the Church. I could see this as an absolute priority before any revival came: 'If my people who are called by my name humble themselves, and pray and seek my face, and turn from their wicked ways, then I will hear from heaven, and will forgive their sin and heal their land' (2 Chron. 7:14). For example, with all the division in Northern Ireland which has perpetuated the violence there for so many years, there can surely be no true healing of relationships until there is first a deep repentance – not just for the sin of violence, but even more for the sin of bitterness which lies at the heart of the troubles there.

The same principle is true wherever we Christians do not

love one another as Christ has loved us, nor welcome one another as Christ has welcomed us, nor forgive one another as Christ has forgiven us. Until we sort out our relationships with one another, our relationship with God is not right; and he waits for us to repent before he can renew us with his Spirit of love and truth.

When I was leading a festival of praise in St. Anne's Cathedral, Belfast, both Protestants and Roman Catholics were warmly invited, and a number of priests and nuns were present. Some rather militant Protestants picketed the service outside the main doors, and handed out tracts to everyone coming in. One of these tracts showed a lot of ants marching towards Rome. They apparently represented us, since we were Protest-ants who had left out the protest in what we were doing. We were therefore only 'ants' heading stupidly in a Popish direction. It was a rather sick joke, except that it was meant to be deadly serious. How much is the spirit of repentance needed among us all!

A further development in my vision of God and his work came in the summer of 1972 when Anne and I left Fiona and Guy with Anne's parents in Cheshire and went for several weeks to North America, on an exchange-of-preaching scheme organised by the British Council of Churches. Among many fascinating experiences, we were particularly struck by the quality of worship that we experienced in an Episcopal church in Virginia. In many respects there was nothing much to write home about: the musicians and singers were not unusually talented. But they had about them a gentle quality of intimate worship which was like a cup of cold water to someone in the desert. It was enormously refreshing. They were obviously singing not just *about* the Lord, but *to* the Lord, and their worship brought a sense of God's presence into the service in a quiet but most effective way.

That was followed shortly afterwards by a morning service at St. Margaret's Community Centre in Vancouver, where the pastor was Bob Birch. Bob was one of those men whom you might not look at twice in the street; there was nothing outwardly impressive about him. But his whole life was totally directed towards Christ, and he was one of the most prayerful and godly men I had ever met. However, what struck us much more than the pastor was the church itself. We had never been anywhere before where we had felt so completely overwhelmed by love. As I looked around that packed church – people were sitting everywhere – I noticed an amazing mixture of ages and backgrounds. All the normal social and cultural barriers were broken down by the love of Christ. Barefoot students in jeans were sitting next to bank managers in pin-stripe suits. And the worship was simply glorious. Everyone seemed totally absorbed in the act of loving Christ through praise and prayer. You could see from their faces that almost all those present were profoundly aware of his living presence in our midst, and once again they were singing *to* the Lord. The service, although non-liturgical, was ordered and dignified; yet at the same time there was a spontaneity and freedom about it so that words of prophecy and singing in tongues seemed perfectly natural and in no way contrived.

The whole hour was broadcast every Sunday through local radio, and calls were coming in all the time from people in need in different parts of Vancouver. Without any fuss, teams would go out immediately to those calls for help, so that the service had an immediacy and relevance about it that was unmistakable. I preached for about twenty minutes and, after another hymn, the service over the radio came to an end. But the congregation in the church went on for another hour or so, with more free worship, praise, prayer and the exercise of spiritual gifts – all of which proved intensely edifying – and then I discovered that I was expected to preach again! Quickly I put a few thoughts together from Ephesians 5, and preached rather clumsily my second sermon. Several people nevertheless came forward for counselling. Then, after the final hymn and benediction, a woman sang exquisitely in a 'tongue', both language and music given by the Holy Spirit, and then sang, equally exquisitely, the interpretation of the tongue. What I found especially moving and humbling was that, in that short sung word in the Spirit, that woman had perfectly summed up what I had been struggling to say in my second twenty-minute sermon! I learnt later that the woman had normally quite an unimpressive voice; but when it was controlled by the Spirit it certainly had a breath of heaven about it. As Anne and I left that church we felt that if God was anywhere on the face of this earth, he surely was in that service that morning.

Through those fleeting experiences in Virginia and Vancouver, God increased my vision to an altogether new understanding of worship, and gave me a fresh glimpse of the body of Christ in action. Up to that point, I was beginning to think that we had now 'arrived' at St. Cuthbert's, because the work had been developing so rapidly. Now I knew that we had so much more to learn, and I was thrilled with the prospects of new horizons opening up. An official report on our church commented: 'Members of the congregation noticed a much more liberated minister when he returned to St. Cuthbert's, and there was greater freedom, joy and spontaneity in worship . . . Praise became the dominant note.' It was not that we had lessened our biblical teaching – far from it. However we were giving a lot of positive teaching about the primacy and nature of worship. I had seen, almost as if it were for the first time, the rich variety of worship mentioned in the psalms. I realised, too, how straitjacketed we had become with our stilted, formal services, or with our hearty evangelical hymns. How little we understood about adoration in worship! How stiff we were in any bodily expression! In the Anglican church we were used to kneeling, as a posture symbolising reverence and humility. But how inhibited we were when it came to clapping, raising hands or dancing. Even as a 'much more liberated minister' I was still quite a long way from all that. At the Guildford conference Michael Harper had tried to encourage us to lift up our hands in praise to the Lord, but inwardly I replied 'Not on your life!' Since I was standing next to the Dean of the Cathedral I told myself that I would not raise my hands anyway, so as not to embarrass him; but I was the one who was irritated by this un-English display of religious fervour. Yet it was a problem which hardly anyone else at the conference seemed to have!

All this fresh stimulus was preparing us for a major step

forward in God's will for us. Numerically by 1971 we had reached saturation-point at St. Cuthbert's. We packed over 200 into our small building – sometimes even more – and anyone who wished to get a seat in the main building for the evening service had to come at least forty-five minutes early; after that it meant a closed-circuit television relay to two large rooms in another building fifty yards away. But for Guest Services especially we had to extend our facilities by arranging for a sound relay to a third building. It was marvellous to see the crowds pouring in and out, but now we also began to hear of those who were no longer coming because there was simply not enough room. We prayed for guidance.

11

St. Michael-le-Belfrey, York

A letter arrived one morning from a friend asking why on
earth the Diocese had not offered me St. Michael-le-Belfrey
Church, just opposite York Minster. St. Michael's was
almost three times the size of St. Cuthbert's, almost empty
and all but redundant. Plans for making it redundant had
been completed after two years of hard work, and the documents were just waiting for the Archbishop's signature.
Rather like St. Cuthbert's, St. Michael's was also destined to
become a museum, this time for the Minster.

Two or three years before, I had tentatively approached
various Diocesan officials about the possibility of moving into
St. Michael's, but had been given a polite but firm refusal. If
the idea was right, the timing was wrong. But now, through
the excellent work of the Archdeacon of York, the Venerable
Leslie Stanbridge, backed strongly by Morris Maddocks, the
Bishop of Selby, and Donald Coggan, the Archbishop of
York, a provisional experimental scheme of moving the
congregation from St. Cuthbert's to St. Michael's went
through within two months – it must have broken all records
in the Church of England! On January 1st, 1973 we moved our
Sunday services from one building to the other. This was to
prove much more significant than we could possibly have
imagined at the time.

One month before that, however, there was another unusual development. I had been waiting for a train at York
station one day, when a good friend of mine, a member of our
congregation, said, 'David, have you ever thought of holding

our Guest Services in York Minster?' To be honest, the idea had never even crossed my mind. I knew that we were packed out at both the church and the relay rooms, but St. Cuthbert's was really a very small building and the Minster was the biggest Gothic cathedral in the world. Even with our Guest Service congregation of about 700, we would be lost in the Minster. Nevertheless, encouraged by this friend, I approached one or two of the Minster canons to discover their reactions. The Minster had recently gone through extensive works, costing about £3 million, when its crumbling foundations were strengthened, a magnificent undercroft opened, the exterior cleaned and the interior decorated. It was now a superb sight, probably in a finer state of glory than it had ever been in its long history. At the Rededication Service of the Minster, after all the repairs and cleaning had finished, the Archbishop of York said that he hoped the building would not just be a monument but the very gate to heaven to thousands who came within its walls.

The Minster clergy I talked to were surprisingly positive about my strange enquiry, and they agreed that we could organise an Advent Guest Service in the Minster on December 3rd. They gave me every possible help in planning this. At times I was afraid that we had attempted an impossible task, and that at least half of the huge nave would be quite empty. However, the media got hold of this extraordinary idea of a tiny parish church holding its service in the vast Minster, and there was a fair amount of free and unexpected publicity from the press, radio and television. The result was that the Minster was not only full to its seating capacity, but extra chairs were rapidly brought in, and many were sitting on kneelers on the floor. It turned out to be a most wonderful service, and that night many gave their lives to Christ.

The Minster clergy seemed just as delighted as we were; and thus encouraged by them, we began a series of Minster services (about six a year), to which coach parties would come from a wide area. Many clergy and ministers closed down their evening services in country areas, and brought most of their congregations with them. It is hard to know quite why they came, but the services had a popular appeal, both in the themes we took and in the way in which those themes were developed. We taught explicitly from the Bible, trying to relate its message to the obvious issues of the day; and we set the teaching in the context of joyful worship, led not only by the organ but also by a singing group accompanied by a variety of instruments. Later our worship was often interpreted by dance, and my sermons were illustrated by drama. We erected a large stage half-way down one side of the long central nave, and arranged all the chairs around the stage, so that there was much better visual contact with everyone in the congregation. Jesus once described the kingdom of heaven in terms of a sumptuous marriage feast, something enormously attractive to hungry people: 'Come, all is now ready!' The great Jewish festivals had been times of marvellous celebration, marked by colour and music and singing and dancing, as the mighty acts of God were retold. It is in this depressing age of today that the Christian Church learns again how to celebrate, so that we not only talk about the magnificent banquet of the Gospel but let people experience it through the joyful and festive context in which the Gospel is proclaimed. Can this really be conveyed by a procession of clergy at the start of a cathedral service? Often this resembles more the awkward shuffling of grim-faced penguins! Why not recapture some of the colourful drama of those superb Jewish festivals, knowing that their hopes and expectations were now fulfilled in Christ? I can easily understand why the psalmist said, 'I was glad when they said unto me, Let us go to the house of the Lord' – it was such a glorious occasion. As we attempted to set the jewel of Christ in the crown of celebration, we found that many wanted to be there. All those special Minster services were occasions of much mutual encouragement, and many hundreds came to a personal knowledge of Christ. It exceeded all our possible expectations, and also gave us an excellent relationship with the clergy of the Minster, which was most important now that we had become immediate neighbours.

We had begun to see, too, that the timing of our move to St.

Michael-le-Belfrey was just right. Not only was the building saved at the last moment from becoming redundant (which in itself would have been a negative witness to the relevance of the Christian faith for today), but the style and setting of the building was utterly appropriate to the next phase of God's work amongst us. In St. Cuthbert's we were out on a limb, experimenting freely with services, largely doing our own thing (trying hard to be meaningful), but paying only lip-service to the Anglican liturgy. In St. Michael-le-Belfrey, however, we were at the heart of a famous city, next to a famous Minster and under the gracious but eagle eye of a famous Archbishop.

Once the costly job of cleaning, decorating and rewiring the building had been finished, we gradually became aware of the new responsibilities that God had given us. York is a tourist city, attracting each year about two and a half million visitors from all over the world, and all of them, with hardly an exception, came to our very doorstep to look at the Minster. Added to that, the growth of God's work amongst us was beginning to be known throughout Great Britain and further afield, and we found an increasing number of visitors joining us for our Sunday services. When members of our own congregation were away on holiday in August, as many as eighty per cent of the 700 present could be visitors.

We saw the responsibility of all this in two complementary ways. First, if the renewing work of the Spirit is of any significance at all, it must be worked out within the mainline denominations. In Ezekiel's vision of the valley of the dry bones, when the wind of the Spirit came, the bones were not blown away as being dead and useless. God could have done that, and created new people in their place. In fact, however, the bones came together, were clothed with flesh, and God breathed his life into them. I was (and still am) convinced that God's purpose is to renew the dry bones of existing Christian traditions, and we should not try to bypass them in favour of something more immediately exciting. It always saddens me when I see Christians leave their denominations to join a new independent church; it is precisely in this way that all the

20,800 denominations in the world today came into being in the first place. Jesus weeps over our self-destructive divisions, which only help to deny the Gospel that we try to preach. In St. Michael's, therefore, we became more consciously Anglican, even though my work was becoming increasingly ecumenical. If the renewal of the Spirit had no place in the Anglican tradition (or in any other mainline tradition), it was of no value at all. So we adopted the new Anglican liturgies since these represented the liturgical renewal of various Christian traditions around the world. We did not want St. Michael's to have an independent identity all of its own. We were not out to build our own empire, with our own order of service different from everyone else. We were a tiny part of the 'one holy catholic and apostolic Church' and felt it important to maintain a clear visible identity with that Church. When the Archbishop came, for example, we did not have suddenly to change our pattern of service; it was just the same format as anyone else might find on any Sunday in the year, with rare exceptions. Only as we came clearly under the authority of the Church could we be of any service to the Church. In fact, the more we willingly and gladly submitted ourselves to those over us in the Lord, the more the blessing of God seemed to be upon us.

Secondly, together with this important development, we learned to discover 'freedom within form'. Once we accepted the form of the Anglican liturgy as our basic identity (everyone has some identifiable form, even the most 'independent' churches), we found that there is plenty of freedom within that form. For example, in this latter part of the twentieth century we should not be tied only to the hymns and music of the eighteenth and nineteenth centuries. Some of those hymns are almost timeless, but many songs and hymns are being written now to express the life of the Spirit in today's Church. Through the marvellous ministry of the Fisherfolk we learned the combination of dignity and joy, depth and simplicity, quality and gentleness, spiritual sensitivity and artistic skill. Countless people today are hurting, often because of the pain of broken relationships; but through the gentleness of worship the Spirit of God can touch and heal those inner wounds. When members of our own congregation later began to write and compose songs, we found that the songs that had that special quality of tenderness about them usually were born out of suffering and tears.

It was in St. Michael's, too, that we learned about the more visual expressions of worship and communication of the Gospel. Most traditional church buildings make drama, mime or dance virtually impossible. Narrow chancels, restricting choir pews, massive pulpits or huge pillars eliminate all but the preacher and choir. It was just the same in St. Michael's; but a careful inspection of the choir pews (by me) revealed some woodworm. Admittedly there was not a lot, but enough to cause us to rip them out altogether, leaving a marvellous space between the front pews and the communion rails – a space that we subsequently used to considerable advantage every Sunday. During a visit to Christchurch Cathedral in New Zealand, I was particularly impressed by a simple design for a large stage which enabled the structure to be erected or dismantled within a matter of minutes. The Dean of Christchurch kindly gave me a copy of the design, and we built a similar one ourselves. It was, and is, in constant use as we began to learn about relevant communication for the world of today, still holding firm to the traditions of the Church to which we belonged.

During this time of settling into St. Michael's, the small congregation that had kept the church from closing needed much grace to welcome the hundreds who came from St. Cuthbert's. It was not easy for them. In spite of being true to the basic Anglican liturgy, the style of music, worship and most other things were clearly different. A few of the original congregation stayed, including Peter Gibson, one of the church-wardens and the Minster glazier, a world expert on stained glass. Peter soon won everyone's affection by his wise diplomacy, a humble serving spirit and a great sense of humour. But others found the crowds and changes difficult and found a quieter home in the Minster. This was sad, but quite understandable. Journalists occasionally tried to draw out from me unfavourable comments about the Minster services since their style was obviously much more formal than our own. Always I resisted this. I refused to say – or even think – that we were right and they were wrong. Their style of worship was no doubt just as valid, but it was mostly for more traditional Anglicans. We were attempting to make the same basic traditions live for those with little or no church background, but who had become spiritually alive in Jesus Christ.

Over the years we had seen many individuals and families brought to Christ and filled with the Spirit. My short visit with Anne to North America, however, had given us an altogether new understanding of worship and of the Body of Christ; and I began to be aware that we had much more to learn in both these directions before we could share more widely anything significant about the renewal of the Church.

Of course, it is one thing to have a vision of all this, and quite another to work out how that vision could possibly be implemented. In many churches, some of the desired gifts seem either to be absent or not yet developed; and anyway those who may be gifted in certain ways are usually far too busy to give more than a very limited part of their time to the work and mission of the Church. We had to discover ways of releasing men and women for the work to which God might be calling them.

12

The Growth of Community

'I think we ought to share our home with others,' Anne said to me one day.

'We've done that already,' I replied defensively. 'All sorts of people have stayed in our house for longer or shorter periods. We've hardly been on our own since we moved to York.'

'Yes, but they've only been lodgers, such as those university students, or close friends. There are so many others whose primary problem is loneliness, who need to belong to a family. And anyway, we must learn to share our lives together if we're ever truly going to be the Body of Christ.'

I was slowly discovering that Anne had a visionary and prophetic ministry, although I usually questioned it very carefully. With some hesitation I agreed to open our home, a little at a time, to those who were willing to come not as lodgers, but as part of what soon became a community. Anne's vision was much wider than she initially revealed. She felt that a community of shared lives would deepen the sense of community throughout the whole church, even though the majority of our congregation would not adopt this lifestyle. We had the obvious model of the early church who had 'all things in common', and the strength and credibility of their witness lay largely in the quality of their corporate life together. 'See how these Christians love one another!' was the cry of the pagan observer.

Anne also saw that extended households could considerably facilitate ministries within the Church. The cry of most churches is lack of money and shortage of manpower (or personpower, to be non-sexist!). Most churches cannot get anything like the workers they could use, and, even if they could find the personnel, they could never pay for them. However, by sharing our homes and possessions, we could release both money and people for the work of the kingdom of God.

It was fascinating to see, in the following years, that both these visions which Anne saw so clearly were fulfilled beyond anything that we had imagined possible when we took our first faltering and feeble steps.

To begin with we had little concept of who should join our family. They just came. The first was a girl with a long history of mental instability, who had for many years defeated the care of doctors and psychiatrists. For almost two years she became a marvellous member of our household, opening up our closed lives towards others in need, welcoming everyone with great enthusiasm and cheerfulness, teaching Anne to cater for the large numbers who rapidly filled our house, and dealing swiftly and firmly with those who had just come off drugs but who were secretly trying to pursue the habit. She had at least one girl down to the hospital in no time at all to have her stomach washed out. As much as we loved her, however, we were unable to help her beyond a certain point, partly owing to her natural strength of personality; and very sadly I had to ask her to leave, and return to her own home. I felt a terrible sense of failure, which haunted me for months afterwards, especially when we heard indirectly that she had been going through some rough times. It was an early and painful lesson that not all community living is 'successful', and before long we had to clarify our aims: did God want us to concentrate on those who had special personal problems, or what?

Others came for a whole variety of reasons. Andrew Maries, a gifted musician who later became our Musical Director, originally brought his washing round for Anne to do, at her suggestion, and stayed for a number of meals. He was living a typical bachelor's existence. Before long it was a

natural progression that he should join us. For several months
I found that he irritated me beyond measure, and no doubt I
did the same for him. Temperamentally we seemed such
opposites, and everything he said and did drew out the worst
in me. I found that community life is not always easy, partly
because in the pressure of sharing our lives together we begin
to see ourselves as we really are, not as we fondly imagine
ourselves to be. Always the Lord is concerned not so much
with the situation, however trying or irritating it may be, but
with our reaction to that situation. 'Lord,' I said, 'I'm not sure
I can stand having Andrew in our house much longer. If you
want him to stay here, you must do something about it.' I am
not sure what God did about it, or how, but I do know that
Andrew stayed in our household for seven years and soon
became one of our closest friends. We felt almost bereaved
when he moved out to marry Alicia, although of course in
another sense we were thrilled to see the two of them come
together. Alicia had been a member of our household for
three years, before moving out to become a District Midwife,
and we had all been extremely fond of her.

Another aim of the extended household was so to develop
the reality of brotherhood in the Church that single people
should not have to spend much of their time wishing and
waiting to get married. In today's society there is such a
pressure on a single person to be married, or at least to enter
into a sexual relationship with someone, that the disappoint-
ments and scars of broken relationships are to be seen everywhere. Jesus, however, called men and women into a new
society where they could be first and foremost brothers and
sisters in the family of God. Marriage is certainly a gift of
God, and to be held in honour by all; but Christ wants us to
enjoy a depth of relationship with one another that is not
always leading towards a sexual union. Many who enjoy
community life find depths of commitment with other people
that can release them from the trap of thinking only in terms
of marriage or sex. However, within those deeply committed
relationships of love and service, we are always delighted
when two people eventually get married, especially when

they have worked through some of the pressures and problems of a single life in today's permissive society.

It was also a joy to see the rapid growth into maturity that Andrew found during his time with us. As Musical Director he now shows a quality and sensitivity which might not have been there apart from all the blessings and traumas of community life. Through his musical leadership many discover in St. Michael's a gentleness in worship, speaking of joy through pain, that they do not easily find in other places. I can see that just as God rubbed off some of my rough edges through my early abrasive encounters with Andrew (and others!), so God may have used both the riches and tensions of living in an extended household to increase his work of grace in Andrew, whom he was preparing as a worship leader to encourage many churches throughout this country.

Others joined our household for shorter or longer periods of time – the shortest was three months, I think – and our roomy Victorian rectory usually had ten or twelve people living in it, our nuclear family being just four. One girl had only recently left the drug scene, and she had to go before too long, as she needed more specialised care than we could give her. However, our children were especially fond of her during her short stay, and it was with immense sadness that we learnt several years later that she had committed suicide. We had to learn humbly that we could not do everything, and that our ministry within the household had definite limitations. We also had to be willing for people to be with us only for a time – perhaps for quite a short time – and then to let people go peacefully out of our household to some other place. This we found quite difficult, and sadly when one or two people left, our relationships with them afterwards were strained, or even non-existent. This was not right, and we had to learn both how to welcome people and how to release people. Several communities find this difficult. Anyway, for many years there was a lot of coming and going, and beds and other furniture were constantly being moved from one room to another.

'Will you go and see a girl called Teresa?' asked a Roman Catholic sister, who had become a dear friend of ours. 'Teresa comes from an impossible home situation, has absolutely no faith, and has just attempted suicide. She is in a mental hospital, and yet she is a bright sixteen-year-old with quite a future. She simply needs a family.' I went to the hospital with another household member to see Teresa, and it was clear to us immediately that she needed to get out of that hospital as soon as possible and find a home. We took her home with us. Her whole life needed sorting out, but most of all she needed to be loved. Within the growing sense of God's family in our house, Terri soon gave her life to Christ, went back to the Roman Catholic Convent in York to continue her studies, and became a delightful member of our household. Naturally Terri had her difficulties; but it brought us immense joy to see her successful in her exams, going to Stirling University, getting married from our house (we were effectively her family), having a child, and more recently settling in South America as a healthy wife and mother, with a strong Christian commitment. Anne had virtually become Terri's adopted mother – and sister in Christ – and we maintain strong links with her to this day. This was one of many encouragements when we saw the healing power of God's love coming through a community of his people.

For the first two years, this new way of living seemed to threaten many in our church, and we felt distinct opposition. It may have been partly because our relationships within the household became unusually deep, as we related to one another as brothers and sisters in Christ, and possibly others in the church were jealous of the special relationship that some had with 'the rector and his wife'. But I suspect that the opening of our home in this way was an inevitable challenge to those who naturally valued the privacy of their own family life. We had taken great care not to press this way of living on to others, but had taught that it was *one* valid way of expressing Christian community – not the only, and not necessarily the best. I fully understood the sense of threat that many felt, however much we tried to avoid putting pressure on other families to follow suit. I found the exercise extremely difficult myself. 'An Englishman's home is his castle' is the old saying, and I was startled to find out how deep this cultural trait went. To begin with I resented others treating my furniture, my possessions, my money, my car, and sometimes even my clothes, as if they were their own. After our first four months, when I was still very unsure whether or not we were doing the right thing, I went to New Zealand for eight weeks, and at the end of that time I was naturally longing to see again Anne, Fiona and Guy – but not so keen on having to see the rest of the household (three or four others at that stage). On my return, I found a practical joke waiting for me. Knowing that I was every inch a typical Englishman who valued his privacy, they put up three camp beds in my study, and strewed with deliberate untidyness, pyjamas and clothes all over my little sanctuary! I was not amused! Indeed after a journey of some thirty-six hours I was exhausted and disorientated, and the little joke threw me into depression for a few days. Fortunately Betty Pulkingham and the Fisherfolk came to stay with us the day after I returned (with people sleeping everywhere in our house – except in my study), and Betty, with her wisdom and experience, told the household in no uncertain terms that they should never do that again when I returned home from a tour. Apparently a group had done something similar to Graham Pulkingham, then rector of the Church of the Redeemer, Houston, Texas, shortly after they had adopted this community style of living, with equally unfortunate results. We all had much to learn.

We soon found that some clear structure was essential to keep everyone from just 'doing his own thing'. We knew that prayer must be the basis of our household, and almost the only time we could meet regularly together was at 7 a.m., when we would spend about thirty minutes sharing together from the Scriptures and praying for one another and for the needs of that day. It was not always easy to maintain this discipline, but we all recognised the importance of it, so kept each other to this commitment. Usually one of the household would make notes of each person's sharing, and then summarise what it seemed that God was saying to us that day. We often found this helpful, and, as a by-product, it encouraged

all of us to read our Bibles on our own in order to have
something fresh to share each morning. We also had lists of
household duties, with everyone on washing-up rotas, etc.
Each person had also an individual assignment: mine was the
simple task of carrying out the dustbins!

Although Anne and I exercised joint headship over the
household, and to that extent were 'house parents', we
worked hard on developing the brother–sister relationship, so
that everyone had the freedom to 'speak the truth in love'. I
sometimes found it difficult and humbling being rebuked by
someone half my age; but the rebuke was usually justified,
and I learnt to take as well as give. Once a week to begin with
(less often later on) we had a household meeting in the
evening, when we would share together at greater length,
raise anything on our minds, even if these were points of
criticism or irritation, and then pray together, often ministering to one another at the same time. Occasionally these were
very painful sessions when some home-truths would be spelt
out, ending perhaps in tears; but it was through these times
that we learnt a lot about ourselves, and the Spirit of God was
able to heal areas of our lives that needed sorting out.

In spite of the threat that we posed to some members of our
church, the obvious value of the household became impressive for several families and individuals; and after two years of
being on our own, six or seven other households emerged,
with families moving in together, or single people joining a
nuclear family, or widows, widowers, or solo parents moving
in to find a larger family to which they could belong. We spent
much of our time trying to encourage and guide them,
although some of them were not successful. There are many
pitfalls in this way of living, and there were so many principles
we were having to learn the hard way that we increasingly
discouraged enthusiastic couples in other places from following our example. Although we did not always keep rigidly to
this, we saw the wisdom of inviting a person to join us for a
'probationary period' of three to six months before they made
a more definite commitment. During that time we would all
sense whether or not that person would be suitable for this

particular way of life, which we knew was not for everyone. We also made quite clear the priorities of household living. First, everyone must support the ministry of that house, which in our case included several growing ministries in St. Michael's, as well as my own wider work. Second, everyone must support the children, and see them as young but vital members of the household. Third, everyone must support one another, expressing this by serving each other in practical and specific ways. Then, if there was any energy left, they could look after their own interests!

The experience, which lasted for several years in York, was frankly mixed, with much pain. But through it all, quite a few people were significantly healed in various areas of their lives, the sense of fellowship within the whole congregation considerably deepened, money and possessions were much more readily shared, and several new and fruitful ministries within the church were created. For about five years, when these households were in existence, we were aware of God's presence among us in unusual ways, and many visitors to our church from all over the world spoke spontaneously about the striking quality of love and joy that they experienced within the whole congregation. Although most of these visitors spoke warmly about the worship, preaching, or whatever, the most impressive factor mentioned again and again was the experience of the living Body of Christ. We ourselves at that time might have been most conscious of pain and tears; but through our own profound and felt weakness, the grace of God was even more clearly seen.

A friend of mine, Ken Gullickson, pastor of The Vineyard, Whittier, Los Angeles, once said that our ability to minister is most effective through brokenness, when we are weak, vulnerable and hurting. This creates, he said, a sensitivity to the voice of God and to the needs of others. Nobody wants naturally to be 'weak, vulnerable and hurting'. However, it is in the opening of our lives to one another, as well as to the Lord, that this is often effected. Naturally we all like to be strong, self-confident and self-contained. It was our experience through household living especially, as well as in other ways of course, that God broke our natural strength and made us extremely vulnerable; and in this way, *his* life and joy were manifested – which others were quick to appreciate. When, through our hurts, we pulled back from this vulnerability and closed our hearts a little to each other (and to God as well) because of the pain of it all, the sense of God's presence among us was not so obvious. If we want to know 'the power of Christ's resurrection' in our midst, we must also be willing to accept 'the fellowship of his sufferings' (Phil. 3:10).

To begin with in our household, everyone paid what they could. Some paid nothing at all, since they had nothing to offer; others, with reasonable salaries as a nurse or a teacher (nothing much to shout about admittedly!), gave more than was necessary for their own keep. In this way we were able to support those who had no other means of support. When two other friends joined us, however, they gently challenged Anne and me about the question of finance. If we were really trying to share our lives together, why not share our money as well, to the extent of no one having a private bank account of his own. Instead we could have a 'common purse', a household account, into which all earnings went, and out of which everyone received exactly the same pocket money. From this, we would have to buy all our clothes, presents (for birthdays and Christmas), and other personal items, such as chocolates, perfumes, or little luxuries. It seemed a natural extension of our lifestyle, and we shared the idea with our bank manager, who was puzzled, slightly impressed (I think) and encouraging. For several years we worked on this principle, and it became a vital means of release, for me at any rate, from the constant desire to possess. Covetousness is perhaps our greatest sin, and also the root of all evil. Community living is not the only way to guard against this, of course, but it proved extremely helpful for many of us adopting this way of life.

Our children had more limited pocket money, but the rest of us received £3 a week, out of which we had to get everything that was not supplied by the household account as basic necessities for life. This meant that I started hunting round Oxfam shops for clothes, which for a rector in his early forties was perhaps a bit unusual. I picked up a few marvellous bargains, some of which I am still using. Otherwise it meant saving up for weeks before buying a pair of shoes. It also meant choosing presents with great care, and those who had time would make their own Christmas and birthday presents, trusting the inspiration of the Spirit, often with much greater satisfaction all round than going into a shop and buying something extremely expensive and possibly unwanted by the recipient. We also tried to eat less, to buy in bulk and choose carefully. We cut out altogether the expense of meals in restaurants, and learnt to celebrate birthdays and festivals at home. These were often marvellous occasions. It is surprising how creative a small community can be!

At the same time, we attempted in some small measure (and we knew that it was only a pathetic gesture) to identify ourselves with the poor in this world. We gave a lot of money for the relief of the poor and for the work of the Church. We were also able, through this shared life and common purse, to release several members of the household for full-time work in St. Michael's. For some time there were only three wage earners in our house, including me, but five full-time workers in the church, entirely supported by the household. Without this means of support, some of the most significant developments in and from the church, which I shall describe in the next two chapters, might never have come into being. For several years there were more than thirty full-time workers in the church, many of them living simply by sharing in these small communities. Some of these workers were developing new ministries; others were lay-pastors, secretaries, youth workers and so forth. In other words, the households, beginning with our own, rapidly became the facilitating ministries that Anne had foreseen, benefiting not only St. Michael's, but the wider Church too.

Naturally there were real problems. Our respective parents found it difficult visiting us in such a full house, and hard sharing us with so many others, as the congregation had also experienced. Our Christmas gifts for them, too, were a little meagre to begin with, compared with previous years, until we started to think through the continued importance of family relationships. Our children responded well to all the new additions to the family, but initially we made the mistake of having too many disturbed people in our home at one time. Indeed, many believe it to be a basic principle that you should have no really disturbed person in your house, if you can help it, when your children are under twelve years of age, as ours were. Thus the time we spent on other members of our house began to tell on our children; and one day my son's grandfather saw him put a few pennies into a box. 'What are you doing with those?' he asked. Guy replied, 'I'm saving up enough money so that we can buy a house where Mummy, Daddy, Fiona and I can live *by ourselves*!' It was amusing, and yet that little remark touched our hearts, and the message got through. However, there were obvious benefits, too. It was other members of our household who gave Fiona some musical skills, and who encouraged her in her work, particularly maths, physics and chemistry, which she is now doing for her A levels. It was others who helped Guy with practical projects in our workshop, and assisted him with his homework. The sharing of our lives with others was by no means all negative, even as far as our family was concerned. I suspect, too, that both our children learnt to relate to others better as a result.

The most serious tensions came in our own marriage. We nearly did not make it at all; and it took us some time before we found anything like the right balance between the special relationship within marriage, and the strong brother–sister relationships we were trying to deepen within the household. Not a few crises developed, and it really seemed that our marriage would fall apart altogether on several occasions. I felt torn in various directions, and began to suffer from quite deep depression, which has afflicted me from time to time since then. None of these problems can be blamed on the 'community lifestyle', but only on the sin in our own hearts. It was especially painful for me (and I suspect for others too) to find that sin was such a reality and not just a theological issue, and that, for all my supposed spiritual maturity, I was as weak as any other person, but for the grace of God.

Miraculously God's grace won through. After numerous agonising experiences, and with the wise, patient counsel of some good friends, especially David and Jean Smith (elders in our church), Anne and I came through to a richer and deeper relationship than we had ever known since our wedding. Once we had passed through such storms, when everything seemed to be collapsing around our ears, we discovered a new and stronger commitment than we had ever known before. We learnt to be much more open to one another, sharing quickly anything that might cause unspoken tensions. Although our eight years in an extended household were sometimes incredibly painful, we now see that, through the tears, God was refining and healing us, and we have both been enriched by that testing time. Also, they were years of such fruitfulness, both in the lives of many individuals and in the life of the church, that I am sure we would do it all over again. It was a period of humbling and chastening, and vital lessons were learnt that I doubt I could have known in any other way; and both Anne and I feel we have become more whole people as a result. We are therefore immensely grateful to all those who shared with us over the years: for loving us, forgiving us, correcting us, being patient with us, and revealing to us something more of Christ. In its own peculiar way, it was perhaps the most important period of our life.

Part of the difficulty of this lifestyle is that you feel as though you are living in a shop-window. When there are problems, everyone knows about them immediately. Those who remained cautious, if not critical of the extended households used to say, 'When you think of households, you think of problems!' But there are often just as many problems within nuclear families (see the enormous tragedy of broken homes today), but not everyone knows about them in the early stages. It all takes place behind closed doors. In an extended household, however, you have to be open since there is not much that you can hide. 'It is not convenient,' said a friend of mine, 'but it is fruitful!' Throughout those years of living in this way, I discovered a quality and depth of relationships in Christ beyond anything I had ever known before. I still have a profound love for all those who lived with us, and I shall always feel a family affinity with them beyond the ordinary levels of Christian fellowship.

Together with moments of great pain, we also had plenty of fun and great joy. We joined together in Israeli dances on the rectory lawn; we went to the sea together and walked on the Yorkshire Moors together. Even the animals felt part of our life: we had a cat, a dog, a rabbit and two budgies! When a bishop came to preach in St. Michael's he joined us for tea in the rectory first. We left him to finish his sermon while most of us went off to church to prepare for the service. When the Bishop went upstairs to go to the bathroom our dog Sam protested noisily. Sam could look alarmingly fierce; so the Bishop fled from the house, accidentally dropping his sermon notes in the process. Fortunately they were discovered before he got into the pulpit.

The rich sharing of lives together in Christ is what I remember most clearly about those years of extended household living. The apostle Paul once wrote to those at Thessalonica, 'We loved you dearly – so dearly that we gave you not only God's message, but our own lives too' (I Thess. 2:8, Living Bible). Such sentiments became a living reality during those years.

Jeff Schiffmeyer, the present rector of the Church of the Redeemer, Houston, Texas, once said that 'the effectiveness of our ministry depends on the fervency of our love for one another'. The experience of shared relationships in Christ proved exceptionally creative in the life of our church, and from this stemmed a number of strategic ministries that God, in his mercy and grace, has used in various parts of the world.

13

Creative Arts

I had been at a student leaders' conference for four days, and my mind was beginning to reel with all the talking and studying that we had done. Intellectually it had been valuable, but spiritually I was feeling distinctly dry, and it was obvious that I was not the only one. I approached the leader of the conference: 'We've been here for four days, and yet we haven't once really worshipped God.' He readily agreed, and announced that there would be half an hour of hymn singing before the next session. My heart sank! Yet that had been my own perspective for many years: worship had been that bit of the service that comes before the sermon – a few hymns and psalms and prayers. My understanding of the nature of worship was minimal.

Gradually I saw the significance of the truth that worship is our primary calling. The chief end of man is 'to glorify God and to enjoy him for ever', as the Westminster Catechism expressed it. The difficulty was how, in practical ways, to develop worship so that it became the most important part of our life as a local church. Our first seven years in York were limited by an organist who was totally reliable and faithful, but did not really comprehend the spiritual aims that we were pursuing. When he left, he was replaced for a short time by a brilliant organist who was absolutely committed to Christ, but who was musically too sophisticated for our congregation. He produced amazing harmonies and I found much of his playing exciting. But I could see some puzzled expressions on the faces of those who were trying to sing the straightforward tune.

I learnt then that a natural talent becomes a spiritual gift only when it both glorifies Christ, *and* edifies the Body of Christ. Many gifted musicians (and other artists too) have to learn how to serve others with their gifts, and not to use the occasion as an opportunity for self-fulfilment. It is no doubt good for congregations to be stretched sometimes in their musical taste, but Jesus taught his disciples to wash each other's feet; and preachers, musicians, singers, actors, writers, architects and others all have to learn exactly the same lesson. Unless our contribution is helping and encouraging others, it will never be a spiritual gift, however brilliant it may be. It becomes 'performance', not 'ministry'. The style of worship that is especially needed today (and is all too rare) is one marked by gentleness and simplicity.

The real start of a new dimension in worship came when I was away in New Zealand for eight weeks. I was having a tremendous time touring various universities with Merv and Merla Watson, two superb musicians and singers from Canada, whose praise and worship had thrilled me during the International Conference at Guildford two years before. Their music also attracted many New Zealand students, and we saw young men and women turning to Christ because they had sensed his presence before listening to his word. At Dunedin we held a lunch-time meeting in the Students' Union, and it was clear from the start that a group of students were out to wreck the whole meeting. They made a lot of noise, and handed out anti-Christian literature that was aggressive and obscene. Through Merv and Merla's continued praise, however, they quietened down considerably, and after I had been speaking for five minutes or so, the leader of the group turned to those who were still talking and said, 'Will you shut up? I want to listen to this guy!' There was a respectful silence for the rest of my talk, and I was able to pray a prayer of commitment for those who were ready to receive Christ. There was absolute stillness, and at least two students found Christ that day.

While we were still in New Zealand, my wife back in St. Cuthbert's brought a small group together to sing something during one of our Family Services, simply to encourage a lay pastor who was preaching his first sermon. The group consisted of Anne, who only sometimes sings in tune, our two children (aged six and four) who played the guitar and triangle, a violinist and two others playing guitars. Significantly they were all members of our household, so that Anne's vision was again being fulfilled. Added to that, this very first 'singing group' developed out of the harmony of their lives together, not just the harmony of their music. This we later found to be a fundamental principle, which can transform any singing group or choir from a musical performance (of whatever excellence) into a spiritual ministry which brings the presence of Christ to other people. In order to back this group wholeheartedly, and to be personally identified with it, I even joined it myself for a Sunday or two, playing a borrowed guitar. I could play only three chords, and gladly stood down a week or two later when another guitarist offered his services; but the congregation loved this fresh approach to worship, and before long a more competent group was established.

Anne stayed with them for some time. Having the vision for this development in worship, she urged them to serve the congregation with their gifts, encouraged and supported the leader of the group, and stressed both the strong commitment and the sharing of lives that such a ministry demanded. All those who were willing to lead the Sunday worship in this way had to commit themselves to an evening of rehearsal each Tuesday, and, as the group became more established, the first hour of that evening was spent in prayer and in sharing together what the Lord had been saying and doing in their lives. Only as they became more open to one another in God's presence could the Spirit bind them together in God's love; and only as they learnt 'to live in such harmony with one another, in accord with Christ Jesus', could they together 'with one voice glorify the God and Father of our Lord Jesus Christ' (Romans 15:5f). Their vision was not just to sing songs, old or new, but to refresh people with the life and joy and love of Christ. Thus, this first hour on Tuesdays for prayer, praise and sharing was an indispensable part of their

ministry on Sundays. Added to that they had to be willing to
come about an hour early on Sundays before each service in
order to pray and prepare themselves for leading in worship.
Any preacher will know the importance of prayerful preparation for his sermon. Yet, if worship is the primary calling for
the Christian, our preparation for worship must be equally
demanding if it is not to degenerate into 'that bit before the
sermon'.

Soon we discovered the necessity of a 'worship committee',
which met each Monday for an hour or two (before the
singing group rehearsal on the Tuesday), to plan in detail
every part of the worship for the coming Sunday. Our aim was
to combine the old and the new, and so to produce the
appropriate blend of the more familiar hymns with the less
familiar spiritual songs that were emerging. Our organist by
this time was Andrew Maries, who was also an extremely
gifted oboist, and again a member of our household. He was
the natural leader of the singing group, and with the financial
support of the household became our first full-time musical
director. In this way we were able to give much more serious
attention to the whole area of worship, and it has undoubtedly
become one of the most essential ingredients in the life of the
congregation. One Anglican nun wrote, after a visit to the
church for a week: 'More than anything I am filled with
thanksgiving for what I saw and heard of the worship of St.
Michael's, not only in the church building, but in the whole
life of the community. I came away with the impression of a
Christ-centred, loving, caring and joyful community.' No
worship can be taken for granted, and of course we had our
ups and downs; but as we set our hearts to glorify God, so the
sense of his presence in our midst touched the lives of
countless people.

Being a musician, Andrew wanted to encourage other
musicians in the congregation in their worship of God. This
had already been done to some extent before Andrew had
become our organist; but under his leadership a Family
Service orchestra developed, consisting mainly of children
who came regularly to that service playing their recorders,

clarinets, oboes, violins, guitars, and even a glockenspiel. Older musicians, apart from those in the singing group, found a regular commitment to the evening service harder, but Andrew drew together a special orchestra for the Minster Guest Services and other festive occasions. It was wonderful to see more and more of the congregation, young and old alike, taking an active part in the service instead of just sitting in their pews.

One further expression of worship that I had not even remotely considered was dance. I knew that the psalmist talked often about praising God's name with dancing, and I remembered that King David had 'danced before the Lord with all his might'. But such Jewish exuberance in Old Testament days was surely not for respectable Anglicans today. Before my conversion I had loved ballroom dancing, but afterwards I felt that dancing was one of the many things that the good Christian did not do. So I cut it out of my life altogether. The thought of introducing dance in any form into worship seemed out of the question. Indeed it was never an issue – until Merv and Merla Watson came to York, at my invitation, bringing with them from Canada a remarkable group of seventy musicians, singers *and dancers*, all of whom were professionally trained. I organised two Festivals of Praise for them in York Minster, and they were two glorious evenings. For the first time ever I saw dance in worship, and found it, to my surprise, quite beautiful and spiritually moving: a descant in movement. Never before had I experienced such a majestic act of celebration. It seemed almost a glimpse into heaven, with the glory of God filling the Minster, and I found my spirit lifted up into exalted praise and joy. I soon discovered that many others had been deeply affected by those two festivals; and a group of women, of varying ages, approached me to see if they could use our church hall to learn how to worship God in dance. Cautiously I agreed.

To begin with, however, I had to be sure that dance in worship was biblical. I could see plenty of references in the Old Testament, but where was there any suggestion that dance was a part of the New Testament Church? Was not this a dangerous area, bringing the world right into the Church? Would not a dance group of attractive girls raise all sorts of unholy emotions in the men, no doubt including me? Surely this would detract from true worship, not add to it? Might we not be setting an unfortunate precedent or example which could lead other churches astray? These were the pressing questions which I had to face before I could possibly encourage a totally new area of worship that was virtually unheard of at that time. My information might have been limited, but I knew of no other church in the world where dance was used in worship.

As I began to study and pray, a number of pointers helped me to see the way forward. First, dance had clearly been part of the worship of God's people for many centuries before Christ; it would be strange if it suddenly ceased at the moment Jesus came to bring fullness of life and joy. Secondly, the New Testament Church used the book of psalms as their 'hymn book'; it would be strange if they sang about praising God with dancing, and never did it. Thirdly, there is no New Testament reference to the use of musical instruments in worship, yet very few Christians would question that dimension of worship. Fourthly, dance is mentioned twice by Jesus, both instances being significant. In the story of the Prodigal Son, everyone was happy when the prodigal came home, except the older brother: 'And as he came and drew near to the (father's) house, he heard music *and dancing*' – and he did not like it. On the whole it has been the 'older brother' in the Father's house who has taken exception to these 'new' forms of worship. Also, Jesus elsewhere said: 'To what then shall I compare the men of this generation . . . ? They are like children sitting in the market place calling to one another, "We piped to you, and you did not dance . . .".' Whatever we do, you respond negatively and critically.

Anne Long has put it in this way,

There are those who are very scared of anything moving in a service – either emotionally (such as the sermon) or physically (such as the kiss of peace or a dance). Some want a service that is safe and completely predictable where they can keep their liturgical masks in position and not relate to others. Certainly meeting each other in the presence of God can be very embarrassing if people are unsure about either God or each other.

That sums up much of the negative reaction to anything new in the Church today. Many Christians are not at all secure in the unchanging love of God, otherwise they would be willing for any fresh approach that sought to glorify him. Instead they try to find their security in the unchanging structures of the Church as an institution. This will always, sooner or later, quench the Spirit of God, who is the Spirit of movement.

What about unhelpful sexual emotions being stirred by watching pretty girls dance? Obviously this is a danger, and the dancers in their dress and movement must aim for modesty. But I am told, on good authority, that some women have the same sexual problems with certain preachers in the pulpit! What should those preachers do? Hide in the vestry and put their sermons on tape? Surely we must all come to terms with sexuality, since God made man in his own image, both male and female. Some men have been so afraid of sexuality that they relate very badly to women altogether. Indeed I would say that the Church in general has become almost gnostic in its attitudes to the body, treating it as though it was evil in itself. Much Western Christianity ignores the body, suppresses the emotions and concentrates almost exclusively upon the mind. But God wants our bodies to be the dwelling-place of his Holy Spirit, and it is by presenting our bodies to God that we offer him spiritual worship.

As I began to formulate these ideas, I encouraged the dancers to prepare an interpretative dance to a song of praise. Like the singing group, they met together each week, and for the first hour gave themselves to prayer and sharing from the Scriptures. It was only the quality of their relationships together in Christ that would make the dance genuinely an act of worship. None of the dancers had any professional training,

although one older member had an obvious vision for this
ministry and was able to help them with exercises and basic
movements. Progress was soon made, and several dances
were choreographed to songs of worship. I tried further to
encourage the group by teaching the whole church more
specifically about worship, referring to the place of dance and
giving it plenty of biblical support. I also went to that first hour
of prayer and sharing every week (as I did with the singing
group), to demonstrate that I was with them all the way, and
would give them the necessary 'covering' should any negative
remarks be made.

At first, most of the congregation were as cautious about
dance as I had been myself. But gradually, as we pressed on
gently with it, explaining all the time what we were doing and
why, this expression of worship was not only accepted but
well received, and often proved a vital means of communication to the hearts of those present. One Baptist minister wrote
in these words: 'I appreciated the worship very much indeed.
Except that I felt like crying all the time! You ought to issue
tissues at the door! One morning when I was practising being
a "block of concrete", it was the dance that the Lord used to
break me up and allow his Spirit to come through.' That has
frequently been the comment from many people whom God
has touched through dance in worship. Every area of life
needs to be redeemed for Christ. Also, since God is Creator
as well as Redeemer, all the creative gifts of his Spirit, such as
the performing arts, can be used to his praise and glory. With
this conviction we went on with the dance, despite some
cautious warnings and negative criticisms, usually from those
who had never seen it. I soon realised that most of these
criticisms voiced fears, and I received very few negative
comments once people had seen for themselves what we
meant by this highly explosive word 'dance'! It was one of
those times when we were sensitive to all comments and fears,
but we felt it important not to be deflected from developing
more effective methods of communication in this highly visual
age which is largely word-resistant.

After a slow and hesitant start, dance became a natural part of our worship almost every Sunday. We also learnt a number of vivacious Israeli dances, which we performed outside the church when the weather was warm enough, and these always attracted quite a crowd of people, including tourists of many nationalities. 'What is going on?' they used to ask. 'Is it a celebration? Is it a festival? Is it a wedding?' It was the golden opportunity to say, 'Yes, we are celebrating that God is among us, and we have come to know him through Jesus Christ.' In this way, many became genuinely interested and wanted to know more, and some were undoubtedly brought to Christ – initially through the dance. During the summer months, for several years when the Spirit seemed to be with us in unusual power, we had lunch together in the church hall every Sunday, with many visitors joining us; and we would then go into a courtyard outside the hall for a time of more Israeli dancing. These proved to be wonderful community dances, and both expressed and increased our sense of oneness together in Christ. Always these spontaneous and joyful moments of celebration drew in the tourists. Although I loved to dance with everyone else (my past love for dance was being redeemed for Christ!) I spent most of the time talking to tourists about the Lord, and had the privilege of leading several to Christ – once again, initially through the dance.

As the Spirit seemed to move freely among us, it was a time of remarkable creativity. Another example of this was the making of many beautiful banners. One girl in our household had obvious artistic gifts, and we encouraged her to use them, in conjunction with several other women similarly gifted, to the glory of God. This small group spent much time in prayer and meditation on the Scriptures; and out of this, one or more of the group would have a picture in her mind for a banner. This idea would subsequently be realised, and the design of the banner often linked up with the theme of a forthcoming service. This was especially so for the great festivals in the Church year. Several banners would be hung on pillars in the church, and their dignity and beauty greatly enhanced the atmosphere of celebration, and the few words on each banner increased the sense of expectancy the moment people came into the church to worship. As more and more banners were made, it became possible to choose just the right banner for the theme of every service. Sometimes those who came with special needs would find meditating on the words and picture of a banner one of the most helpful aspects of the service.

Perhaps the most striking development of artistic gifts came in the area of drama. While leading several university missions I began to experiment with methods of communication other than just speaking. I came across one or two short dramatic readings, and at various universities asked if there were any Christian actors who could do them for me. During a mission at Oxford University in 1973 there was one student who did one of these readings brilliantly, and it made a considerable impact on all those present as well as enriching my talk that evening. His name was Paul Burbridge, and we began to strike up a personal friendship. At about the same period I was preaching in Cambridge University, and had dinner with a close and long-standing friend of Paul's, Murray Watts. We had an immensely stimulating conversation over dinner about the arts in general, and I discovered that Murray had already written one or two plays and was a dramatist with obvious potential. Moreover, both Murray and Paul had just started a street-theatre group called Breadrock, and with a group of like-minded friends spent part of their summer vacation performing their sketches – mostly enacted parables – at a seaside resort in North Wales. In this way, they were able to go among the crowds of holiday-makers and present the Gospel in attractive, humorous and lively ways that were much more readily accepted than the old-fashioned open-air evangelistic service.

Although I had not yet seen their group in action, I was fascinated by the concept, and saw the potential for marvellous communication in this generation that has been so influenced by the 'drama' of television. I could see that Christian artists today could become front-line missionaries in our modern culture, since they had learnt the language of communication for the mass of ordinary people who were right outside the Church.

I was also very much aware that Christian artists were under enormous pressure from the secular world in which they spent most of their time, and that the Church in general neither understood them nor did anything much to encourage them. The Arts Centre Group in London had been formed a few years before, and was doing excellent work in trying to reach artists for Christ, and then seeking to strengthen them in their faith; but the need for supportive churches was obvious. I wondered if in York we could perhaps start another Arts Centre Group for the north of England; and now that we had moved our main services from St. Cuthbert's to St. Michael-le-Belfrey, I wondered if St. Cuthbert's might be used for such a centre, maybe even becoming a small theatre where people like Paul and Murray could perform their plays. We spent some time thinking, talking and praying together about the possibilities.

I kept closely in touch with Paul during his time in Oxford, and when he got his degree he came as yet another member of our household to live with us for a year. We all became very fond of him, and he was a wonderful, creative member of the community. I especially enjoyed taking him with me on most of my visits to schools and universities during that year, and we had some marvellous fellowship together in Christ. He was both sensitive and caring, and his infectious sense of fun helped to release some of the tensions in the work or in the household. Even though Paul was my junior I found it extraordinarily helpful sharing closely with a Christian friend in this way, and over the years I have treasured one or two such friendships where I can be completely open and honest about my own needs, questions and problems.

Wherever we went, I would speak, and Paul would illustrate my talks with some very effective short, punchy pieces of drama. Occasionally Murray would join us. I led another mission to Oxford University in 1976, and before each talk to a packed audience in the Union Debating Chamber, Paul and Murray would perform one of their sketches. The undergraduates simply loved these. A wonderful rapport was established, with spontaneous applause at the end of each sketch.

After these sketches I found it so much easier speaking, and it was an exceptionally profitable mission, with about 150 students finding Christ. I was increasingly excited about the value of drama in evangelism. It had its own immediate appeal, and cut quickly through the barriers of communication that are often huge between the Church and the world. Of course, it is only the Spirit who can bring anyone to Christ, but I could see the Spirit was using this method of presenting the Gospel with considerable effect.

Paul and Murray were beginning to think seriously of developing a theatre company, and could see that York could be the ideal base. It had a long history of arts festivals, including in particular the medieval mystery plays, and was not saturated by other theatre companies as was London. Added to that, they could see that St. Michael's could give them the spiritual support that they would need; and indeed the households that had been established could provide for them financially also. This, in fact, was just what happened, and it proved the crucial factor in everything else that followed. But for the households which supported the members of the company in every way for the first year or two, the venture would never have been born. Once again we saw the vital facilitating ministry of these households, and most of the best creative moves of the church came into being because of them.

I was as excited by the vision that Paul and Murray were forming as they were themselves, and gave them every encouragement I could. In order to achieve some credibility in the eyes of the Church for what they were about to do, both of them went for a year to St. John's Theological College, Nottingham, for a post-graduate diploma in theology; and it was during that time that their vision began to unfold further. As the original street-theatre group Breadrock they were invited to perform a number of their sketches at the Nottingham Evangelical Anglican Congress (the Congress where I was almost lynched by some delegates who had misunderstood my remarks about the Reformation!), and their drama was extraordinarily well received by the large number of

Christian leaders who had gathered. Many of these leaders gave them much personal encouragement, and it became clear that their work would receive much wider Church support than just from us in York. 'Your sketches are hermeneutically sound!' said a Professor of Hermeneutics, with even a hint of enthusiasm in his remark.

During that year at St. John's, Paul and Murray, together with others from St. Michael's, joined me on one or two missions that we led in Belfast, Leeds and other places. These missions demonstrated the effectiveness of our 'multi-media' approach; and we could see that God was beginning to open up for us a sphere of ministry that was much wider than any of us had conceived.

On September 1st, 1977, after that year at St. John's, the Riding Lights Theatre Company was born. Together with Paul, the Director, and Murray, who was mainly an associate member and freelance writer, three others joined them from the start. Nigel Forde had lived in York for a number of years, and he and his wife Hilary had been converted about a year before through our church. For ten years Nigel had been a professional actor, writer and director of the Humberside Theatre, Hull, and therefore gave them just the necessary professional experience that they needed at this stage. Dick Mapletoft was another: a social worker who was a 'natural' in many of the comedy sketches, and who had the gift of quickly winning people's affection. Sarah Finch was the third, an extremely talented young actress who had recently finished her training at Manchester, possessing vitality, a marvellous voice, and unusual sensitivity for someone of her age. Two months later, an American friend working in our church, called Geoffrey Stevenson, joined them; and after several years with the company he has since become an accomplished and well-known mime-artist. Then, on January 1st, 1978, the company was completed by Diana Lang, who had taught drama at Roedean, the girls' school. Diana also had obvious talent and versatility, and was a perfect match for Sarah Finch. To begin with, all of these were living in households, apart from Nigel and Hilary Forde who had two children and a house of their own; and they all saw that their close links with our church in York were fundamental if the company were to have any spiritual ministry as well as artistic effectiveness. Paul came back to live in our own household, much to our delight, and remained with us until his marriage to Bernadette in July 1978.

During the next year or two, Riding Lights came with me everywhere, as I began to lead Christian missions, or 'festivals' as we increasingly called them, in many parts of Great Britain; and with six other talented members of my congregation, gifted in music and dance, we made many trips together. However, as the work of Riding Lights became more widely known, invitations came pouring in to them from all over this country and from abroad, and sadly I had to release them more and more from the team that I had formed for Christian festivals. I could see that a theatre company must fulfil its particular call to the theatre, and we were not able to make the best use of their time and energies on these festivals. We have always remained in very close touch, and after going through all sorts of experiences together – some exciting, some hilarious, and some very painful – our relationships became unusually deep. However, it was necessary in every way for them to develop their own work; and the wide popularity of it has been seen by the excellent sales of their books on drama (suitable for church drama groups), *Time To Act*[1] and *Lightning Sketches*[2]. Since then literally hundreds of drama groups have sprung up all over the world, some as a direct result of the vision of Riding Lights; and increasing recognition for this company has been given in the secular theatre. They won two awards for fringe theatre in the Edinburgh Festivals of 1979 and 1980, and have recently performed a full-length play for Yorkshire Television, which was well received.

Further, this means of communication has enabled them to bring the Gospel to a variety of situations: churches, cathed-

1. Hodder & Stoughton, 1979
2. Hodder & Stoughton, 1981

rals, city halls, schools, universities, shopping precincts, market-places, theatres, bars, car parks, seaside resorts, tourist centres – virtually anywhere. Drama is one of the outstanding means of presenting Christ to those who would normally have no contact with the Christian Church. At a recent mission to Oxford University (1982), and after the very positive experience of the previous mission in 1976 when Paul and Murray came to help me, the whole of Riding Lights took an active part. Each lunch-time they performed a brilliant revue in one of the colleges, which helped to dispel the false but common misconception that Christianity means a narrow form of religious piety. Then, each evening during the eight-day mission, they performed three of their sketches to illustrate the theme of my address. It was so popular that after two nights we had to move to a larger building, and an average of at least 1,000 students were present on each occasion, with many turning to Christ as a result.

As Riding Lights became less available to join me, however, I had to form another team who could travel with me. Although they were less experienced and perhaps less gifted than Riding Lights, we discovered that God was nevertheless able to use us in many unexpected ways.

14

The Mustard Seed

'Why not open a shop as part of the continuous witness of the Church in the city throughout the week?' Many of the ideas that we have are like passing dreams: they fade with the morning and are forgotten. Occasionally there will be a seminal thought which, like the tiny grain of mustard seed growing into a huge shrub, can become surprisingly influential in the kingdom of God.

Anne and I had been aware that most of the recent creative developments at St. Michael's were directly relevant for the Sunday worship; and although these were affecting the lives of a great many people, there was not much witness in the city during the week, apart from the lunch-hour service during the summer and of course the indispensable daily witness of every Christian at home and at work. We had a number of workers involved with young people, and gave strong support to a coffee bar called the Catacombs and the Detached Youth Work, both of which tried to help youngsters who were in and out of prison and often on drugs. However, God had placed us in the centre of a famous city and we were doing little to reach the tourists for Christ. We also saw the need for a centre where Christians from different churches could meet together, thus breaking down some of the barriers existing between those churches.

As a direct result of much prayer about this, we believed that God had given us a prophetic vision, if that does not sound too presumptuous, of a shop staffed by a small community of Christians from our congregation. They would live together in the same style as our own extended household, but with the specific task of serving people in the context of a restaurant and gift shop. The confirmation of this vision came from a study of Isaiah 58, and this had also been a theme at a recent parish weekend. In that chapter we read about the calling to share our bread with the hungry and to satisfy the desires of the afflicted. We also read, 'And your ancient ruins shall be rebuilt; you shall raise up the foundations of many generations; you shall be called the repairer of the breach, the restorer of streets to dwell in.' York had recently been a restored city, with much rebuilding of ancient ruins, and this, together with its history going back to A.D. 71, had made it a tourist attraction. But it was difficult to 'dwell' in the city shopping centre without owning a shop. We also felt that God was calling us to encourage the spiritual restoration of the city, to match its material developments. It seemed desirable in every way to run a suitable shop where the work would be dedicated to God as an expression of his kingdom. Steadily God pressed this vision on us.

As we were praying about this, we heard unexpectedly about some premises, almost opposite St. Michael's, that could be ideal. On enquiry we discovered that the property was owned by the Church Commissioners of the Church of England, so that we could not buy it, but could rent it at a straight commercial rate. The building was in a poor state of repair, but in the heart of the city centre. We were aiming for a non-profit-making organisation (or any profit would be ploughed back into the work of the church), attempting in a gentle way to make Christ known in the city. Also the shop would be run entirely by members of the Church of England. I confess that I was disappointed that the rent was so high considering the purpose for which we wished to lease it. No doubt the Commissioners have their own responsibilities to be businesslike with the vast areas of property that they own, but I tried hard, in vain, to persuade them to reduce the rent. Considerable sums of money were also needed to put the building into working order, including the addition of stringent fire precautions, since part of the shop would be used as a restaurant. All in all it required a considerable financial commitment.

Having found the possible building for the project, the next vital task was to discover someone who would run the business and who could respond to the immediate financial needs. The idea was that they would live above the shop and lead a small community who would be willing to serve there. The members of that community, or staff, would receive their keep plus a small amount of pocket money for their personal spending. This was in line with the simplifying of lifestyle that a number in the church were attempting, and it also meant that the overheads of the shop could be kept to a necessary minimum. All this, we felt, would be one valid expression of the kingdom of God.

We clearly required a couple, therefore, who had vision and the willingness to accept a considerable sacrifice of their own. As Anne and I prayerfully pursued this further, we found the ideal couple in Philip and Wendy Wharton, who had either been converted, or come into assurance of their conversion, a few years before in the days of St. Cuthbert's. Philip worked for the National Coal Board in Doncaster; Wendy had obvious artistic flair, had worked as a buyer in a department store, and was developing evangelistic gifts. Their three children were now grown up: Judith, their daughter, was working in our home at that time, and was one of the leaders of the dance group in our congregation; Michael and David were mostly away from home. The Whartons lived in a lovely house a few miles out of York: they had a beautiful garden, which Philip especially found a source of great joy, and Wendy had made the house most attractive in every way.

As Anne and I shared our vision with them, they responded in a marvellous way. After further thought and prayer Philip and Wendy, with the total support of their family, told us that they were willing to sell their home in order to rent the property from the Church Commissioners, and pay for all the extremely expensive alterations that were necessary before they could move in. As it happened, once they had sold their house, they had to squeeze into another already full household for about nine months before the shop was ready. It was an extraordinary testing time for them all, but through much prayer and holding firm to the vision they all survived.

In May 1976 the Mustard Seed, as the shop was appropriately called because of its potential influence from small beginnings, was opened. Philip continued with his job at the Coal Board, to provide some stable income (even though they had sacrificed their property and security to make the venture possible); Wendy managed the shop; Geoffrey Stevenson, the American who was later to join Riding Lights, became the chef; and five or six girls committed themselves to serving there, four of them living above the shop in a small community with the Whartons. They began and ended each day with prayer, asking God to bring into the shop those of his choice, and praying for wisdom to know when to speak openly about Christ to the customers and when to be content simply to serve them with his love. It was extremely hard work, especially as most of the staff were actively involved in other aspects of church work, notably the dance group. Some of them also came regularly on the teams I was taking with me to lead Christian festivals in many parts of the country. Occasionally tensions would arise, as was inevitable when most of the staff were working and living in the same place, sharing their lives openly together, and often under much pressure. But visitors and customers frequently spoke about the striking atmosphere in that shop: it was so full of love and peace. Indeed, it was through the fragrance of Christ in that place, mediated through the depth of their relationships together and created through constant prayer, that many people, directly or indirectly, found the Saviour. Sometimes, after the hectic day was over, they held evangelistic supper parties for friends and business contacts; and these were some of the best that I have ever experienced.

The vision of the Mustard Seed as a meeting-place for Christians from widely different traditions was also being fulfilled. The Whartons and the staff had excellent relationships with Roman Catholic priests and nuns; the Anglican sisters from the Minster used to come regularly, and both ministers and members of various churches used to meet over coffee or lunch. I enjoyed the opportunity of taking journalists there for lunch, when they wanted to interview me for some article, and always they would ask me, 'What is there about this place? It is so friendly, and there is such a sense of peace here!' It was natural for me to explain briefly the basis on which the shop was created, and then go on directly to speak about Christ. On more than one occasion I took my guest across the road to St. Michael's after lunch and had the privilege of leading him to Christ.

With Wendy's creative imagination, there were many other positive aspects to the work. Members of our church with appropriate talents made banners for sale (mostly smaller versions of the ones we had in our church). Others designed notepaper and an attractive mural for the shop itself. Local craftsmen were given orders for their pottery, artists for their paintings. There was also a good sale of books and albums, some of which came from our fellowship. It was a venture which involved many more than just those working at the Mustard Seed. Anne and I felt that this was one of the most exciting projects we had so far seen during our first eleven years in York. In spite of some tensions in relationships, which occur everywhere when people work and live in close proximity, the entire work was creative and wholesome, a marvellous expression of the kingdom of God in contemporary and relevant terms. It was used for evangelism, renewal and reconciliation – the three burdens that have been closest to my heart for many years. Many visitors spoke warmly about their experiences of the Mustard Seed, and increasingly Wendy was asked to guide similar ventures in other towns and cities. It was encouraging also to see the staff maturing spiritually, and most of them are now active in various forms of Christian service.

It was therefore all the more shattering three years later when Anne and I heard, while on holiday with our children in Cornwall, that the Mustard Seed was in danger of total closure. We could hardly believe our ears.

The Archbishop of York, Dr. Stuart Blanch, had encouraged me to have something of a 'sabbatical' in 1979, but with our children still at school, and as I was frequently away from home on missions and festivals, we felt that the most we could do was to spend all the school holidays away as a family, and this included three weeks in a tiny cottage in Cornwall – for what turned out to be one of the wettest summers on record! A telegram arrived from Philip and Wendy asking us to ring them at once. We had grown very close to them indeed, and they knew well the pressures we were under; so for them to cable us in such a way meant that the situation, whatever it might be, was serious.

Having no telephone in the cottage, we stopped at the first call-box and got through to Philip and Wendy. Thus began the first of two lengthy calls every day for the rest of our holiday as we heard about the developments. I was tempted to fly or drive back at once (and maybe should have done so – I am still not sure), but my sense of responsibility to Anne and the children, together with the Archbishop's instructions, kept us in Cornwall. Also, my 79-year-old mother was far from well, and had to be admitted to hospital in Winchester. We knew it was important to stay in the south of England and to visit her for several days on our way home.

By the time we returned, however, the problem in York had reached the point of no return, and the Mustard Seed had all but closed. What had been one of the most fruitful and imaginative enterprises I had ever been associated with, had been virtually destroyed in one swift blow. It was almost impossible to believe.

This is not the place for recriminations, and to this day I still do not fully understand the reasons for what happened. I suspect that a number of complex factors were at work simultaneously: personal frustrations and guilt projected into open criticism; a negative attitude on the part of some towards women leaders, especially those with a strong personality; different views of spirituality beginning to emerge within the leadership; a general awareness of some of the problems in the Mustard Seed since, as with every extended household, those problems were readily observable. It is worth adding, however, that those 'problems' seemed to me to be very little different from those of any going concern, especially where relationships are open and committed.

Nevertheless, the next two weeks became a nightmare. It all seemed rather like a trial. Wendy and Philip came before the elders, about twelve of us. We asked searching questions and made critical comments. Some questioned the whole vision of the Mustard Seed. Others cast doubts on its prayerful origin (though prayer had always been one of its most significant factors). Increasingly a vote of 'no confidence' was given. All future hopes were utterly dashed.

Even more serious, Philip and Wendy themselves were all but destroyed through the process. Having been with them from the start, Anne and I could feel at least something of the incredible agony they went through for many months to come; and even three years later, I could not pass by the premises without feeling the profound ache of past grief in my spirit. The stock in hand, of course, had to be sold cheaply, and the property passed on for other purposes. Philip and Wendy were able to stay in their flat above the shop for another two years until they were able to buy a small house for themselves. But they lost thousands of pounds through their obedient response to the vision which I firmly believe the Lord gave them. It was nothing less than a miracle of God's grace that they were eventually able to forgive, and once again become active members of the church which had hurt them so much.

It never helps to apportion blame. The whole sad saga was a vivid and painful reminder that, however 'renewed' individuals or churches may feel themselves to be, we are still sinners, in constant need of the Lord's forgiveness, patience and love. We still hurt one another, sometimes unbelievably so, and still have to go on forgiving one another, as much as seventy times seven, as Jesus taught. The message of the Gospel is that of God's grace through human weakness; but human sin can quench the Spirit and hinder God's work, so that Satan, temporarily at least, appears to triumph. Philip and Wendy had always felt it important to submit to the recognised leadership in the church, whether they felt those leaders to be right or wrong. Through their humble submission, astonishingly painful though it was, God later blessed them both with a wider and richer ministry than before. Even the whole church eventually experienced the resurrection that follows crucifixion, when God is in control. But the crucifixion was agonisingly real.

The rise and fall of the Mustard Seed brought many of us to our knees, as we repented of all the sin and folly that made the nightmare happen. Thus began a refining, chastening process within the whole congregation, although we did not yet know that the most severe fires were still to come.

15

Shared Leadership

It was through the recognised leaders in the church that the Mustard Seed came to a sudden and tragic end. Yet whatever were the rights and wrongs in what happened (and it was difficult not to feel that we had all been wrong), the shared leadership that I encouraged in St. Michael's was an indispensable part of its growth over the years.

Often I think that I lack vision (Anne is the visionary in our partnership), and usually I have been prodded into action either by Anne's prophetic insights or by murmuring within the church. I am encouraged to think that even Moses was sometimes spurred into taking a lead through the murmurings of the children of Israel. When the problems became too numerous for him, he wisely consulted his father-in-law (which suggests how serious the situation had become!) and shared his leadership in an orderly and impressive way. He had 600 leaders over thousands, 6,000 leaders over hundreds, 12,000 leaders over fifties, and 60,000 leaders over tens – making 78,600 leaders in all. That must have eased his personal responsibilities considerably, providing he was on good terms with all his leaders.

After five years in York, and with my university work around the country taking me away increasingly, some of the congregation were complaining that I was not sufficiently at home to see to all the pastoral problems in a rapidly expanding work. From 1967 onwards we had held an annual residential parish weekend away from York, and these had always been significant times for welding our congregation close together and for discerning God's direction for us in the coming year. In 1970, 126 came away for the weekend, and I put them to work in small groups to review the entire work of the church and to pray for the Spirit's guidance. Partly as a result of this, it became clear to me that I had to ask others to share in the pastoral load of the church.

In Acts 6, when there were complaints about Greek widows who were being neglected, the apostles asked the congregation to choose seven men 'of good repute, full of the Spirit and of wisdom', to help with this pastoral need. Once they reorganised in this way, we are told by Luke that 'the word of God increased'. I therefore preached about the need for others to share in the work I was doing in the church, and asked the congregation to suggest, in writing, those who might be suitable. I noted that in Acts 6 the apostles kept the right of appointment of the seven in their own hands, even though the congregation was asked to make the choice. This seemed to be a wise procedure, as I did not believe that I should opt out of the God-given responsibility that I had over the congregation as a whole. I was sharing my leadership, not dividing the authority of it into a number of equal parts. Further, before taking any action at all, I consulted with the Parochial Church Council, since that is the legally elected governing body in any local Anglican church, and they unanimously agreed with the suggested development.

Naturally I prayed much about the choice of 'elders' (as we called them), and it was greatly encouraging for me to see that the choice of the congregation exactly coincided with my own personal feelings. In October that year, six men were commissioned by the Bishop of Selby to serve as elders in the church. To begin with the appointment was only for a year, since it was obviously experimental. I had heard of one, or perhaps two, Anglican churches that had done something similar, but the whole idea in our tradition was a relatively new one. The six elders happened to include the church-wardens and readers, but there was no automatic or 'ex officio' qualification. At that time, I was still a curate, and therefore could not have another clergyman to assist me in the growing work. Thus I had to call in the support of laymen to take on some of the burden of pastoral leadership. We met regularly together, once every two weeks in those early days, and I found this group immensely supportive.

Although Anne totally agreed with this new move, the practical implications of it all were painful for her. Up to this point, in spite of many strains, Anne and I together had been the effective leaders of the work, as we tried to discern God's guidance for each new stage of development. Now that the elders had come into being (and for many years they were strictly all men), Anne was excluded from this leadership group. She therefore had to work indirectly through me, trying to impart through my thick skin some of the creative ideas that she was constantly having; and then I had to work them out for myself before sharing them with the elders. In the first-century Church in Antioch, the leadership of the congregation consisted of a group of prophets and teachers. On reflection, it was ridiculous that we should have excluded for many years the one person who had such a growing prophetic ministry. Indeed it would have been most healthy if that prophetic ministry could first have been exercised within the eldership. But our prejudice against women leaders was strong, and the thought of Anne, or any other woman, joining that group never even entered our heads. An official report on our church by the Archbishops' Council on Evangelism (a most thorough report that was extremely searching and helpful) commented about our fellowship: 'It is male-administered, female-attended, mother-and-family and student orientated . . . It is directed by men, women being excluded from the eldership, but playing a leading role through prophecy. There is a real danger of compromising prophetic vision where it does not tally with the going concerns of the eldership. A determined individualist would find the whole set-up frustrating.' I did not realise at the time just how frustrated Anne and several others would find the male domination that had emerged from this otherwise necessary move.

In spite of all that, the experiment was clearly successful, and the elders were subsequently appointed for three years at a time, subject to reappointment. This allowed within the eldership a certain turnover, determined partly by age, health and other commitments. We were always on the lookout for those whose primary ministry was pastoral. The Church Council was the governing body within the church, and therefore its main function was administrative; but it happened that most of the elders were also on the Council so that there was never any friction between the two groups. The Council met only five or six times a year, but the elders were soon meeting every Saturday at 7 a.m., and about every six weeks we spent the whole of Saturday morning together (later we met at 6.30 a.m. each Tuesday). I was quite certain that the Council as a whole had no desire for that demanding commitment! In Anglican terms, the eldership was virtually the pastoral subcommittee of the Church Council, but that was a clumsy title and it was never used. Always the elders were commissioned by the Bishop of Selby or the Archbishop of York, so that we tried to bring the whole scheme under the authority of the wider Church. In effect, the commissioning of the elders was a local ordination for ministry within our church.

In July 1972 we went one stage further, and one of the elders, Peter Hodgson, was commissioned as a full-time Lay Pastor. Peter had been licensed as a Reader for some twenty years, and while running his own radio and television servicing business had enjoyed increasing conversations about Christ in the homes where he went on business. Our task as a Church Council was simply to recognise the obvious pastoral gifts that God had given him, to hear his own sense of calling to full-time service within the church, and then to commission him for that purpose, accepting the financial responsibilities of a married man with a wife and three growing children. Peter was an invaluable helper since he had lived in the area all his life, and knew intimately some of the needs of those who came to us.

One almost impossible task facing the elders was to put a brake on my own outside engagements. I was slowly learning to say 'no' to invitations, but too quickly responded to opportunities both for evangelism (especially) and also for the renewal of the Church. Some invitations I refused with minimal thought; but the others I brought to the elders' meetings, and perhaps a disproportionate amount of time was spent sifting through those invitations to see how I should reply. However, for me it was immensely helpful submitting to the combined wisdom of the elders; and since one of them was my doctor, Walter Stockdale, who looked after my asthmatic problems with great care and skill for many years, they had good reason for trying to prevent me from doing too much. Further, since my outside engagements often increased the tensions at home, the elders had a primary pastoral duty to perform towards us – which was not always easy for them.

Even with the establishment of elders, which greatly eased the pastoral load from my own shoulders, we heard further murmurings after a year or two. The congregation was growing too big, especially after our move into St. Michael-le-Belfrey in 1973. It was hard for people to know one another in any depth; and, more than ever today, most people need to belong to a relatively small and identifiable group. Our Thursday fellowship, which had moved out of the rectory into St. Cuthbert's, had levelled off at about 150 or more, which was still far too big for any intimate fellowship. Consequently, a few small groups had formed spontaneously so that people could enjoy more relaxed fellowship within the informal atmosphere of individual homes. The time had come, however, to organise these groups in a more structured way; and a half-day parish conference one Saturday confirmed the widespread desire for this to happen as soon as possible.

One area that needed immediate strengthening was the young people's group. So in April 1973 I went to see the Archbishop of York, Dr. Donald Coggan, to ask if I could have a curate. 'But you are only a curate yourself!' he replied. 'Are you asking to be made a vicar?' I detected a slight twinkle in his eye, so I dutifully and accurately answered, 'Well, I have been a curate for fourteen years, and I just thought that perhaps . . .' The Archbishop was very gracious. On September 19th, the day of our wedding anniversary, I was instituted as vicar of St. Michael-le-Belfrey, and four days later my first curate, Andrew Cornes, joined me. I had been used by God to help Andrew find Christ at Oxford University, and I had subsequently come to respect Andrew immensely during his placement with us, as part of his training for ordination. He had an astute mind, obvious drive, gifts of leadership, and showed all the marks of becoming an outstanding preacher and teacher. Added to that his Christian experience at the camps that I had attended gave him excellent training to develop the youth work almost from scratch. One particular problem, however, had to be worked through with honesty. Andrew could not identify with the charismatic renewal, as it was now commonly called. However, my burden was already growing for the reconciling of Christians over this issue; and since Andrew's teaching was crystal clear about the heart of the biblical Gospel which I constantly sought to proclaim, I felt that it might be good deliberately to invite, as curate, someone who was definitely not a 'card-carrying charismatic', partly to demonstrate that our unity is always in Christ, and not in any particular spiritual experience.

As it happened, Andrew had three marvellous years with us. Immediately he was loved by everyone, and his gifts widely appreciated. His sermons were a model of careful and spiritual exposition, his sense of humour was infectious, his concern for individuals was full of the compassion of Christ, and, above all, his pioneer work among young people was brilliantly effective. Not only did many young people find Christ through Andrew's ministry, but his follow-up system, based largely on what he had learnt at those boys' camps, enabled them to grow rapidly in the faith. Each young Christian was attached to a family (which helped to bridge some of the generation gap), and the father or mother of that family would spend an hour a week reading the Bible with the young Christian, as well as extending hospitality through meals. By the end of those three years, the young people's fellowship, called 'Eureka' (meaning 'I've found it – or him') had grown from nothing to about 140, most of whom were steadily maturing in their faith.

In 1976 Andrew left to become Director of Training at All Souls, Langham Place. I am not sure that he changed his views about charismatic renewal as such during his time with us; but he was totally loyal, and our relationship was always one of the utmost harmony and mutual respect. Andrew was replaced by Patrick Whitworth, who had also found Christ during a time I spent at Oxford University; and Patrick took on the excellent work that Andrew had established as well as becoming more widely involved in the whole church. Andrew had spent about ninety-five per cent of his time with young people, since I saw that as a priority; but I was concerned that Patrick should receive more general training, and it soon became obvious that God had gifted him in both evangelism and teaching. It was a joy to share these aspects of the ministry with him; and once again he was much loved by the whole congregation.

The young people's group was not the only one developed at this stage. We saw that most people wanted, and needed, to belong to a small group (the ideal number being about twelve) where they could get to know one another informally. We therefore divided the regular congregation into more than twenty *area groups*, as we called them, since the determining factor for almost all of them was a geographical one. We wanted these groups to build up a sense of community in a given small area, with the opportunity of establishing good relationships 'seven days a week'. For example, although the focal point was a meeting in someone's home every other week, for the purpose of praise, prayer, study, sharing and ministry, we wanted the relationships in each group to become much deeper than that. It was a natural practice in our group for members to walk in and out of each other's homes without needing to knock or ring the door bell. If the visitor saw a young mother struggling with washing, cooking and babies, immediate practical help might be offered, followed by a helpful chat over a cup of tea and then specific prayer.

Mothers with very new babies found that all their meals were provided for them and often their other children were looked after, sometimes staying in the homes of nearby families. There was also much sharing of property such as cars, washing-machines, lawn-mowers. Two women in one group might do a weekly shop for the whole group. Offers for baby-sitting would frequently be made, and meals cooked for any who were ill. We wanted to encourage the sharing of the whole of our lives, not just Bible study and prayer. Some people could not come to regular meetings, but they were still important members of the 'community of God's people' in that area, and we wanted as many as possible to feel that they belonged.

Each area group had its leader, and ideally an assistant leader too, since it was our hope (not always realised) that if these groups grew healthily they should be willing to split, multiply or 'bud' every year or two. Some groups, like individuals, were more gifted in evangelism than others, and thus tended to grow more quickly. Others were more committed to ministry within the church. Sometimes the groups were encouraged along specific lines of Bible study, and a number of them had particular prayer projects, such as the support of certain missionaries. But all groups were designed for the sharing of lives. Normally this 'sharing' would consist of personal thoughts drawn from the Scriptures, but occasionally it would emerge from the ordinary events of life. We knew that God is always trying to speak to us, through his word but also through every circumstance of life, and we encouraged each other to listen to God, to hear what he was saying and then to share it with one another. In this, it was important to be open and honest, so that within the small group of committed Christians there could be freedom to mention quite personal needs, thus drawing out the love, prayer and support of others in the group. It was in 'speaking the truth in love' that we were trying to grow up into Christ in every way.

Another vital aim of these groups was pastoral. When needs of any kind arose – and they were always doing so of course – the members of the group (not necessarily the leaders) tried to help one another in spiritual or practical terms. Further, each elder had the oversight of two or more of the groups, so that if the pastoral need lay beyond the combined experience of the group, it was passed on to the elder. And then, if that elder felt inadequate to deal with the problem, he could, with permission, share that need with another elder of greater experience. In this way, it was obvious that the pastoral load of the church was being borne by a growing number of men and women, thus easing the enormous strain that any clergyman will feel when his congregation is increasing in size.

All the elders, by virtue of their living in some area, were members of an area group, as well as having responsibility for one or more others; but they were never leaders of those groups, except in emergency, so as to encourage more and more lay-leadership within the church. On one snowy occasion, when I was present at my own area group, a young wife apologised that her husband had been delayed from work because of the snow, and she explained that he should have been the leader for that night. 'Oh well,' she said, 'I suppose that I had better lead it instead of Colin.' I was delighted that she did not think of handing the group over to me, even though I was the only clergyman present. Moreover she led it extraordinarily well, and I was greatly refreshed by the whole evening.

Group leadership is a skilled and demanding role, and very few of our leaders were naturally gifted in this. We later developed, therefore, a number of 'support groups', consisting of two or three elders together with the various area group leaders for which they were responsible; and these support groups met every two or three weeks. They also were expected to share their lives together, since the way in which they did this, in a group of leaders, would be likely to determine the quality of the area groups which they were leading. Also, of course, they were able to raise difficulties they were experiencing within their groups, or share certain aspects that they had found valuable; and then they prayed for one another. As with every structure like this, some groups went better than others, and no system is perfect. But the sense of fellowship within the whole congregation grew almost visibly as a result, and the individual needs of the majority had much more chance of being met than if the whole work depended on the feverish activities of one or two hard-pressed clergymen.

It is significant that virtually every major movement for spiritual renewal in the history of the Church has been marked by the development of the small group. The amazing missionary impact of the Moravians lay in their constant attention to relationships, based on small groups. John Wesley, who largely owed his conversion and evangelistic zeal to the Moravians, organised his 'class-meetings' or 'nurture cells', and these became a vital part of the extraordinary influence he had on the whole of England in his day. The remarkable growth of the Pentecostal Church in South America is also due, in part, to the emphasis on the cell structure. Numerous other illustrations can be given. Naturally there are dangers. Unless the leaders develop close relationships with one another, these groups can become independent or divisive. Unless the groups see that part of their function is evangelism and service, they can degenerate into unhealthy introspection. Unless the members of the group develop friendships outside the church altogether, the groups can tragically become safe and comfortable religious ghettos, useless as a witness to the wider world. Unless there is constant training and encouraging of leaders, some groups will soon die a natural death. Yet, given these and other areas of concern, the sharing of leadership became an indispensable part of the growth and witness of St. Michael's Church.

Even this degree of shared leadership, however, was not enough for the growing work. Throughout the seventies, my ministry had been steadily widening to various parts of Great Britain and to other countries in the world, and I found it increasingly hard to cope adequately with the demands in York as well. The wider ministry seemed to have the backing of church leaders of most denominations, and we could see that God was using our Christian missions and festivals in many towns and cities; but I could not sustain the pressure indefinitely. My health was not good: my asthmatic attacks required frequent courses of steroids. And the travelling work always imposed strain on our family relationships. It was clearly not easy for Anne, nor was it much easier for me.

We had invited the Archbishops' Council on Evangelism to study our parish in depth and to make a detailed report on their observations, and in November 1977 a team of nine spent a week with us all. They studied our worship and prayer life, our evangelism and pastoral care. They looked into our finances and practical administration. They examined our preaching and teaching, our work among children, young people and students. They spent time in our households, and asked searching questions about the area groups, the creative arts groups and methods of communication. Every aspect of the work was carefully researched. Most of the comments were exceedingly encouraging. Concerning the creative arts, for example, they stressed that 'man does not learn by words alone'. They commented that

> there are so few congregations as free to experiment in these forms, yet dance, movement and drama are the very warp and woof of the TV age, the media whereby most adult public communication now takes place . . . Most important of all, since the subject here is the communication of Christ to the world today, the team pleaded for the continued examination of the most effective blendings of dance, music, movement, drama, participation in liturgical prayer, and preaching and everyday witness *as expressions of the Word within the Body of Christ.*

Helpfully, the team also revealed a number of weaknesses in our church life which needed immediate attention.

It was hard not to feel threatened by the exercise, and yet we all knew that it was extremely healthy for us to be 'examined' in this way, especially as so many visitors were coming to learn from us. During the week I talked with Canon John Poulton, the leader of the team, and he made a suggestion that was exactly in line with what I had been thinking. 'Why not bring in someone as vicar, to run St. Michael's under your overall leadership, while you become rector, with a greater freedom for travelling?' I had already considered this seriously as a possible solution, so this extra confirmation was just what I needed. I knew that a slightly similar arrangement had worked with John Stott at All Souls, when Michael Baughen went there, so at least the idea had a precedent.

The question was, who should become vicar? If a newcomer came in, it might be years before he gained the confidence of the congregation, and I knew of no one who was an obvious choice from outside York. However, we had a young clergyman in our congregation, who was a travelling secretary with the Church Pastoral Aid Society, Graham Cray; and increasingly Anne and I felt that he might be exactly the right person. He was already an elder of our church in his own right, and he and his supportive wife Jackie were thoroughly accepted and liked by all in the congregation who knew them. As part of the week with the Archbishop's Council on Evangelism, we had a residential weekend with our elders and Church Council members; and during that time Anne and I talked to Graham and Jackie at length about the ideas that were beginning to form in our minds. They were somewhat overwhelmed at first, but warmed positively to the idea, and it became obvious to us that they shared our vision for the church exactly, as well as being able to introduce some fresh and helpful elements. I discussed all this with the elders the next day, and it seemed right to approach the Archbishop, Dr. Stuart Blanch, for his advice.

It so happened that the Archbishop was due to preach two weeks later, and I had an opportunity on that evening to raise the issue with him. Immediately he saw the value of the scheme; and so plans were put into action, and on July 1st, 1978 Graham began work as vicar of St. Michael's, the official service being conducted by the Bishop of Selby on July 20th. Thus began a wonderful relationship between Graham, Jackie, Anne and myself, as we shared together the primary role of leadership in the church. It seemed as if an immense weight had been taken off my shoulders, and Anne and I valued the gentle loving wisdom of Graham and Jackie more than we could say. Increasingly we were impressed by their maturity of vision, their grasp of the Gospel in today's world, and their shrewd understanding of the kingdom of God. At times I have found Graham's teaching quite brilliant, and I have personally learnt much from him over the years.

Sooner than I expected, I found myself phasing out of the main role as leader, and, with complete confidence, letting Graham take over from me. Changes of leadership, however, can be disturbing, especially after a lengthy ministry in a church, and our church was no exception to this general rule. What followed proved to be the most painful experience in my entire ministry.

Tensions and Division

The three common stages of any community are *honeymoon*, *nightmare* and then *reality*. Much the same is true also of a new ministry in a church. To begin with, the congregation were overjoyed with our new arrangement. The fresh depths of Graham Cray's teaching touched many people's lives; his constant presence in York was a refreshing change from my increasing absence; and a variety of loose ends in the church were beginning to be tied up. It was largely through Graham's initiative that the area groups were reorganised into manageable sizes, and support groups for the leaders came into being. Time and again I was impressed by his mature grasp of the pastoral needs in the church, and he was clearly a gifted counsellor – a fact that many came to appreciate for themselves in the following months.

Nevertheless, the changeover of leadership is a time when various negatives come into the light, particularly any frustrations and criticisms which might have been suppressed out of deference to the previous leader. After a year or so, I became aware of new influences from one or two leaders (not Graham) beginning to creep in, which were pulling the church in a different direction. Graham was aware of this as well, but I was not always around to support him. There were some severe prophecies about God's judgment on our church, and these instilled an unhealthy fear and critical spirit into parts of the congregation. I personally questioned whether those prophecies were from the Lord; but, significantly perhaps, they were all given when I was away, and I heard only a recording or report of them when it was too late to do much about them. The boat was beginning to rock, and the storm was still only on the horizon.

A little later, I heard that a number within the church were quietly visiting a non-denominational fellowship in Northern Ireland, and going back there on several other visits, taking their friends with them. There was nothing wrong about this in itself. Indeed, many from throughout Northern Ireland had visited our church on several occasions, and apparently were blessed by those visits. But then I discovered that a small group in our church were putting themselves under the authority of the leaders of that Ulster fellowship, and their leaders, in turn, were coming under the authority of other leaders in Florida, U.S.A. They were apparently looking for a much stronger authority structure, involving more rigid discipling, shepherding and submission. Moreover this group in our church were advocating a slightly different aspect of spirituality, which had all the dangers of becoming a super-spirituality, and they were questioning the developments of the creative arts within the church, which God had been using with much obvious blessing.

It was possibly due to these emphases that an investigation was held into Anne's ministry. One or two elders felt that she had been too strong and dogmatic, which, if true at all, was doubtless due to her having spiritual maturity and vision beyond that of most of the elders – particularly frustrating, since she was a woman with no voice in the eldership. Up to that point Anne had been a much valued leader of the area group and area fellowship (a larger body comprising about six area groups), a prominent member of the worship committee for years, and the founder-leader of the Children's Workshop – an exciting and creative group treating children as members of the Body of Christ and encouraging them, at their own level, to take a full part in the life of the church. Anne had also initiated a number of women's groups, which had proved an enormous support for many women, some of whom were under much pressure domestically.

The result of the investigation was that Anne was required

by the elders to leave *all* the groups in which she had been involved, without exception, for a period of six months at least – although it was difficult to see how she could go back into them after that time. Part of the reason given was to strengthen our own marriage relationship, which actually had been steadily improving at that stage; but since I was shortly to go off to Australia and New Zealand for ten weeks (almost half those six months), the decision was pastorally disastrous. In spite of a vigorous protest from both Graham and me, the recommendation somehow went through, and for Anne the spiritual and emotional effect was like an amputation of both her arms and legs. It was exceedingly traumatic, although I was amazed to see how well, after an initial struggle, she managed to accept it, since she always determined to submit to the elders whether she felt that they were right or wrong. I was far more angry than she. I wrote a furious letter from New Zealand to one elder, and later apologised for my outburst.

The tour in Australia and New Zealand was an exhausting one, though with numerous encouragements throughout. I shall always remember the best street theatre we have ever experienced, in the Cathedral Square of Christchurch. An estimated crowd of 1,000 gathered and the sense of communication was excellent. An aerial photograph of the event is certainly impressive. Likewise I shall remember our final night in Auckland where, despite my fears and misgivings, the Racecourse Grandstand was booked. I felt it was the wrong time of year: cold, dark, windy and threatening to rain. However, the confident faith of the organisers was justified: a crowd of between 6,000 and 9,000 turned up (the estimates varied), and streams of people came forward in the dark to say that they had committed their lives to Christ. Altogether in that tour I preached 150 times in fifteen different centres, and the team I went with worked equally hard – Phil and Joy Potter, Liz Attwood and Pauline Hornby, with local additions helping us out. Our final stop was in Canberra where we had packed meetings in the Big Tent directly in front of Parliament House. Imaginative publicity added to the festival, and I found myself described as a 'gentle-mannered rector' and the

team as 'energetic musicians, dancers and actors who have
leaped across the British scene with a burst of Spring Fever
which lasts all year round'. I think the spring fever was sagging
a bit by that stage, but everywhere we were startled to see how
God was using our varied presentation of the Gospel. Even in
the two most discouraging meetings (from our point of view)
we heard later how people's lives had been changed by the
Spirit of God.

My telephone calls to York each week, however, were in
sharp contrast to the blessing that we were continuously
experiencing. I found Anne to be increasingly depressed not
by her removal from all the groups to which she had given her
life, but by the tensions and splits developing in the church,
particularly within the leadership. There had been more
stringent prophecies, and one or two leaders were clearly
trying to swing things their own way. They were accepting
neither Graham's leadership, nor, by implication, my own.
Indeed, it was during my tour that I came to understand more
clearly one crucial principle in shared leadership.

In one city I met a minister who told me, after one of my
seminars: 'David, for years I have been trying to share my
leadership. But now I find that they are all pulling in different
directions.' This very fine man had been the pastor of his
church for fifteen years, and God's work there had been an
inspiration to Christians all over the country. Now, amazingly, he was experiencing just the same problems that we were
going through in York. At the next seminar we discussed in
greater depth the whole issue of shared leadership, and saw
that the main leader (vicar, minister, or pastor) has a God-
given 'apostolic' role to play, in the way that Timothy was the
apostle of the church at Ephesus. Now, shared leadership
begins with the sharing of lives and building up deep relationships of love, commitment and trust. Unless that quality
of relationship exists, shared leadership is fraught with dangers through the spirit of competition and self-seeking. But
even when the fusion of lives has genuinely taken place, there
must still be the leader of leaders, and others must respect
that God-given call. The other leaders may, in love, question,

challenge or even rebuke if necessary; but they must, in the long run, submit to the one who is over them in the Lord. The tragedy of the Church today, not least in 'renewal circles', is that 'every man does what is right in his own eyes' – which was the mark of spiritual degeneracy in the Old Testament, and the sign of carnality in the New.

On my return from Australia, I found our church more like the Corinthian Church than at any other time during the previous fifteen years. At Corinth, various factions formed round the different personalities of Paul, Apollos and Peter. This was tragic, wrote Paul, since those leaders were only servants through whom God worked to bring life to others. They were nothing in themselves. Moreover, he said, the one and only foundation for any church is Jesus Christ; it can never be the personality, gifts or even teaching of a particular leader. Paul went on to say that it is therefore extremely important how we build on that one foundation of Christ. The whole theme of the chapter (I Cor. 3) is that of the unity of the Church, so that if we build up anything which becomes divisive, we are building with 'wood, hay, straw' – materials which will not stand the fiery test of God's judgment. Indeed, if anyone destroys the temple of God, God will destroy him. Paul could not have been more emphatic about the sinfulness of divisions within the Church.

I had one brief day off after my ten-week tour, recovering from jet-lag and total exhaustion, before plunging into a number of intense meetings and discussions as we tried our utmost to avoid a split. However the splinter group, as it was rapidly becoming, was preaching a dangerous idea, currently taught in some circles but with no theological basis, a distinction between the *logos* and *rhēma* of God (both words being used interchangeably in the New Testament for the word of God). They held that the *logos* referred only to the general word of God in the Scriptures; but the *rhēma* was the prophetic word, God's word for now. Further, although there may be general agreement about the *logos* of God, our unity and fellowship depends in practice, they claimed, on our response to the *rhēma* of God. One of the leaders of this splinter group

wrote to me: 'Unity is not built on a relationship with my
brother, but on a response to the word of God. Thus you may
have as much unity as you have agreement on the *rhēma* of
Jesus Christ.' If there is a disagreement in our response to the
rhēma of the Spirit, it is virtually impossible to maintain any
working fellowship. Thus, they concluded, they had no choice
but to separate themselves from us.

The subtlety is that all this may sound plausible for the
Christian who genuinely wants to be obedient to God, and I
did not doubt the sincerity of this group. I had known them,
loved them, prayed for them and worked with them for many
years. The trouble was that the basis on which they felt they
had to withdraw was entirely fallacious. Our unity is, quite
simply, in Christ. The New Testament permits us to separate
from others *only* if they deny either the divinity of Christ, his
death for our sins, or his resurrection from the dead. All this
we tried to explain as clearly as we could, both publicly and
privately. Graham, again entirely with my support, even
asked the main leader of this group to be an elder again, when
the time came for the reappointment of elders. This was a
final attempt to avoid division, but the invitation was not
accepted.

Perhaps the final straw came when Graham gave a masterly
series of four sermons on leadership and, as vicar but with my
total agreement, included three women in the next body of
elders, one of those women being Anne. Many of us felt that
the inclusion of women was long overdue, but that particular
group found this altogether unacceptable. About twenty left
the church. Although we were thankful that a much larger
group did not leave us (we had been told that 150 would go),
the pain was still enormous, especially as we had enjoyed such
close fellowship with them for many years.

Looking back, I can see that the considerable overlap
between my leadership and Graham's was extraordinarily
important, and but for that factor the split might have been
much worse. I wonder if this should not be the pattern for the
handover of the leadership in any church, especially where
the previous leader has been there for a long time.

In spite of the prophecies of God's judgment upon us, the shaken and chastened congregation found a new unity in Christ, gave Graham full support once again in his role as vicar, and became hungry for further spiritual renewal. Through the visit of a gifted pastor and a great friend of mine, John Wimber (from Yorba Linda, California), we had another Pentecost. At their own expense, John brought over a team of twenty-nine from his congregation, and the Spirit of God worked through them with unusual effectiveness and power. There were some wonderful healings and conversions, and many were filled with the Spirit. Those who had recently separated themselves from us kept away; but within the rest of the congregation there was a marvellous healing of relationships where tensions still existed. John Wimber, whose own church had grown from nothing to 4,000 in four years and who has wide experience of churches in many places, told me that he had never found any other church like ours that was hurting so much. The sense of grief was acute. Because of the special depth of shared relationships that God had given us in Christ, the split had caused terrible wounds. Through this we felt, no doubt in very small measure, the pain that Christ must feel over the divisions in his Body, the Church today.

Those who leave their churches to form 'non-denominational' fellowships need to realise what they are doing. As soon as those fellowships become more structured and administer the sacraments of baptism and the Lord's Supper, they virtually become churches; and when those 'house churches' have some affiliation with one another, another denomination is born. This is the sad but constant witness of church history, but we never seem to learn the lessons of the past. Often I say to those who are impatient with the stuffiness of their traditional church: 'If you want more life, give your life; if you want more prayer, give your prayer; if you want more love, give your love . . .' It is only as the grain of wheat falls into the ground and *dies* that it will bring forth a harvest.

Significantly, when the Spirit came, in Ezekiel's vision of the valley of dry bones, he did not blow the bones away and start with something entirely new, as he could easily have done. He worked on those dry and dusty bones, bringing them together, clothing them with flesh, and instilling new life into them. This is what I see God is doing with all the denominations throughout the world today. There is often an unholy impatience when Christians divide, often on some minor issue, to do their own thing. It is worth reflecting that Jesus continued worshipping in the synagogue and Temple for some thirty years, patiently bearing with its spiritual deadness, before his incredible and brief ministry took place. The only divisions that are in any way justifiable are when Christians are literally driven out of their churches through active persecution, as with Wesley and Whitefield (though they did their utmost to remain within the Anglican Church throughout their lives), or when the institutional church has apostasised by denying the most fundamental tenets of the Christian faith. All other divisions are wrong and sinful, and they grieve the Holy Spirit of God. We need only to see the urgent apostolic appeals for unity within the New Testament epistles to understand how important this is.

If we really followed the Spirit we would be willing to go through suffering and crucifixion if need be – no doubt at the hands of religious people – in order to bring life to others. To form another church of like-minded people, thereby impoverishing the lives of our brothers and sisters who are working hard for renewal within their own churches (however slowly and imperfectly), is an easy option and not the way of Christ. Indeed, it is a sad twist that those who genuinely want to 'obey the Spirit' can so easily 'grieve the Spirit' by their actions, which are contrary to the word of God.

Naturally there were faults on our side too. No doubt we should have been more renewed, more prayerful, more committed, or whatever. In one sense this will always be true. In any painful split like this, no one can point the finger; everyone needs the mercy and forgiveness of God. We are all in the wrong. The amazing truth is, that in spite of our sinful divisions God can so overrule what we do to one another (and to him) that his kingdom grows even more. The apostle Paul once had an argument with his great friend Barnabas. Luke tells us in Acts 15 that 'there arose a sharp contention, so that they separated from each other; Barnabas took Mark with him and sailed away to Cyprus, but Paul chose Silas and departed . . .' It seems that the Church expanded still further as the result of God's mercy and grace in the midst of human sin.

17

Renewal Weeks

'Go on talking,' I said. 'I think the Lord is saying something through you.' I began to scribble notes as fast as I could. I was at the sharing time of the dance group, and one member of that group was talking quietly about her thoughts concerning possible future developments in York. As Sue talked, I sensed that what she was sharing was prophetic in its quality. That was in the summer of 1976.

During the previous three years, since our move into St. Michael-le-Belfrey, many church leaders from Great Britain and overseas had visited our church to see what we were learning about evangelism, renewal and church growth. Occasionally those visits, brief and seemingly insignificant, had resulted in the transformation of people's ministries, much to our surprise. However, although we felt it right to give time to clergy and other leaders, the same questions were being asked over and over again; and it was a time-consuming business repeating the same answers. I seemed to be available even less for my own congregation, and though the time spent with one visitor after another was nearly always profitable, the demands being made on me and on some of the other elders were proving a problem.

'Why don't we plan a special week, perhaps twice a year,' asked Sue, 'when we invite lots of leaders to our church, let them stay in the homes of the congregation, experience the life of the fellowship, and see for themselves its strengths and weaknesses, and hold seminars so that we can share what we are trying to learn?' The whole vision excited me. Not only would this concentrate our time with visitors into two main weeks in the year (apart from some exceptions for overseas visitors), but those who came could see God's work among us in much more depth than I could ever begin to explain in the course of a few hours. It had many obvious advantages; and instead of the congregation finding that much of my time was being absorbed by those outside York, they themselves would be directly involved in sharing any vision that God had given us.

The elders were enthusiastic about the idea, and two prophetic words were later given confirming that God wanted to use us as a source of encouragement and renewal for other churches. But for this initiative from the Lord (as I took it to be), I would never have dared to launch these weeks for local church renewal. Without some conviction that we were obeying the leading of the Spirit, the whole idea would have been presumptuous. Who were we to tell other churches what to do, even by implication? Those of us in the hot seat of leadership were profoundly aware of numerous weaknesses in our own congregation. We ourselves were in constant need of spiritual renewal and greater maturity. In fact, I was delighted later on when I received a letter from a Swiss pastor: 'We had heard that St. Michael-le-Belfrey was an almost perfect church. We could hardly believe it, but we praised the Lord. Now we have been to York personally, now we have seen. It is not perfect, and now we praise the Lord even more. If the Lord can use sinners such as the people in St. Michael-le-Belfrey, he can use us too!' That was clearly the good news we had to share: if God could do something among us, he could do something anywhere!

In many ways, this proved the strength of our Renewal Weeks, as we called them. The first took place in April 1977. Although we did not advertise it at all, word got round and we were inundated by bookings. We organised two a year (each April and September, for six days at a time), and held twelve in all, with some 1,500 coming from all over the United Kingdom and from many countries overseas. Most of the participants were leaders – since we always stressed that these

weeks were for that purpose – and those who came represented many traditions and denominations. The main difficulty
we had was finding sufficient hospitality to accommodate
all those who wanted to come. There was an undoubted
momentum of the Spirit, which confirmed our discernment of
God's initiative in the whole venture. Apart from those from
England, especially large numbers came from Northern Ireland, Wales and Sweden.

These weeks took a simple form, and were superbly managed by a businessman Douglas Greenfield, who was one of
our elders, and by his wife Joan. Normally guests arrived on
the Friday evening and settled into the homes where they
were staying. Some of the hosts had never received guests
before, and one or two embarrassing situations had to be
sorted out quickly. We had the occasional complaint of
impossible beds or bedroom doors that could not shut. But
other hosts were so generous in their hospitality that their
guests found this experience of loving relationships the most
refreshing part of the week. On the Saturday morning we
took time explaining some of the biblical principles behind
renewal, particularly giving an indication as to what the guests
might expect in the Sunday services, since our developments
in terms of music, dance and drama would have been quite
new, if not revolutionary, for some of them. On Saturday
evening we usually had an entertainment, often led by Riding
Lights and supported by others in the church, to show that we
were not desperately intense and pious, but knew how to
laugh and enjoy ourselves in God's presence. This frequently
relaxed the more nervous guests who were anxious lest they
had come into a wild spiritual hot-house!

The Sunday services were always times of special joy.
When you add 100–150 leaders, all hungry for spiritual
renewal, to an already packed church, the sense of anticipation is considerably heightened. Both the Family Service in
the morning and the evening service of Holy Communion
were invariably times of unusual blessing, and helped to put
into some clear context the teaching of the seminars during
the next few days. One couple expressed it in this way,

although we had numerous similar letters from most of the participants: 'We praise our living Lord that his Spirit was so powerfully evident in the praise and worship, and in the overflowing love of the fellowship. Since coming home, we have wept together in the joy of the Spirit, and for someone who is not given to weeping, like so many men, that can only be of God!' For most people, these weeks were primarily times of personal renewal, which of course is a necessary prelude to local church renewal; and often the Spirit of God touched our visitors deeply through the worship of his people. It was not uncommon to see some, including strong and mature men, in tears. The services provided a visible and tangible expression of what we were talking about, even though later in the week we touched on numerous aspects of renewal and evangelism that were not immediately obvious in the services.

From Monday to Thursday, we met together each morning for worship and teaching, followed by a choice of seminars, covering subjects such as ministry, healing, evangelism, small groups, music, dance, drama, creative arts, youth work, counselling, children's work, catering. A team of helpers organised lunches each day, and this was so carefully and beautifully done that often it made an impression of its own, indicating that renewal touched every area of our lives, not just singing choruses! The Bishop of Selby, Morris Maddocks, came to most of the weeks, and gave an excellent seminar on healing, which was followed by the ministry of the laying on of hands, with the elders assisting the Bishop in this, and most of the guests came up for prayer. We became aware of the deep personal needs that most Christian leaders have; but who can minister to them in their churches? Where do they find for themselves the counselling that they so frequently give to others? Those healing seminars, together with many other opportunities for personal counselling, became a vital part of these weeks. Further, the presence of the Bishop also helped the guests to see the approval of the wider Church for these weeks, and indeed bishops from elsewhere were even sending their clergy to us for renewal!

The strength and weakness of such a week lay in the fact that it was hosted by a local church, instead of the more usual conference organised by a specialised team of experts. This meant that the quality of teaching on the part of seminar leaders was admittedly varied; but unless renewal could be seen to work within the context of an ordinary congregation – and we were a very ordinary congregation, with a complete mix of social and educational backgrounds – it had nothing much to say to the Church as a whole. Indeed, although the teaching and worship was generally appreciated, it was the impact of the church as a living fellowship, with all its obvious faults and failings, that almost always made the most impact. One church leader, who encouraged several other clergy to attend, wrote afterwards: 'I have seen all the people who attended the recent Renewal Week . . . They have all been blessed beyond words. One person put it beautifully: "It was a glimpse of heaven". This is precisely what our Lord means his living Body to be.' That, and countless similar letters, gave us enormous encouragement. From our perspective as elders, we often seemed to be limping from one crisis in the church to another. 'What next?' we often asked ourselves gloomily. We wondered if those who came to our church would have a glimpse of hell instead of one of heaven! But the Gospel always speaks of God's grace in the midst of human weakness, sin and frailty. There was no doubt about our weaknesses – one of our best Renewal Weeks came immediately after the traumatic closing of the Mustard Seed – but somehow God's grace was still there among us, which is why those who came continued to be blessed.

The leader of one of the many Irish contingents put it in this way:

The value of a course like this lies chiefly in the encouragement and stimulus it gives. People coming from local situations which seem fairly hopeless, can return home to weigh the biblical principles to see how they can be applied in their own churches. If God can do in such unpromising soil what he has manifestly done in 'redundant' churches in

York he can do new things in any place, if his people open
up to him and in the power of the Holy Spirit respond where
they are. This is the main message of the York Weeks of
Local Church Renewal.

Another said, 'Here we *felt* God's love in action. He was really
among us. We go back believing he goes with us.'

It was always a special privilege to pray with those who
were longing for personal renewal. One older Norwegian
pastor, who was also a gifted theologian, was so hungry to
meet with God that he did not sleep at all during the night
before he came to York. I have hardly ever met a man who
was so 'hungry and thirsty for righteousness'. Naturally God
met him with unusual power. We did not say anything very
much to him. God did his own work, and it was wonderful to
see it happen. We never quite knew why those weeks proved
to be such a turning-point in the lives of many who came, not
least clergy and ministers, but that is what happened time and
again. At a recent leaders' conference for renewal in Wales,
seventy out of the eighty leaders present had been to our
Renewal Weeks.

It is important, however, to be sensitive to the momentum
of the Spirit. When the wind of the Spirit seems to be blowing
in a certain direction, we need the courage to hoist our sails
and to move as the Spirit leads us. But when the wind changes
direction, we need equal courage to change with it. In our
churches, we must be willing not only to start some ventures
we have never tried before, but also to stop them when their
immediate purpose seems to have ended. Recently we
noticed a slackening of momentum in the Renewal Weeks,
and I am glad to hear that the present leaders of St. Michael's
have had the courage to stop them – at least for the time
being. Perhaps these weeks will start again at some later date,
possibly in a different form. We need always to be open to the
Spirit of God, who is the Spirit of movement.

Constantly we need renewal. The Holy Spirit will never let
us stay in one place for too long, lest we become stale and
stagnant. Always he is moving us on, to make us fresh and

relevant for the needs of people today. We can never cling to what is relevant only for the people of yesterday – or if we do cling to those patterns we shall soon become spiritually sterile. 'He who has an ear, let him hear what the Spirit says (*lit.* is saying) to the churches.' The greatest hindrance to the work of the Spirit is not tradition, since tradition can have a vital stabilising effect in a confusing world of constant change, but *traditionalism*, or the clinging to tradition for tradition's sake. The history of the Church could be characterised by the breath of the Spirit of God breathing new life into the Church. Man then comes to regiment and institutionalise it; and the Spirit of God quietly withdraws. The institution, devoid of any real spiritual life, may continue to rumble on unperturbed, sometimes for generations. Occasionally I come across certain church events which perhaps were highly relevant at one time, but over which you now see written the word *ichabod* – 'the glory of the Lord has departed'. It is then that we need to cry out with the psalmist, 'Wilt thou not revive us again, that thy people may rejoice in thee' (Ps. 85:6).

18

Teams and Travelling

'Someone has told us that a bomb has been planted in the theatre. Will you get everyone out immediately!' I was leading the Merseyside Festival with a team I had taken with me from York. It was Youth Night, and the Empire Theatre in Liverpool had at least 2,000 young people in it. It was only ten minutes before the programme was due to begin when the bomb scare came. We asked everyone to leave as quickly and as quietly as possible, and within four minutes the theatre was empty.

The police cordoned off the area while the theatre was searched, and there was confusion in the streets. Someone found a suspicious package near the electrical wiring system, and so we were all ordered back to a safe distance while the Bomb Disposal Unit from the army was called. So we had 2,000 young people standing on the steps of St. George's, looking like a typical football crowd. Alan Godson, an enterprising vicar in Liverpool and a great personal friend of mine, persuaded the Fire Brigade to erect some lighting, and the team did some drama, interspersed with the singing of Christian songs and choruses by everyone. Alan then guided a police van to where we were standing, and Bishop David Sheppard and I climbed in. Bishop David led in prayer, and I preached – all from the police van, using their loud-hailer! It was the strangest pulpit I had ever used! After well over an hour, the suspicious object was found to be only a hoax, and we went back into the theatre to begin the Youth Night. 2,000 youngsters had gone onto the streets; but the impromptu street theatre had been so effective that 2,500 youngsters went back in for the main event, which went extraordinarily well. In fact it was so successful that the following week, when we had another Youth Night, the theatre was packed with over 3,000, and more than 600 were turned away at the doors! Many young people found Christ on both those occasions, and we saw how marvellously God can turn any situation to his glory.

This was one of the many unusual incidents in the work I was now doing for much of the time. Six years before, in 1973, five respected Christian leaders had written to me over the course of a few months, and as far as I know they all wrote independently. However, each letter said roughly the same thing: 'I wonder if God might be calling you to lead city-wide missions in the future?' I had for years been leading university missions, but this was quite different. To begin with, I dismissed the idea without much thought. I knew that God had blessed the big events of the past, such as the Billy Graham Crusades at Harringay and Wembley in the mid-fifties. But I felt sure that such events were not for Great Britain in the seventies, even if they were still fruitful in other parts of the world. The whole pattern of evangelism had changed, I thought. Today, 'small is beautiful', and I had been impressed by the value of the small evangelistic home meeting. It cost nothing, required minimum organisation, genuinely reached the 'outsider', and through such meetings many had been brought to Christ. I was not interested in any more 'big events'.

It was hard to ignore those five letters, however, especially when I received invitations to lead united church missions in Tonbridge, Bristol and Sheffield in 1974–5. I could not ignore the possibility that God *might* be saying something to me through all this, however unlikely it seemed to me at the time. Tentatively I accepted the invitations, and was pleasantly surprised when we had three thoroughly good missions. At Sheffield, for example, 13,000 people attended the meetings and at least 400 gave their lives to Christ. Further, Christians came together from widely different traditions and denominations, and undoubtedly there was some spiritual renewal both for individuals and churches. We soon changed the name of these events from missions to 'festivals'. I could see the value of the occasional celebration, especially with all the gloom, depression and hostility of today's world.

It is commonly said that Christians need three sizes of group for healthy growth into maturity – sociologists speak of this as of general importance for everyone. The Christian ideally needs the cell, the congregation and the celebration. The *cell* is the small house group, where there can be an intimate sharing of the faith. The *congregation* is what most Christians know about, when we come together each week for worship, teaching and the sacraments. But there is also value in the occasional *celebration* when we come together in much greater numbers but still as members of one family in order to worship God, to proclaim the Good News of Jesus Christ, and to encourage one another in our faith. Even in secular terms we all benefit from celebration: birthday parties, weddings, anniversaries, and so forth. The Royal Wedding in 1981 was a time of rejoicing for the whole country: everyone felt better for it. We need these special events to lift us out of the drabness of much of our daily lives, and to remind us of some of the good and positive values in today's negative society. So it is with the Christian family. It is easy to get engulfed by problems, personal or otherwise. But God's people are called to rejoice together in his presence, and to encourage others to do the same: 'O magnify the Lord with me, and let us exalt his name together!' (Ps. 34:3). In no way could these festivals ever replace the mission and evangelism of the local church. But if they could be used to encourage the local churches in their necessary and continuing work, they would be eminently worthwhile.

At Tonbridge, Bristol and Sheffield I worked with the Fisherfolk, a singing group gifted in leading people in worship. For several years I had been convinced of the value of setting the proclamation of the Gospel firmly in the context of joyful worship. In this 'feelings' generation I knew that most people needed to feel God's presence and sense his

reality before listening to his words. We found repeatedly in
York that those who came to Christ in our services were
initially aware of God's presence through the worship of his
people. It was then my task as a preacher to say, in effect,
'That which you have seen and heard I declare to you.' This
had been the method of Jesus and the apostles when people
realised that God was among them through healings or signs
and wonders. I knew that joyful and sensitive worship is a
wonderful way of opening people's hearts to the Spirit of
God.

As much as I enjoyed working with the Fisherfolk, however, I looked forward to the time when I could travel with my
own team. Slowly I built up a group of young people from St.
Michael's who were gifted in music, dance and drama – the
drama section initially filled by those who later became
Riding Lights.

Our first really major commitment came in response to an
invitation from the Bishop of Down and Dromore in Northern Ireland to lead a Campaign for Renewal in his Diocese in
1977. We went as a team of twelve and although inexperienced had a remarkably good time, especially during the
closing five days in St. Anne's Cathedral, Belfast. One strict
Calvinistic Presbyterian minister wrote to say,

> How my eyes were opened! What a new lease of life I am
> enjoying in Christ! It is almost like experiencing my rebirth
> once more. On the Sunday morning following your depar-
> ture I felt I had to be man enough to stand and let my people
> know that God had blessed me at your services with a
> baptism of his Spirit. Many told me afterwards that I did not
> have to tell them because they could see the difference.

Since then he has experienced deep fellowship with Roman
Catholic priests who have themselves been renewed – something unthinkable previously. Others spoke of our time in
Belfast as, in the words of one of them, 'the most spiritually
rewarding experience I have ever known'. All that was an
important confirmation that God was with us in this new

development, and we could see both clergy and laity come alive in the Spirit.

Once the basic vision of the work had been established and a regular full-time team had come together, the invitations to lead festivals came in (and increasingly do so) much faster than we could possibly manage. It soon became apparent that all these invitations needed careful researching. Which areas were ready for a festival? Were the Christians in that area beginning to work well together, especially the leaders? Did the proposed festival have the backing of the bishop and other denominational leaders? Was the Spirit causing a fresh hunger for God and a desire among Christians to make Christ known? Were we the right team for what was wanted? Obviously there are many different approaches, and ours may be one valid way of communicating the Gospel, but not the only one. It was clearly impossible for me to do the necessary research as the invitations grew in number. Providentially an elder in St. Michael's, Douglas Greenfield (who ran the Renewal Weeks) felt that God was calling him to help us in this, and, as consultant to an export pharmaceutical company, he was given flexibility of time to combine his business with this research. Douglas over the years has proved indispensable, and without his careful investigation and practical planning we would have wasted many thousands of pounds and endless time and energy in fruitless work.

The simple plan is for Douglas to follow up an invitation with a preliminary visit, in order to discuss plans with church leaders. He then submits a report, giving some indication whether a town or city is ready for a festival. If the report is favourable, we arrange a 24-hour visit for the whole team, leading a festival of praise in the evening and holding seminars the next morning – seminars usually on evangelism, small groups, music in worship, dance in worship and drama. By the end of that visit both the local church leaders and we as a team will have some idea whether a festival is right in the future. If we feel this to be so, much praying and planning begins.

When the festival arrives, the focal point is an evening celebration each night of the week, marked by joyful, corporate worship and then preaching illustrated by drama or mime. These are always festive occasions, even when we take very serious and challenging themes. The rest of the time is taken up with a wide variety of activities: visits to schools, universities, colleges, prisons, hospitals; lunches for business-men, seminars for clergy, special meetings for ladies, the elderly or the sick; street theatre in shopping precincts, children's services, workshops for local churches – anything that is relevant in the area.

Our overall aim is threefold: reconciliation, renewal and evangelism. As far as *reconciliation* is concerned, it is thrilling to see Christians of all traditions come together, usually with very few exceptions, and discover one another in Christ. After an encouraging festival in Manchester in 1978, one prominent leader in the City wrote: 'I have now been working in the City for over twenty-eight years and I can honestly say that there has never been anything like it . . . One of the outstanding features has been the way in which so many churches have worked together (250 of them), plus the note of celebration and just a real joy in the Lord himself.' In Birmingham (1981) over 600 churches committed themselves to the festival, and once again there had never, in living memory at least, been such co-operation between the churches. If new love and trust can be found within the Body of Christ in a given area, that alone would make the festival well worth all the time, money and effort involved. It is where 'brothers dwell together in unity' that the Lord 'commands his blessing' (Ps. 133).

Obviously the theme of reconciliation is foremost in our minds when leading festivals in Northern Ireland and South Africa, and we make it clear in all our meetings that all people, no matter what tradition, race or culture they belong to, are welcome. Reconciliation, however, is never easy. In Northern Ireland, for example, we have been openly opposed by militant groups. In South Africa, one attempted city-wide festival was frankly a disaster. One of our biggest disappoint-ments, however, was in Malta. In January 1978 Douglas and I spent a week in Malta at the invitation of several leaders in the

Roman Catholic Church to see if we should lead a mission for renewal in the island for Roman Catholics. Douglas knew Malta well through his business, and although I had an extremely heavy cold through the week, I found it a fascinating time. We had many sensitive discussions and we knew that it was remarkable that we, an English Anglican team, should be invited for such a purpose. On the last day, when everything looked set and all the plans were fully made, there was an objection from a totally unexpected non-Roman source. There was nothing that could be done but to call off the whole mission, and they (and we of course) were extremely sad about it.

Our second main concern is for *renewal* – that is, encouraging fresh spiritual life both for the individual Christian and for the local church. The advantage of a special week, such as a festival, is that it gives everyone the motivation for doing what should be done in the normal course of the church's life. Christians come together to pray; they learn how to talk to their friends about Christ, and start doing it; they meet for studying the faith; for worship; for projects in the area, both evangelistic and social. In fact such good work takes place before we arrive in a town or city for the festival itself that I am frequently told on the opening day, 'If you had died before the festival had started, it would all have been worth it!' It is a curiously ambiguous remark (since I had not died, was it worth it after all?), but I know what I hope they mean by such a remark, and am delighted that we become the excuse for so many good Christian initiatives in the area.

There can also be renewal in other ways. Many people find renewal in worship: 'For the first time in my life I am learning what it means to worship God,' wrote one person after a festival. Others discover a new confidence in God, a new understanding of the faith, a new assurance of God's forgiveness and love. One of the most frequent and significant results is the renewal of relationships. In the summer of 1978 we led a mission (as it was called) for the whole of Cornwall, based mainly on Truro Cathedral. The Dean of the cathedral, who was nearing retirement, said that in all his long ministry he had never sensed such a powerful presence of the Spirit of God as during those ten days in the cathedral. One night I urged all those present who felt that they needed to put right some relationships to do so before they went to bed, if possible. 'Talk when you get home,' I urged. 'Make a phone call; write a letter.' Outside the big west doors of the cathedral are many telephone boxes. I heard later that after the service was over there were queues of people waiting to make a telephone call, and I understand that many relationships were put right that evening. I did not know all this at the time. What I did know was that, in the cathedral the next night, the sense of God's presence was almost electric. The Spirit of God was no longer grieved through long-standing bad relationships, and was thus free to move in unusual power. This is an experience known to Christians throughout the world in times of revival.

In Ipswich (1981) the hunger for God throughout the whole area was so great that we could not deal adequately with the crowds that came. The Corn Exchange was booked for the main meetings, with overflows in the Town Hall nearby. But on the opening night some 600 had to be turned away, many of them having come in coach parties from some distance. The next night extra relays were provided, and the meeting was broadcast to a crowd of 200 standing in the cold, dark streets, with cups of coffee and tea being taken to them. Eventually the Christians had to say to one another, 'Don't come unless you have to!' Not many churches say that today. From Ipswich we went on to Northampton where we saw tremendous joy in God's presence as we came together from a variety of traditions. 'The gift of joy has almost overwhelmed us' is how one Anglican leader expressed it. We also visited Wellingborough Borstal when we were there. The prison chapel was packed with young lads, over fifty of whom committed their lives to Christ that morning. During the Leeds Festival (1977) we saw a particularly unusual healing. As the final hymn 'The Lord's my Shepherd' was being sung, a woman with multiple sclerosis realised that God was healing her. She got out of her wheelchair and, supported lightly by a member of my team, walked all round the Town Hall. In the course of a few months her healing became more complete, and she later married the Bishop of the New Hebrides, now the Bishop of Glasgow. These are only a few samples of the renewing work of the Spirit of God, and stories similar to these could be multiplied many times over.

My third and primary concern has always been *evangelism*. The reason why I travel with a team, gifted as they are in the performing arts, is that they are able to communicate the Gospel much more effectively than I could with mere words. It was in 1977 that we first went to Crumlin Road Prison in Belfast, and had two wonderful services for the prisoners, most of whom were terrorists. The Chaplain said to us before we went in, 'You will probably see more murderers in the next hour than in the rest of your life put together.' We were decidedly nervous, but found that the combination of drama, music and dance, and short simple preaching, created an instant rapport. When I led the prisoners in a prayer of commitment to Christ there was total prayerful silence. Many professed conversion that day, and the commander of one of the leading terrorist organisations wrote to tell me that he had been considering for some time becoming a Christian – which was an interesting point in itself. 'But,' he went on to say, 'after seeing your team I no longer had any doubts, and have now been saved by the blood of Christ.' Later he told his prison chaplain, 'For the first time in my life I feel free!' I have many such letters from prisoners, including a number of terrorists, and most of those letters comment specifically about the vitality and communication of the team, and also about the experience of feeling free once they had found Christ. In another prison in Canada, the prisoners wanted an 'encore', so we had to sing more songs, perform more sketches and even preach more of the Gospel. Once again many prisoners came to Christ in that prison, and as they were leaving one prisoner said, 'You have brought us much joy in this prison today.' Such remarks and letters are some of the most precious I have ever received from anyone.

I find that the team is effective almost anywhere, especially

with those who are right outside the Church. In 1978 we held a
festival in Newcastle-upon-Tyne, called 'Celebrate the
Faith'. It was an exciting week and the crowded City Hall each
night was filled with a sense of joy in God's presence. The
vicar and curate of an Anglican church in the city centre had
found it impossible to attract men to their church. It was a
rough working-class area, with only a few elderly women
attending the services. But the festival gave the two clergymen an opportunity to take lots of men they knew to the City
Hall. The men were thrilled with the sense of action: drama,
dancing, humour and vitality. It seemed like the atmosphere
of a football match, one of them reported. The result was that
a number of those men gave their lives to Christ, and the
whole work of that tough parish took on a new lease of life.

During that week in Newcastle we also held a service in
Durham Jail, one of Britain's maximum security prisons. We
were allowed to take with us into the prison various props for
drama, including a large step-ladder. It was a strange sight
seeing the team marching into the prison armed with a ladder!
Once again we had a most fruitful service in terms of prisoners
committing their lives to Christ.

We soon found that this threefold emphasis of reconciliation, renewal and evangelism is at the top of most church
leaders' agenda, and invitations to lead festivals became even
more numerous. In 1980 alone, for example, I went (nearly
always with the team) to Pasadena, Kansas, Vancouver,
Calgary, Edmonton, Saskatoon, Winnipeg, Bedford, Roch-
dale, Poole, Chelsea, Cambridge, Wellington, Dunedin,
Christchurch, Auckland, Brisbane, Launceston, Hobart,
Melbourne, Sydney, Armidale, Tamworth, Canberra, and
Sheffield. Almost all the places have vivid memories for me,
and always we were aware of God's presence with us, both in
times of blessing and in the moments of depression or exhaustion. Increasingly it was obvious that God was using the team
as a catalyst. A catalyst is nothing much in itself, but it either
precipitates change or speeds up what is already taking place.
We as a team know that there is very little we can do in a
major city during one short week. But frequently God has

used these festivals, superficial though they are at one level, to stimulate the work that is already happening in that area. If we did not see clear evidence for this, we would have stopped them a long time ago. The apparent glamour of jet-setting around the world disappears within a few days.

It is not easy sitting in cold and draughty cathedrals, waiting for the stage or sound equipment to be erected before rehearsals can start. It is not easy travelling from one place to another, so that when we wake up in the morning we sometimes have to think hard to remember which country we are in, let alone which town or city. It is not easy working in halls or churches where the facilities leave much to be desired. It is not easy living out of a suitcase for weeks on end. It is not easy sleeping, or trying to sleep, in strange beds for roughly half of each year. My particular trial is damp beds. I have endured these so often that I now automatically carry with me a 'survival kit for damp beds'. If I suspect that the bed is damp, I put a mirror between the sheets. If the mirror mists up, I am left in no doubt! I then put on a black nylon mackintosh, which I always carry with me, over my pyjamas, pull on thick socks and climb carefully into bed. It is not the last word in comfort, but infinitely preferable to lying in a damp bed when you get chilled to the bone and find sleep out of the question. In one vicarage where the bed was damp – vicarages are nearly always the worst, and I usually stay in vicarages! – I wore my mackintosh as usual. I was taken by surprise, however, when the vicar came in early in the morning with a cup of tea. I had to sit up in bed to take the tea, and I think he was taken a little by surprise when he saw me in my black nylon mac! A travelling ministry is not always easy; but it does have its humorous moments!

Above all, it is not easy having to say goodbye to my wife and children so often, and it is not easy being away for weeks on end. It is even more difficult for them. In order to retain some stability for our children Anne virtually never travels with me, and we have accepted the constant separations as necessary for the present time. We work hard to maintain communication, however. Anne and I write to each other about every other day, and I write to Fiona and Guy twice a week. I also telephone every day when in this country – once a week when overseas – and we try in various ways to encourage and support one another. Anne helps, for example, by seeing to a lot of correspondence in my absence, making decisions where necessary and, with my secretary, trying to avoid a mountain of demanding mail waiting for me on my return. Sometimes they hide the mail from me so that I cannot even see it until I have partially recovered from a tour.

After those ten gruelling weeks in Australia and New Zealand, however, I have resolved never to be away for more than five weeks at a time, if I can possibly help it, but even so the work places strains on us as a family. In spite of this, however, God's grace is there for every human need, and our family life today is richer than it has ever been before.

I have the privilege, of course, of travelling with a team, and the mutual support we receive is tremendous. All team members commit themselves for at least a year at a time, and I am always glad when some choose to stay longer. So many people have spent time with me over the last eight years that it is difficult to mention any names in particular. All have played a special part in the work, and indeed in my own personal life. Most important, perhaps, is not the individual performances of gifted people, but the sense of Christ's presence through our oneness in him. The depth of our relationships in Christ depends on the degree to which we are willing to share our lives openly with one another, and such openness brings pain as well as joy. For example, sometimes I battle with depression. I never know all the reasons for this 'dark pit', as it seems to me. Some of it may be hurt pride. Sometimes it is obviously exhaustion, physical, mental, emotional and spiritual. At times, when I am tired and strained, I can get angry over an incident that may be quite trivial in itself; and then I get angry with myself for getting angry. As I suppress both forms of anger, depression is the result. I am then even more difficult to live with than usual. I do not want people to get too near to me, but I hope very much that they will not go too far away either. My team members have always been extremely supportive when I have gone through these difficult times; and naturally others in the team have had their ups and downs as well. In this way, by our mutual caring the sense of our belonging together in Christ increases.

At the end of the day we know that we have nothing to offer anyone of ultimate importance apart from Christ himself. If he can be manifested more clearly in our lives through our conscious weakness, we are content to remain weak and vulnerable. I find both the travelling and the team work demanding in every way, but I am thankful to God for having drawn me into it against all my initial prejudices. I sometimes say that God sucked me in backwards into this work: I have neither wanted it, nor been ambitious for it. Fortunately God is able to use even reluctant servants to accomplish his sovereign will. I have also discovered, together with the team, a great sense of privilege and tremendous times of joy both in our fellowship with one another and in seeing God at work through us.

19

Move to London

July 26th, 1982 closed a major chapter in our lives and opened a blank page. After seventeen years in one house in York we moved to central London. The transition was not easy, and as I write this six months later we are still suffering profound bereavement. We knew that our relationships in York had been deep – perhaps more so a few years ago than recently – but we had little idea how deep they were until they were severed. Next to literal bereavement within one's own family, this must surely be one of the most traumatic events in one's life. The sense of loss has been acute; and, as I have often counselled those who are bereaved, we have to let time do its own healing work. It is not that the Christians in London have lacked in kindness and generosity. Far from it. We know that we are a part of God's family wherever we go on the face of this earth; and the sensitive caring of many Christians here has encouraged us with God's love time and again. But deep relationships are forged through suffering and pain, as much as through joys and blessings. Without both warp and woof, no tapestry is made.

'Joy and woe are woven fine' are the memorable words of William Blake. God spoke to us through a close friend in London that the riches we would find here would be 'the treasures of darkness'. Richard Wurmbrand once said, 'The most distant object you can see in the bright light of day is the sun. But in the dark of night you can see stars which are millions of times further away.' We shall doubtless discover many of God's treasures through all our difficult experiences.

Outwardly we have not been suffering at all, but the inward grief has taken us by surprise, and that is why I mention it. Many thousands of others must experience the same pain of parting, especially where the relationships had been bonded together by the super-glue of God's love for many years.

'Why did you leave York at all?' is the question I am often asked, and it is not always easy giving the answer. I had always said that God called us to York in such a convincing way, despite all adverse circumstances, that it would require a spiritual bomb to get us out! It did not happen like that. Nor did we leave on account of the closing of the Mustard Seed or the split in the congregation. Indeed, while those problems were still around, nothing would have taken us from St. Michael's. It was only when the church had come together with a new unity and love, and when the Holy Spirit was manifestly blessing God's work there again, could we even contemplate the idea of departure.

The marriage ordinance in Genesis 2:24 is clear: 'Therefore a man leaves his father and his mother and cleaves to his wife, and they become one flesh.' Leaving always comes before cleaving. Now that our spiritual children had grown up into maturity, and were more than competent to take over the family business, it seemed that the time for leaving had come. No parents should hang around their children when they get married and start having a family of their own. Occasional visits are one thing; to live in the same house is quite another. We felt that the time had come for us as 'parents' to make room for others to take over, without us looking over their shoulders all the time to see how they were getting on. Apart from any other reason, it was primarily for the future health and growth of the congregation at St. Michael's that we knew we ought to move. The challenge for us of a major move at this stage would no doubt be good, even though we did not relish the thought of it.

Besides all that, there were other considerations. More of my time was taken up with travelling, including many trips overseas, and London was an obvious centre for this. Increasingly I received invitations also to consult with church leaders, and nearly all of these took place in the metropolis. I also needed more time for writing, and for preparing for the many speaking engagements I had throughout the year. As rector of St. Michael's I still had *some* parochial responsibilities, and crises were often awaiting my return from some overseas tour. Added to that, our children were at an age when a move was comparatively easy in terms of their educational progress; if we did not move now, it would have been much more difficult during the next five years. Cautiously, therefore, we responded to a tentative suggestion from one or two leaders to base ourselves in central London.

It was not a sudden decision; and I have to remember that when agonising doubts often assail me as to whether or not we did the right thing. Over the course of nine months or more, we spent much time in prayer and asked the advice of several discerning Christian leaders, from the Archbishop of York to friends in different parts of the world. Increasingly we heard the same conclusion, 'It makes sense.' One or two prophetic words, from those whose ministry I deeply respected, confirmed that God wanted us to be available for him to work in the wider Church.

So we moved. Undoubtedly it was a step of faith. Although the bishops seem right behind the work we are doing, there is no ready-made job with salary for the work I am doing, and I have therefore become a 'non-stipendiary clergyman' – which simply means that all my salary, house and expenses must come from 'other sources'. Housing in central London is not cheap, and I have the further responsibility of paying and housing a team of about nine others, although we have seen encouraging answers to prayer about this. In York our team had been undergirded by a Trust that had been formed through the generosity of one couple who, after being renewed in the Spirit, had given both money and property 'for the advancement of the Christian religion by the proclamation of the Gospel of Christ and the building up of his Body the Church'.

With our move to London, new Trustees were appointed to manage what was now to be known as The Belfrey Trust for our support and the team's. Even though we received a gift from the previous Trust in York, the budget was more than four times as great as anything we had known in the past, and therefore – together with many Christian organisations – we have to depend on the Lord month by month. Over the years I have never worried about money (perhaps partly because I never understand it!) and I always remember Hudson Taylor's principle that God's work done in God's ways will never lack God's supplies. If in the future we ever find ourselves in financial difficulties, it will be a clear sign that we need to re-examine the whole work very carefully indeed, since I have no desire to perpetuate beyond its usefulness what God seems to have raised up for the present time. He may well have quite different ideas in the future, although I expect we shall have some warning of this.

I sense that one reason for my freedom from parochial responsibilities is to concentrate more on writing. I have never considered myself a writer, which is probably obvious by this stage; but through the encouragement originally of Bishop Timothy Dudley-Smith and Gavin Reid, formerly of the Falcon Press, and more recently through the stimulating wisdom of Michael Green, Edward England (my literary agent) and Hodder and Stoughton, I have had several books published. Although the whole process is a nerve-racking business, I have been amazed repeatedly by the way God has used these publications to touch the lives of individuals and churches. One woman wrote to me saying that, after reading my book *In Search of God*, she knew that she must give her life to Christ. So she had a shower, dressed, did her hair, put on her make-up, and then knelt down by her bed to ask Christ into her life! She argued that, if she had an audience with the Queen, she would have done all that and more besides. So why not be presentable when meeting, for the first time, the King of kings and Lord of lords? It was fair logic, even though God would have received her just as she was, because of her repentant and believing heart. I do not know if any other of my books has ever had such an unusual response; but I do know – and for this I am profoundly grateful – that through them God has touched the lives of many thousands whom I shall never see this side of heaven.

One immediate joy in our move to London has been the creation of a new team. In York we had developed such close relationships in the various teams I worked with that I had been tempted to think it could never be the same again. For example, Phil and Joy Potter had been with me for four years and we had travelled round the world together – Phil as a gifted singer and worship leader and Joy as a dancer and constant encourager. When they both left to go to Trinity College, Bristol, to train for ordination in the Church of England, they left an obvious gap which I knew would be hard to fill. It was not easy recruiting a new team but we managed it, and in a remarkably short time we found that the Spirit of God was creating among us that same quality of shared relationships that I had known in the past. There is much talent in the present team – several of them have had professional training, and the quality of performance is good. But we all know that what finally counts is the reality of our life together in Christ.

We came together as comparative strangers at the end of August 1982, and our first festival was in Dartford two weeks later, based on the brand new Orchard Theatre. The festival went wonderfully well and we were all encouraged. That was followed almost immediately by a five-week tour in Montreal and Ontario, Canada, and again I was excited not only by the specific contributions of the team but also by our fellowship in Christ. Quickly the new team has learnt how to care for one another, pray for one another, worship God together and work well together. The quality of what we do off the stage determines the value of our ministry on the stage.

Opportunities for Christian ministry abound on every side. We continue to receive more invitations than we can possibly accept, and are currently investigating about thirty-five potential festivals both in this country and overseas, together with numerous other requests. London itself is also a vast and endless mission field. Many clergy and churches need encouragement and increasing renewal. Other churches have the potential to send out lay teams, some of whom could prepare the way for our forthcoming festivals, or else return for the purpose of follow-up. There is constant need for reconciliation, both within the Church and in the wider circles of society. Repeatedly I detect a growing hunger for God. There is no possible unemployment within the kingdom of God. In the words of John Wesley, we need to keep 'a cool head and a warm heart'. The prospects for the future are like the beginnings of spring – bursting with potential for new life.

As a family too we have had encouragements. Although the memories of all that we loved in York are still very fresh (at times disturbingly so) we thank God for the clear provision of a house which has a considerable measure of privacy about it – something which we find particularly helpful with all the demands of a public ministry. It has also been fun exploring new places together, from Battersea Park where I enjoy rowing on the lake with Guy, to Wimbledon Common, where Fiona rides and Anne exercises the dog.

Life is full of changes, some joyful, some painful. What is of inestimable comfort is to know that God himself never changes. His steadfast love endures for ever and his mercies are new every morning. These are the rock-like certainties we must hold on to when everything else may seem to be tumbling about our ears. There are many questions for us as yet unanswered. I do not know at present what my priorities should be, and where to give my limited time and energy. I am not clear which invitations to accept. All of us as a family have found the move much more difficult than we had imagined, and it is easy to dwell on the negatives. What we do know, however, amidst all our doubts and uncertainties, is that we cannot trust God too much.

Anne and I know that through the fires of past trials God has brought us into a much more complete marriage, and our family relationships are closer than they have ever been. God can use even our sins and mistakes, when surrendered to him, to increase the beauty of his pattern in our lives, and to make us more useful in serving others. Nothing is outside his sovereign control and constant love. He is the One who turns

our negatives into positives, especially in the darkroom of
suffering. That is the confidence we always can have when we
pray 'Our Father, who art in heaven . . .'

Having written these words I heard only yesterday and
unexpectedly, that I have to go into hospital in two days' time
for a major abdominal operation which is expected to knock
me out of action for the best part of six months. This has come
as a total surprise, but I know that the matter is both serious
and urgent. I cannot say that I have no fears but I do know
that 'trusting God in every situation' is a reality and not mere
words. Over the past few years I have been teaching large
numbers of Christians all over the world the 'festal shout',
based on Psalm 89:15, 'Blessed are the people who know the
festal shout . . . For thou art the glory of their strength'. Over
the centuries God's people have often been exhorted to shout
praises to God, and the great liturgies of the Church have
echoed these acclamations of faith such as 'The Lord is here –
his Spirit is with us' or 'Christ has died, Christ has risen, Christ
will come again'. These glorious words should not be mum-
bled, as is sometimes sadly the case, but shouted out with
ringing confidence since, if we genuinely believe the truth of
those words, they represent the greatest good news that we
could ever know on this earth: whatever may happen, *the best
is yet to be*! One particular festal shout that I have taught,
which has rung through many cathedrals, city halls, theatres
and in the open air, is the repeated acclamation in the psalms,
'*The Lord Reigns!*' When once we gave this festal shout in
Belfast Cathedral (on the day after a particularly horrifying
bomb disaster in a crowded restaurant) you could almost see
the faith of the large congregation rise above their fears and
sorrows into a fresh confidence in the God who has the whole
world, and therefore our own personal lives, entirely in his
hands. That is the same festal shout with which I now encourage myself on the eve of my operation. I do not know what I
shall experience nor what the prognosis will be, but I can rest
in the marvellous certainty that the Lord reigns. Nothing is
too great for his power, nothing is too small for his love.

Facing me, as I write this in my study, is a simple banner

made by Janet Lunt who was once a member of our household and who started the Banner Group some years ago in York. She, her husband Colin and their children, have all been very close to us. The banner I can see now consists of words in the shape of a tulip: 'TODAY my grace is sufficient for you.' God calls us to live one day at a time, each day trusting in the sufficiency of the Father's love.

One of my favourite songs is a fine one we often sang in York, since through the background of pain there is a ringing confidence in God himself. It is based on Psalm 16, and I quote part of it:

> For you are my God;
> You alone are my joy;
> Defend me, O Lord.
>
> You give wonderful brethren to me,
>   the faithful who dwell in your land,
> Those who choose alien gods
>   have chosen an alien band.
>
> You show me the path for my life;
>   in your presence is fulness of joy.
> To be at your right hand for ever
>   for me would be happiness always.
>
> For you are my God;
> You alone are my joy.
> Defend me, O Lord.[1]

Fear No Evil

Facing the final test of faith

Foreword by
James I Packer

Hodder & Stoughton
LONDON SYDNEY AUCKLAND

Fear No Evil

Acknowledgements

When Edward England, my literary agent and personal friend, suggested that I should attempt a book of such an intimate and painful nature, I was unsure. Increasingly, however, I felt that it is important today to talk openly about cancer, especially from the standpoint of the Christian faith. Edward's advice, and that of Ann, his wife, has been marvellous throughout. I am so grateful.

Hilary Saunders, my indefatigable secretary, has not only typed several drafts of the manuscript admirably, but has constantly encouraged me, gently corrected some of my writing and throughout has helped us all as a family during the most difficult year of our life. My gratitude to her is profound.

Other readers have helped considerably: Carolyn Armitage of Hodder and Stoughton, John and Gay Perry of Lee Abbey, the Very Reverend David Edwards, Provost of Southwark Cathedral, and Teddy and Margaret Saunders whose personal support, together with many others (especially in London and York) has been of the utmost value.

Especially I thank my Team: Mark and Carol Slomka, Sandy Campbell, Alison Charles, Margot Evans, Shaun Islip, Mark Jennings and Diana Nairne. Not only have Mark and Carol made many perceptive comments about the manuscript, but the whole Team's constant prayer and love has been quite extraordinary.

The debt I owe to many other friends is almost endless. Most of all I thank God for showing me his love as never before.

To John Wimber, Blaine Cook, John McClure,
Bishop Morris and Anne Maddocks,
together with countless Christians throughout
Great Britain and overseas who have prayed, loved
and encouraged us as a family.

Contents

Foreword

When David Watson, evangelist, author, and renewal preacher, died of cancer at the age of 50, a great man fell in Israel, as the thousands who poured into his two memorial services in York and London attested. But David's ministry is not over; though dead, he still speaks by his books, and not least by this, his final piece of writing. *Fear No Evil* is, quite simply, marvellous: poignant and radiant, matter-of-fact and sublime, modest and heroic, heart-rending and heart-warming in equal measure, and all the more overwhelming for being understated in David's very British way. To introduce it, as I have been asked to do, is the privilege of a lifetime. In doing so I want to pinpoint what seems to me to be its real greatness.

'Our people die well,' said John Wesley (a leader, incidentally, with whom David bears comparison in a remarkable way). Wesley was celebrating God's grace among the Methodists. Until recently a good death was seen as the godly man's crowning achievement, the climax of his good life. That is why tracts on the 'art' of dying were among the first printed books in all European languages; that is why William Perkins, the Puritan devotional writer (with whom also David bears comparison, though whereas Wesley died at 88, Perkins died at 44), composed *A Salve for a Sicke Man (The Right Way of Dying Well)*; and that is why from the sixteenth to the nineteenth centuries, when most adults died in the presence of family and friends, great importance was attached to a Christian's deathbed sayings. Things are, of course, different today: death has replaced sex as the great unmentionable. All stress among Christians is laid on present knowledge and enjoyment of God, and the old awareness that only one who is ready to die can live to God's praise has been generally forgotten. The discipline of what Alexander Whyte called 'forefancying your deathbed' is in abeyance, and anyone who were to hint that he wanted his death to edify others would be thought unbalanced for thinking about his death at all. But we are the unbalanced ones, and there is something here that we need to relearn.

Readers of *Pilgrim's Progress* will recall the unforgettable last scene in which the pilgrims crossed the river of death to the Celestial City. Mr Stand-fast, the last to go, experienced 'a great Calm in the River': 'when he was about half-way in, he stood a while and talked to his Companions,' and this is what he said.

'This River has been a Terror to many, yea the thoughts of it also have often frighted me. But now methinks I stand easy . . . The Waters indeed are to the Palate bitter, and to the Stomach cold, yet the thoughts of what I am going to, and of the Conduct that waits for me on the other side, doth lie as a glowing Coal at my Heart.

'I see myself now at the end of my Journey, my toilsome Days are ended. I am going now to see that Head that was Crowned with Thorns, and that Face that was spit upon, for me.

'I have formerly lived by Hear-say, and Faith, but now I go where I shall live by sight, and shall be with him, in whose Company I delight myself.

'I have loved to hear my Lord spoken of . . . His Voice to me has been most sweet . . . His Word I did use to gather for my Food, and for Antidotes against my Faintings. He has held me . . .'

While Mr Stand-fast was saying this, Bunyan tells us, he was taken. 'But Glorious it was, to see how the open Region was filled with Horses and Chariots, with Trumpeters and Pipers, with Singers and Players on stringed Instruments, to welcome the Pilgrims as they went up, and followed one another in at the beautiful Gate of the City.'

To any Bible lover with a full-grown Christian imagination, Bunyan's pictures in these paragraphs and those that surround them trigger joy and tears, ardour, adoration, and assurance, with a power that no other Christian literature can match – though some things in Charles Williams and C S Lewis, all modelled (I think) on Bunyan, come close. But few of us in this century know our Bibles very well, nor have we full-grown Christian imaginations, and Bunyan's diction may strike us as merely quaint. Must we then miss the ministry that his lyrical prose has had to so many in the past? Not necessarily. For God in grace has given us our own Mr Stand-fast, who paused during his own dying to model for us in contemporary terms faith face-to-face with the last enemy. That was David's final role, and his blow-by-blow record of a losing battle with cancer is his equivalent of Mr Stand-fast's last speech. The same certainty of God's love is voiced; the same victory of faith shines forth. That is the greatness of *Fear No Evil*.

The fact that David, right to his last page, hopes for supernatural healing that never comes is not important. In the providence of God, who does not always show his servants the true point of the books he stirs them to write, the theme of *Fear No Evil* is the conquest of death – not by looking away from it, nor by being shielded from it, but by facing it squarely and going down into it knowing that for a believer it is the vestibule of glory.

David's theology led him to believe, right to the end, that God wanted to heal his body. Mine leads me rather to say that God evidently wanted David home, and healed his whole person by taking him to glory in the way that he will one day heal us all. Health and life, I would say, in the full and final sense of those words, are not what we die *out of*, but what we die *into*. Whichever notions fit, David's or mine (and differences will continue about that), there is profound wisdom in David's maxim that the *what*-question (what, Lord, are you saying to me, doing for me, asking from me?) gets one further than the *why*-question (why,

Lord, has this happened?). To ask God to give us an account of himself and his actions is a dead-end street, as Job found, for God doesn't do it. However, to know God in Christ – that is, to know that God is Jesuslike – is to know that he is always ready to tell us how he loves us and how we are to love him, even when he will tell us nothing more about his present plans. But to know this, as David knew it, is to be unsinkable – whatever the enemy, the battle, and the wounds. David lived and modelled this even more tellingly than he verbalised it: read this book, and you will see.

Samson, we are told, did more for God by his death than he had ever done in his life. In character terms, one could hardly imagine a person less like Samson, the lifelong juvenile delinquent as he has been called, than the tidy, disciplined, courteous, poised, genial, and humble Cambridge man that was David. Yet he may well be like Samson in this one regard. Could it be that his dying testament will minister more widely, helping more needy people, and at a deeper level, than anything he wrote before? Could it be that God has accomplished more for his kingdom by taking David home as he did than he would have done by any alternative pattern of events in David's life? Most certainly it could. I know no book better fitted to impart to twentieth-century Christians in the West the lost wisdom about death than this one. I am more thankful for it than I can say. I must not keep you from it any longer.

James I Packer

Introduction

All of us, I think, have deep-seated fears about something in our life, even if they are seldom expressed. We may be afraid of all sorts of things: spiders, mice, moths, snakes, injections, loneliness, exams, feathers, failure, the dark, the dentist, flying – the list is endless. Most are frightened of death. And of all the terminal diseases that may afflict us, none causes such anxiety as *cancer*.

When I first heard earlier this year (January 5th, 1983 to be precise) that I had cancer, the news hit me like a thunderbolt. All human hopes and securities were suddenly shattered. 'It *can't* be true,' I said to myself foolishly and anxiously. 'That sort of thing doesn't happen to me!' But it did, and my deepest fears were realised.

Often I say, as a Christian, that I am not afraid of death but I am sometimes afraid of the process of dying. In my mind I think of several people I've known who have died painfully and rather horribly from cancer. My fears have not been groundless.

With the fear of cancer so widespread in society, I was encouraged to write this book, giving an honest account of my feelings and reactions and how I have come to terms with cancer over these last eleven months. I write unashamedly as a Christian, although I hope that my thoughts will be of some interest whatever faith a reader may have.

One test of any religion is how far it will stand up to the crises of life, especially the final crisis of death. The shock of having to come to terms with death made me examine again the whole basis of my Christian faith.

I have tried to mingle my personal story with my own

wider reflections, because such thoughts have all been with me since the diagnosis was made. The experiences of this year, although mild compared with the pains and traumas endured by others, have made me ask searching questions about life and death. I have been candid about my doubts and fears, even though I struggled through to a restful trust in God and in his healing power. Even now, eleven months later, I am quite vulnerable to further fears, especially in the middle of the night.

It has not been an easy book to write, partly because I am still standing too close to these events. At the same time I record my thoughts as someone who is right in the middle of the trial, with no certain security about the future – apart from faith in God and in his healing power.

The problem of suffering is always a baffling one, devoid of simple solutions, and yet the experience of that suffering is all around us. The question is, how can we live with it, face it, overcome it, and reach that position where we *fear no evil*?

1

Anxious Moments

'Have you got any spare room in your cupboard for a chest of drawers?' I asked Fiona. 'And Anne, where on earth can we put these two chairs?'

'Hang them in the garage, with everything else!' replied Anne. The garage was already looking like a warehouse for old second-hand furniture, with chairs, tables, old carpets and mirrors hanging on its walls.

'There's just *not* enough room!' complained Guy, as he heaved his bed into another corner of his room.

It wasn't really as bad as all that, and in fact we are extremely fortunate to be in such a pleasant house in central London. But it was the first time we had ever moved as a family. For seventeen years Anne (my wife) and I had lived in York, and since Fiona was sixteen and Guy thirteen, it was the only home they had known. I am an Anglican clergyman and we lived in a large and typical mid-Victorian rectory – not very attractive, but it had fourteen main rooms and a considerable garden which usually looked wild since we had little time to spend on it. However, it was *home*.

Suddenly, all our roots had been pulled up, as though all our teeth had been pulled out in one go. It really hurt! We moved from north to south ('They've got such funny accents!' said Fiona and Guy), from one of the most beautiful small cities in Great Britain to the heart of a huge metropolis, and from a rambling house that had been almost a part of our lives to a small house in a mews. Even though we gave away masses of tables, beds, wardrobes, desks, chairs, carpets and clothes, we still carried far too much with us, and it was quite a game squeezing it all in. Anne and I saw it mostly as the next adventure in our lives. Fiona and Guy longed to be 'back home', in York.

Sam missed the big house and garden as much as anyone else. Sam was our dog – a friendly mixture of every breed you could think of, though appropriately fierce with intruders. But Sam wasn't well. The difference between York and London hit us hard when Sam had an operation two months after our arrival. Virtually the identical operation had cost us twenty pounds in York; in London we paid one hundred and thirty-four pounds – considerably more than my week's salary! And a few weeks later Sam died. Anne sobbed, the children were upset, and I really missed him too.

The move to London had not been easy in all sorts of ways, and I found it hard to answer Fiona's constant question, 'Why did we leave York?' Basically we had moved because of my work, and because Anne and I believed that God had called us to London, but it wasn't easy convincing our children, who were missing 'home'.

Then came the biggest shock of all.

I had gone to my doctor, William Robarts, for only another prescription concerning my asthma. Since I had learned to live with asthma for eighteen years it was no more than a brief routine visit.

'One little question,' I asked him as I got up to leave, 'Does this medication have any side-effects? I seem to be going to the loo rather a lot these days.'

'How long has this been going on for?' He startled me by the serious tone of his question.

'Well I'm not sure. I haven't paid much attention to it until the last few weeks. But looking back I suppose it might have got gradually worse over this last year. As you know I travel widely, and any problems I've put down to changes of food and water. I remember having a little trouble in Sweden nine months ago . . .'

'Do you mind if I have a look?'

After a slightly uncomfortable examination he looked thoughtfully at me across his desk. 'You have an ulcer in the colon. I would like you to see a specialist because you might need an operation. It could be serious.'

'I'm afraid that is impossible,' I replied, beginning to feel uneasy. 'I'm just off to California with my team for five weeks, and of all the events in the year this is one that I simply cannot cancel. It's out of the question.'

I spend much of my time travelling to many parts of the world with a team of about eight men and women who are gifted in the performing arts: music, song, dance, drama and mime. In five days' time we were due to leave for our most demanding tour of the year: five intensive but enjoyable weeks based at Fuller Theological Seminary in Pasadena, California, with weekend engagements at San Francisco, Phoenix Arizona, Fort Leavenworth Kansas, and one or two other places. I was already booked to lecture over sixty times (including a few preaching commitments) and I knew that over eighty pastors were coming from all over America and from as far away as Australia for those lectures. I teach in California at the same time every year, and I always find it totally exhausting but wonderfully stimulating. It stretches my capacities to the full, yet I always come back with a renewed vision of God and of his work in different parts of the world. No, that was one engagement I definitely could not cancel! My doctor, however, seemed unmoved by my protests.

'Are you saying it could be – malignant?' I asked, a little nervously.

'It's possible.'

I did not know what to say. My heart thumped away beneath my outward poise.

'I'll just make a phone call,' said my doctor; and within a couple of minutes the appointment with Mr Beard, a consultant, was fixed for the day after next.

'This really *is* serious,' I thought to myself, almost as

though I was dreaming, expecting to wake up at any moment to discover it was only the start to a nightmare. But no, I was wide awake. It was no dream.

As I stepped out of the doctor's surgery I could not really believe that anything was seriously wrong. It is true that I was shaken, but I could not accept the possibility of an operation. I wove my way through the January sales' shoppers streaming in and out of Peter Jones department store. It was late afternoon, and the lighted streets were thronged with brightly coloured punks from King's Road and fashionably dressed ladies from Belgravia.

Sloane Square seemed alive with colour and bustle, shopping bags bulging with bargains and bright lights from Christmas decorations still shining from the trees. I always love the start of a new year. From earliest childhood I have thought of it as a season of promise and hope – a new start and fresh expectations. It is Epiphany, the manifestation of Christ to the world when the wise men from the East brought their priceless gifts to honour the infant King. Every year seems to herald the dawn of a new age.

I felt sure that my doctor was only being cautious. I felt remarkably fit. How could I have a malignant ulcer? Indeed, what exactly *was* a malignant ulcer? I noticed that neither my doctor nor I had used that dreaded word 'cancer'. As I looked into the faces of the shoppers hurrying home for tea I wondered how many of them carried in their hearts secret fears, anxieties and sorrows? I walked through the quiet elegance of Eaton Square into the jostling crowds around Victoria Station. I was going to buy a brief-case with some money that had been promised me for that purpose. And it would be a brief-case for California. I really could not cancel that trip. I was almost certain that I would be going with my team on the Tuesday as planned. The talk of a malignant ulcer was surely no more than a sobering scare. In fact, purchasing the brief-case for the journey became for me a symbol of faith. Or was it of fear? I found just the one I wanted and I hurried home.

'How did you get on at the doctor's?' asked Anne once I had displayed my brief-case.

'All right. He thinks I may have an ulcer,' I replied cautiously.

When our children, Fiona and Guy, went out of the kitchen to watch television, I closed the door and related to Anne what had happened.

'What actually did he say?' pressed Anne. She had been trained as a nurse at Guy's Hospital and would not be satisfied with anything less than the full details.

'He thinks it could be malignant,' I replied, speaking in short sentences since I wasn't far away from tears. 'Got to see a specialist. Mr Randolph Beard. Friday morning, nine o'clock.'

I sat there, choking back my emotions and watching her face. Anne had been through some rough times in our marriage, and a few lines on her face and the wisps of grey hair spoke of pain and tears. But she was still beautiful, with open searching eyes.

'Mr Beard is the best!' she said enthusiastically. 'He was loved and respected even when I was a nurse.'

'I'm glad,' I replied weakly.

We held each other's hands and prayed.

'Heavenly Father, we know you love us and are fully in control of our lives. Help us to trust you, and keep us in your peace. We really need your help. Amen.'

Anne cried a little. We gave each other a hug, and then I went to join the children in case they wondered what was going on.

'What did the doctor say?' asked Guy immediately.

'Just that I've probably got an ulcer, and may need an operation,' I replied as casually as possible.

'An operation? Gosh!' Guy was puzzled, since the only ulcers he had known were in his mouth and had not needed an operation. But I didn't try to explain.

We spent the rest of the evening watching a film on television. It wasn't a good one and I couldn't concentrate, but at least I was with my family and I relaxed.

That night I took a mild sleeping tablet, committed my life, my family and my future to God, and slept well.

The next morning I met with the team as usual, mainly for a time of worship and prayer. I began by telling them the news of my visit to the doctor, the possibility of an operation, and the uncertainty of my going to America. They were all shaken by the news. For weeks we had been preparing for this trip, but essentially the team were going to illustrate *my* lectures. Apart from packing, we were all set. Now, at the last moment, everything looked precarious.

Much more important, I knew they were very worried about me. Although the members of the team were all half our age Anne and I had come to love them dearly as our Christian brothers and sisters, and we were not surprised by their immediate and enormous concern. We joined together in several songs of gentle praise, expressing our faith in God's ultimate control and unceasing love; and then we prayed for one another. They gathered round me and laid hands upon me, praying that God's peace would continue to fill my life. I felt immensely encouraged, and returned home, leaving the team to rehearse for California, but without much enthusiasm.

Back in my study, I tried to work further on my lectures. I had not written the material for two of my subjects and others needed tidying up. But my mind was not in it! My natural apprehension unsettled my stomach more than ever, and I seemed to spend much of the day in the smallest room in the house! Some work, however, was accomplished. In the afternoon I made good progress on the two lectures whilst spending an unusually long time in the dentist's waiting-room – a wonderful place for gathering one's thoughts!

That evening I was restless and anxious. There was still plenty to do in preparation for California, but the possibility of my going seemed to diminish hour by hour, and I really wanted to spend more time with Anne, Fiona and Guy. So we had a quiet evening together doing nothing in particular.

Friday, January 7th was a bright and fresh January morning. The air was crisp and the winter sunshine seemed full of hope. I went to see the consultant, Mr Randolph Beard. Arriving early, I walked through the streets until my appointment was due. I was surprisingly peaceful as I rang the doorbell and was ushered upstairs to meet Mr Beard. At once he impressed me with his quiet and encouraging manner; I could see why Anne had enthused about his outstanding reputation as a consultant-surgeon.

After a brief examination he spoke gently. 'You're in real trouble. You have a malignant ulcer and you need an operation at once.'

I was stunned. My worst fears were confirmed. I felt my throat getting dry with tension. Feebly I told him how difficult an operation was at that time, with over sixty lectures to give in California in a few days, and with many pastors coming having already spent hundreds of dollars on this course. How could I possibly cancel the engagement at this stage? Mr Beard smiled kindly, but was unbending in his decision.

'I cannot overstress how important this is,' he said.

I had no choice but to accept his guidance. He told me that, in anticipation of my visit, he had provisionally reserved a bed for me in Guy's Hospital and that I should be there first thing on Monday morning. He warned me that almost certainly I would need to have a colostomy (I had only the vaguest idea of what this meant), but that many active people learn to live with one. He made it clear also that I must be off all work until Easter at least, with no international work for six months.

As I left his surgery my head was spinning. I still could not quite believe that this was happening to me. I was worried about Anne and the children. How would they take it, I wondered? And what about my trip to America? How on earth could I sort that one out? What about all the pastors coming at considerable expense to themselves? And what about all my other numerous engagements? How could I disappoint so many thousands of people? We had been planning Christian festivals in various towns for months. Everything seemingly depended on my remaining fit and well.

What on earth did the future hold? Indeed was it 'on earth' at all?

2

Roots

I remember little about my father. He was away in the Army for long periods of time, and died in India in 1943 when I was ten.

My earliest memories go back to the North-West Frontier of India, now Pakistan, where my father was commanding a mountain-battery of guns. I have childhood impressions of gunfire over our bungalow, topis and polo-ponies, Indian servants and beautiful saris, and even finding a hooded cobra in my bath! We came back to this country in 1937, when I was four. I must have been a romantic child for I proposed to a five-year-old girl on Victoria station having just crossed the ocean seas with her. To my dismay she refused me, and it took me another twenty-seven years before I summoned up the courage again – but it was not to the same girl!

My father's death was particularly tragic since he was a Christian Scientist and, according to his beliefs, refused all medical help when he was seriously ill with broncho-pneumonia. My mother, stunned by the effects of such convictions (which she never shared) had me baptised and confirmed in the nearest Anglican church, although I understood absolutely nothing of what was going on.[1]

This confusing religious start to my life, coupled with the dull monotony of formal school chapel, caused me to explore a variety of religious paths. Having rejected Christian Science, I dabbled in spiritualism to see if I could make

[1] I have written my story more fully in my autobiography *You Are My God*, Hodder & Stoughton, 1983.

contact with my father. My uncle, however, was a devotee of
Rudolph Steiner, and I went on to study the Law of Karma.
This led to forms of Buddhism and to belief in reincarnation,
which for me at the time was the only logical solution to the
problem of suffering. For those afflicted in this life, there was
always the promise of a better reincarnation another time.
Not that there is any scrap of real evidence for this, of course.
It was purely one interesting theory. I also tried several more
obscure religious philosophies as well.

Becoming increasingly disillusioned, however, and react-
ing strongly against the hypocrisy (as I saw it) of Army
religion during my two years of National Service, I turned
my back on God and became an atheist or humanist. I went
up to St John's College, Cambridge, with mathematics and
science as my subjects, but switched instead to philosophy,
psychology, logic, ethics and metaphysics. This was effectively the humanist faculty in the university. We felt that
the only hope for mankind was for us to work out our own
destiny in the best way we understood with our rational
minds.

During my first week at Cambridge I sampled all the
societies, whether I believed in them or not, primarily to get a
feel of university life. I was amused to find myself at a
tea-party organised by the Christian Union, but I was
impressed by the speaker, a clergyman called John Collins. It
was not so much *what* he said but the *way* in which he said it
that struck me. He seemed obviously genuine as though he
was speaking from a first-hand experience of God.

I talked to him briefly afterwards, and the next day we had
breakfast together whilst he explained very simply, step by
step, how I could find God in my life. What he said made
sense, although I knew he could not prove it. I also knew that
I could not prove my atheism. He spoke warmly about the
reality of God found through a personal relationship with
Christ. I realised logically that it might be true and equally
that it might not be true. If it were not true, forget it; but if it
were true, it was quite simply the most important truth in the

universe. The honest thing to do was to conduct an experiment in the realm of faith.

That night, having read a helpful booklet covering much the same ground as that which John Collins had explained to me, I knelt down by my bed and asked Christ, if such a person really existed, to come into my life. I meant what I said, although I was disappointed that I felt exactly the same immediately afterwards. Later I came to see how that simple unemotional step of faith became the most important turning-point in the whole of my life, eventually affecting every area of my being as I deepened my knowledge of God.

Certainly I needed help, which was wonderfully given in my first year by David Sheppard, who had recently been the Captain of England's cricket team and is now the Bishop of Liverpool. I had to think through carefully my new-found faith, for much of my academic studies challenged every basic Christian belief. It was a testing time, and I waded through plenty of doubts before I gained a better intellectual grasp of the integrity of the Christian faith. During my university days I found such joy in leading some of my friends to Christ and seeing them built up in the faith, that it was hard to do justice to my philosophical studies (although I did tolerably well in the exams).

It was not long before I believed that God was calling me to the ministry of the Church of England; and after two years training at Ridley Hall in Cambridge I was ordained in Rochester Cathedral and joined John Collins at St Mark's Church, Gillingham in Kent. I had three marvellous years in that predominantly dockyard parish, and saw the power of Christ changing the lives of people who had come from a very different background to that of Cambridge.

After three years, however, I went back to Cambridge, this time to the Round Church where I was gradually drawn into further work amongst students. That period in Cambridge was marked by three major personal events. First, I was one day consciously filled with the Spirit of God and felt the love of God enveloping my whole being – I fell in love with Christ.

Secondly, and nearly a year later, I fell in love with a beautiful girl who is now my wife. And thirdly, a short time before our wedding, I developed severe asthma which has been with me, on and off, ever since.

Partly because of the asthma, but there were other reasons as well, the first few years in our marriage were particularly stormy, and we both have a lot of sympathy for those with broken marriages. But for the grace of God ours would have been exactly the same. However, we worked through those storms to a much more mature and open relationship, and I think we have become more whole people as a result.

Then on Friday, January 7th 1983 I learned that I had cancer.

3

Quick Change

The weekend was a whirlwind of telephoning, rearranging, discussing and praying. High on my priorities was the question of how I could salvage my lecture tour in California, with so many clergy and ministers coming for an intensive course for which they had been studying and preparing. My team was ready to go since we had prepared ourselves carefully for our most challenging commitment so far; but we urgently needed one or two experienced Christian teachers whose understanding and approach would be almost identical to my own. Knowing the pressures on my own diary it seemed inconceivable that anyone with the necessary qualifications and experience would be available at this last moment.

Added to that, I was profoundly disappointed about not going there myself. This was to have been my fourth visit but my first time with our new team, and the first extended teaching period of a month (the previous periods had been only two weeks). There were visits arranged to San Francisco, Phoenix Arizona, the Grand Canyon and Kansas, not to mention the growing number of friends I knew out there. I really wanted to go. And now some instant re-thinking had to take place.

There is no doubt that I was worried about this as I made my way home from the consultant's surgery, although I prayed as I walked and believed that God knew all about the problems I faced and had his own solution for me. I am naturally impatient and I like to be in control of situations.

Through my Christian life I have always found it difficult to obey the instruction in the Bible to 'be still before the Lord, and wait patiently for him' (Psalm 37:7). If I do not have the immediate answer to a problem, I like to work it out myself as soon as I can. Some of my close friends tell me that I need to learn how to be still, how to listen to God, how to trust him when there are no apparent solutions, and how to wait for his guidance. As a born activist I confess that I find all this difficult, and yet I appreciate the wisdom of it.

On this occasion I did not have to wait long for an answer to my urgent prayer. By the end of that Friday morning, almost miraculously, I had found two outstanding replacements for those five weeks in North America. They were two friends of mine, David Prior and David MacInnes, both extremely gifted communicators and much in demand for their teaching and preaching skills.

'David,' I said to each of them on the phone, 'can you help me? It's rather an emergency. You see, I've got cancer and can't go to Fuller. Can you take my place?'

Both Davids were dumbfounded by my news and request. I could tell that they were shocked about the cancer and were trying their utmost to respond positively to the cry for help.

It was unbelievable that they could both be free and willing to accept such a massive teaching assignment at this eleventh hour, and equally remarkable that their wives were prepared to let them go. But it happened, and an enormous worry rolled off my back.

Later that day Fiona photo-copied all my lecture notes, Hilary, my secretary, sent them off to the two Davids, and I rewrote the closing paragraphs of my autobiography *You Are My God*. The manuscript was almost finished, and I sensed the urgency for completing it before going into hospital on the Monday, otherwise it might not be concluded for months. 'I heard only yesterday and unexpectedly,' I wrote, 'that I have to go into hospital in two days' time for a major abdominal operation . . . This has come as a total surprise, but I know that the matter is both serious and urgent.

Suddenly everything in the future has become uncertain, even life itself . . .' I still was avoiding the word *cancer*.

That word is still a highly emotive one in our modern society, and for most people it is inseparably linked with fear and death. It is sometimes called 'the Big C' or 'that dreaded disease'. There are no real answers at present to cancer. The word is almost synonymous with helplessness and hopelessness.

Later that day I rang a number of praying Christian friends to ask for their support. They were all stunned by the news. In particular I phoned through to a special friend of mine, John Wimber, the pastor of an outstanding church in Yorba Linda, California, where their healing ministry is one of the most impressive I have seen anywhere in the world.

John is a large, lovable, warm and gentle person, reminding me of a favourite teddy-bear. He also has an able mind, wide Christian experience and shrewd spiritual discernment. Every now and then in my travels I meet someone whom I feel I can really trust – someone who loves me and accepts me as I am, who is not trying to use or manipulate me, and who is full of godly wisdom. There are not many like this, but John Wimber is one.

His secretary answered the phone and explained that John was away on a staff retreat for the weekend and could not under any circumstances be disturbed.

'The thing is,' I said with the word sticking in my throat, 'I've got cancer, and I need help.'

'John will call you right back,' she replied gently and reassuringly.

And John did.

He listened as I told him the facts.

'David,' he said, 'the first thing I want you to know is that we love you. Secondly, I don't accept this cancer and I believe that God wants to heal you. Thirdly, I'm going to call the whole congregation immediately to urgent prayer.'

Both his words and his tone of voice were so encouraging that I just cried.

'Thanks John. I love you all too.'

That weekend John called his 3,000-strong congregation
to commit themselves in prayer and fasting for my healing.

On the Saturday morning I was joined by Teddy Saunders, Vicar of St Michael's, Chester Square and Chairman of
the Belfrey Trust (which finances and guides our work), and
Douglas Greenfield our team Administrator who researches
and plans all our festivals. Teddy, Douglas and I went
through the diary in detail, looking at the many engagements
fixed for the next eighteen months – most of which required
complex planning – to see which ones we had to cancel
outright, which ones could be 'put on ice', and which ones
could go forward with some rearrangements. In the following
six months alone we were booked for a mission in Wands-
worth London, and festivals of various lengths in Brighton
and Hove, Plymouth, Exeter, Bristol, Harlow, Norfolk, Bedford, Oldham and Folkestone. As well as that there was a
Lent series of seven lunch-hour services at St Lawrence
Jewry, in the City of London, and many other preaching
engagements. How could I cancel all those? Or what alternative plans could possibly be made at this stage? I am not a
brave person and am naturally frightened of pain; yet at that
moment I was far less concerned about my own future than
about letting so many people down. At the same time I was
increasingly sad about not being able to lead those missions
and festivals which I had been looking forward to for months.

I hated the thought of having to rearrange all those events.
For years I have loved this work. It has been a vital part of my
life. Suddenly to be stripped of it all was personally very
painful. I also felt as deeply committed to my team as they
were to me, and the thought of not being with them for at
least six months was distressing, and I was concerned that
they might be out of work because of me. My heart sank
continually as the implications of my illness hit me.

However, Douglas had come from an evening in Guildford
with the marvellous news that a good friend of mine, Bob
Roxburgh who had recently become the Pastor of Millmead

Baptist Church in Guildford, was almost sure that he could make himself available for several months to take festivals in my place together with the team. This was another great burden off my shoulders since I knew that the plans were well advanced for major festivals at Harlow and Bedford at least. I could feel the tensions within my body relax as the diary was cleared and as I realised that the vast majority of people involved would not be let down.

Anne and I found it difficult to know what to say to our children. With cancer being such an emotive word, we decided to leave it for the time being as 'an operation for an ulcer', and only fill in further details as they became necessary. I was amazed at the calm way in which they seemed to take it, although of course they were anxious – and no doubt picked up our tensions as well.

Throughout this time, Teddy and Margaret Saunders, who lived just round the corner from us, were marvellous, and so was Hilary, their daughter and my secretary. Our respective families had been on holiday together in the summer and, as family friends, we planned a relaxed afternoon to relieve the tensions of the last few days. We had a delightful lunch in their home, and then piled into our cars to go to Leicester Square, where a *Pink Panther* film was being shown.

It was a grey Saturday afternoon, and driving through the London streets seemed once again like a dream. 'I *still* can't believe it's all happening to me' was the constant thought going through my mind.

At the Odeon, Leicester Square some young man recognised me. 'Aren't you David Watson? How are you?'

How do you answer a throw-away question like that? 'Well actually, I've got cancer. How are you?'

Inevitably I made the usual polite comments and sat down to enjoy the film. Every now and then my mind turned back to the fact of cancer, and I was afraid. But on the whole I forgot everything with the hilarious actions and accents of Peter Sellers. Laughter is one of God's great gifts and a delightful means of relaxation. Life is not always very funny, and my own situation was far from humorous, but laughter can save us from the deadly snares of self-pity and self-importance. It can also act as a powerful antidote to disease by turning negatives into positives. As we emerged from our two hours of happy escapism I felt better equipped to face the major battles still to come.

4

Getting Ready

There had never been a Sunday like it.

As usual I woke early, washed and dressed, and spent some time reading my Bible and praying. After breakfast we went as a family to a Communion Service at St Michael's Chester Square.

Ever since I was twenty-one I have put my trust firmly in Christ, convinced that he was and is the Son of God and therefore the supreme authority in matters of faith. The substantial evidence for this has always seemed totally compelling. When it comes to the most critical issues that ever face us, I would rather trust Christ than any other person in the history of the world. And we all have to trust someone, because nobody knows what happens at death. Who else, apart from Christ and his resurrection (the evidence for this being overwhelmingly powerful) can give us any solid hope for the future? There is no one. Yet one day we must all die, and then what? We remain agnostic in the face of death only by ignoring the many promises and warnings given to us by Christ. Everyone, without exception, has faith in one direction or another: either faith in Christ, with all the weighty evidence for that, or faith in supposing that what Christ said is not true or not important. Sadly, it is often only when our faith faces the final test that we begin to consider these questions seriously.

Brendan Behan, the Irish poet, once confessed, 'I'm a daylight atheist.' It is easy to say 'there is no God' when there is no immediate challenge for personal atheistic views. But

the atheist has faith – he cannot *prove* there is no God. In fact
the atheist has far greater and more daring faith than the
Christian, since he must hold to his non-belief against all the
teaching of Jesus Christ. Moreover, Christ not only taught
with astonishing authority about the vital issues that affect us
all – life and death, God and man – he also vindicated the
truth of what he taught by the matchless character of his own
person. The Christian has faith, yes, but his faith rests firmly
on the historical facts of Christ and his teaching. The atheist
has to believe that all those things are not true – where is the
evidence for that?

For many years I had been telling people that I am not
afraid to die. I know the reality of Christ in my own experience. He has made God real in my life, and has promised that
one day he will welcome me into his home in heaven. At the
same time, with the sudden and alarming discovery of
cancer, I realised that the time had now come to place the
whole of my life into God's hands once again and to renew my
trust in him for all that lay ahead of me.

That simple Anglican Communion Service in St Michael's
said it all. When all the false promise of the world is stripped
away like old wallpaper (or at least threatened), the only
solid reality that matters before God is that Christ has died
for us to bear all our sin, and has been raised from the dead,
giving us a living hope in the face of our last enemy.

There were not many in the church that morning, perhaps
sixty. But here was all that I needed as I faced a future that
was suddenly insecure and uncertain.

> God so loved the world that he gave his
> only Son, that whoever believes in him
> should not perish but have eternal life.

Quietly I confessed my sins to God, thanked Jesus for
dying for me, and told him that my life – and the future of my
family – was in his hands.

Christ has died:
Christ is risen:
Christ will come again.

I took the bread and the wine, tokens of Christ's ultimate sacrifice for my sins and the guarantee of God's unchanging love and mercy. I knew that I belonged to him for ever. Not even death could separate me from his love.

Through him (Christ) we offer you our souls and bodies to be a living sacrifice.

'Lord, I'm yours. You can do with me whatever is your perfect will.' In that surrender I found his profound peace. I was ready.

After lunch, a number of Christian leaders had been invited to the home of Teddy and Margaret Saunders to pray for me. We knew it could be a prolonged time of prayer, so Anne felt it best to take Fiona and Guy out for the afternoon, to avoid any undue anxiety on their part. Fiona rode on Wimbledon Common, and Anne and Guy went for a walk at the same time.

I was amazed that such extremely busy Christians could make time on a Sunday afternoon to spend time with me. I looked around the spacious drawing-room at mostly very familiar faces, men and women whom I had loved and trusted for many years. I knew they were all 'full of faith and of the Holy Spirit' (a description given to some New Testament Christians), and we had an immensely encouraging time of worship and prayer, during which they anointed me with oil in the name of the Lord. This was simply following the New Testament instructions: 'Is any among you sick? Let him call for the elders of the church, and let them pray over him, anointing him with oil in the name of the Lord; and the prayer of faith will save the sick man, and the Lord will raise him up' (James 5:14f). Often I had done this for others, but now it was my turn to be at the receiving end of this loving

and caring ministry. Although the purpose of this gathering
was serious it was a relaxed and peaceful time, and we still
knew how to laugh!

Since these were all mature and experienced Christians I
listened carefully to what they had to share with me. One
said that she had been woken at 3 a.m. with a clear impression (which she took to be from God): 'This experience will
not diminish David's ministry, but will in fact increase it.' I
puzzled over this, since it seemed that exactly the opposite
would happen, if not end my ministry altogether. However,
others shared various verses in the Bible that had come to
them as they had been praying for me: 'What I am doing you
do not know now, but afterward you will understand' (John
13:7); 'You are my servant . . . in whom I will be glorified'
(Isaiah 49:3); 'I will remove disaster from you' (Zephaniah
3:18). All those present seemed fully convinced that God was
not only fully in control, but that he would glorify his name
even more through what was going to happen and would add
a further dimension to my work. I could not see how this
could happen, and I experienced an inward struggle between
faith ('Lord, I believe this and thank you for it') and *fear*
('They're only trying to encourage me, and anyway God
could be glorified through my death!'). However it was not so
much their words that helped me but their obvious love and
concern. They really cared.

That evening I rang my elderly mother. Over the years
since my own conversion at twenty-one, she had come into a
living faith in God – a faith that was often surprisingly strong
in difficult circumstances.

'Hallo,' I said, 'it's David.' I knew my mother was surprised to hear from me on a Sunday.

'Is everything all right?'

'Well, I've got to go into hospital – tomorrow in fact – for
an operation.'

'You haven't! Is it serious?'

'I'm not sure. It could be.' I went on to explain, as gently
as I could, the events of the last few days. Although my

mother, aged eighty-two, was obviously shaken by it all, she seemed full of faith, believing in God's power to look after me.

'I'm sure you will be all right. God will take care of you, and I shall be remembering you constantly in my prayers.'

It was not an easy phone call. I kept simply to the basic facts, but I was glad that she took it so well.

That evening I packed a few basic requirements for hospital, including my *Good News Bible*, which I knew would be the source of enormous comfort and strength in the coming days.

It could not have been an easy time for my family either. Guy was due to return to his boarding school the next day, so he was a bit tense anyway. Anne was packing for him, and trying to support me at the same time. Fiona was endeavouring to encourage us all!

We prayed, and went to bed.

5

Into Hospital

After breakfast on Monday morning I left for Guy's Hospital. It was hard saying goodbye to the children. Fiona, who like me is naturally rather fearful about hospitals, was outwardly calm but inwardly anxious. Guy was going off to school later that day, and so we would not see each other again for several weeks. Anne was marvellous in her support for us all, however, and Teddy Saunders drove us in his car, he and Margaret having postponed their sabbatical leave to South Africa until our immediate crisis was over.

'Well, there's no turning back now,' I thought to myself. 'The adventure has now begun!' I was much in prayer to God, and constantly aware of his presence with me as we entered the hospital.

I was immediately impressed by the pleasantness and quiet efficiency of the Sister in charge of the ward, and her manner set the tone for all the nursing staff there. Their cheerfulness and professionalism gave enormous encouragement to any nervous patient like me! I had been in hospital only once before for an operation (that was about thirty-five years ago) and all my life I have been ridiculously squeamish about such things as tubes sticking in or out of people's bodies. Because of this, hospital visiting has always been something of an ordeal for me throughout my ordained ministry, and only genuine compassion for those who are sick has helped me to overcome my fears.

Anne was on her old home ground at Guy's, and was wonderful in getting me settled into a little side room just off the main ward. When she was sure I was all right, she returned home to take Guy to school, but came back to the hospital later that evening and again first thing the next morning. I was now off all food since the biopsy was booked for the Tuesday afternoon.

The days of both the biopsy and the operation are little more than a blur to me now, although a number of features stood out. In the first place, contrary to my usual expectations, I was struck by the efficiency of the Church of England! The hospital chaplain came round twice, giving Anne and me Holy Communion on the second occasion and once more anointing me with oil in the name of the Lord – *not*, for the uninitiated, to be confused with the Last Rites! And my first visitors outside my family and close friends were the Bishop of Fulham coming on behalf of the Bishop of London, and the Bishop of Kensington. The two Bishops missed each other by half an hour, and I marvelled at being the object of such episcopal concern. I found both their visits encouraging; and letters, telegrams, cards and flowers began to pour in, assuring me of the prayers of God's people from countless different places. It was all quite extraordinary, but terribly moving. Most of the flowers had to be taken back to our home because their beautiful and powerful fragrance gave me a touch of hay fever. Anne replaced some of them with such realistic silk flowers that someone kindly watered them for me!

Most treasured of all were the letters from Fiona and Guy, which I read over and over again. They were mainly chatty letters, but Fiona wrote almost every day, which was amazing! I thanked God for them both and for the love of all my family.

The biopsy confirmed that the ulcer in the colon was malignant. I had already resigned myself to this fact, so it did not come as a shock. But the implications of the cancer had to be thought through, especially the ominous warnings about a colostomy. (In my layman's terms, a colostomy involves the sealing of the normal passage of the bowels, with an artificial opening being made instead in the side of the abdomen, to which is attached a plastic bag.) I tried to imagine myself at home and in public lavatories trying to deal with a colostomy bag. How would I cope with this in the homes of other people? The whole idea was repulsive to me in spite of reassurances of how well people adjusted to this. Anne and I had helpful instructions about the nature of a colostomy, and how the bags should be used; and mentally I tried to prepare myself for this structural alteration in my anatomy. The cancer was so low in the colon that it seemed certain that I would have a colostomy, and a bag was even attached to me before going down to theatre, to give me some idea as to its feel and position. I cannot say that I relished the thought of it all, but I had a remarkable sense of God's peace as I faced the unknown.

As I lay in bed I thought of all that had happened during those seventeen years in York, the happiest period in our life. When we arrived in 1965 we moved into a large but filthy rectory, needing urgent redecoration in all its fourteen rooms, with no money available for the purpose. My own salary was £600 a year! The church, St Cuthbert's, had a tiny congregation and was soon to be closed – probably to be made into a museum. I thought of all the struggles as we worked and prayed that God would bring new life into that church: the time of Anne's deep depression and the time when I nearly died from asthma.

And yet the work grew! I thought of those amazing Thursdays when roughly 140 people would come into our home, filling six rooms, for the purpose of Bible study and prayer. This was the heart-beat of the new life that was steadily developing. I remembered more than sixty university missions, which I had the privilege of leading, although my continued absence from home was not easy for Anne.

My mind moved on to that extraordinary further growth in the church when we moved to St Michael-le-Belfrey (another church about to be closed and three times the size of St Cuthbert's), when we held regular services in York Minster with packed-out congregations, when we lived in an extended household, when we developed music, drama and dance groups and learnt how to express and communicate our faith through the arts. Above all, I thought of the incredible sense of love that blossomed in the congregation and the wonderful quality of worship. Although people came from all over the world to see what was going on, they were usually struck most by the love and worship.

It was far from perfect, of course. We made numerous mistakes and learnt a lot about forgiveness. But the church was alive and real. God was in that place. As I lay in my hospital bed, I knew that hundreds in York would be praying continuously for us as a family, and I thanked God for the incredible love and support they had constantly given us over the years.

When on my own, I spent as much time as possible reading the Bible, especially the Psalms, mingling prayer and praise. Psalm 16 has for a long time been a favourite of mine. I preached from it for my farewell sermon at York, and I have always loved a song based on this psalm:

> For you are my God;
> You alone are my joy.
> Defend me, O Lord.

The translation in the *Good News Bible* is particularly helpful:

> You, Lord, are all I have,
>   and you give me all I need;
>   my future is in your hands . . .
> I am always aware of the Lord's presence;
>   he is near, and nothing can shake me.
> And so I am thankful and glad,
>   and I feel completely secure,
> because you protect me from the power of death,
>   and the one you love you will not
>   abandon to the world of the dead.

> You will show me the path that leads to life;
>> your presence fills me with joy
>> and brings me pleasure for ever.

Quietly, as I leant back on my pillow, I meditated on those words and let them sink deep down inside me.

'*You, Lord, are all I have.*' I knew that when death comes we have to leave behind everything and everyone. So as an act of the will I handed everything over to the Lord – something I have done almost every day from that time on: my work, my future plans, Anne, Fiona and Guy, other friends and members of my family, my health, my life, my all. One by one I released them to God until I could say in my heart: 'You, Lord, are all I have.' I had already found such riches in Christ that I knew that I would be more than content with that. No one else could offer me complete forgiveness. No one else could be with me day and night throughout my life, and even through the valley of the shadow of death. No one else could give me a new heart and a new life. No one else could give me an abundant hope in the face of death. There is no one like Jesus! If we try to hold on to the temporal pleasures we enjoy now, we may lose everything. But if, in our hearts, we lose everything to the Lord, we have nothing more to lose – in fact we gain our life, said Jesus.

'*You give me all I need.*' At this moment I was experiencing a deep and untroubled peace, on the brink of the biggest trial in my life. If Jesus could meet my very real needs now, I could trust him with everything. I knew that he would never fail me. I sometimes worry about possible future problems which seem far too big for me to handle should they ever arise. In the Bible we are promised that we shall find 'grace to help in time of need'. God's grace, meaning the resources of his love, is there when the need is there, but not in anticipation of that need. I surprised myself by the unusual degree of calm I experienced when even life itself was threatened. This is God's grace *in time of need*.

'*My future is in your hands.*' This was especially reassuring at a time when my future was completely unknown and perhaps distinctly limited here on earth. Often I had taught people, in Festivals of Praise, to give what the psalmist called 'the festal shout'.[1] God's people have always been encouraged to shout acclamations of faith, to encourage one another in the Lord. One festal shout I have taught many thousands of people all over the world is 'The Lord Reigns!' I have seen the faith and confidence of people rise up visibly by acclaiming the truth that God has the whole world in his hands. He is the sovereign Lord. He is ultimately in control. We cannot trust him too much. Now I could rest in the certainty that *my* future was in his hands, whatever the outcome of the operation might be.

In this way I went through the whole of Psalm 16, letting every expression take firm root in both my mind and heart.

'*I am always aware of the Lord's presence.*' To be truthful, I cannot always *feel* his presence – indeed I seldom feel it. But I am always *aware* of it, mostly because of his repeated promise that he would always be with me, but also by many years of proving that in my own life.

'*He is near.*' I 'practised' his presence with me, right by my bed, day and night, until I knew that nothing could shake me. I could honestly echo the words of the psalmist, 'I feel completely secure.'

As I spent time chewing over the endless assurances and promises to be found in the Bible, so my faith in the living God grew stronger and held me safe in his hands. God's word to us, especially his word spoken by his Spirit through the Bible, is the very ingredient that feeds our faith. If we feed our souls regularly on God's word, several times each day, we should become robust spiritually just as we feed on ordinary food several times each day, and become robust physically. Nothing is more important than hearing and obeying the word of God.

[1] Psalms 89: 15, RSV.

'*Your presence fills me with joy.*' My spirit was almost buoyant as I prepared for the operation. I knew that God was with me, right beside me, and I felt ready to tackle this new adventure with him. Quietly I rested in the assurance of his presence as I was wheeled down the corridor towards the operating theatre.

6

Death Sentence

My first conscious memory after the operation was feeling for the colostomy bag. To my amazement and immediate relief it was not there! Mr Beard had avoided a colostomy after all, though he later admitted that they had 'sweated' a little over it during the three-hour operation. I was profoundly grateful.

The next day, when I was a little more aware of what was going on, Mr Beard came with his retinue of medical staff. He explained how they had cut out the malignant section of the colon and had managed to staple me together with a Chinese staple-gun! My mind boggled at the thought of it. But, he went on to say, they had discovered that the cancer had spread a little into my liver. He looked at me straight in the eyes and said gently, 'This is inoperable, I'm afraid. And I'm very, very sorry.'

I smiled weakly, but it felt as though I had received a death sentence. Cushioned perhaps by post-operative drugs, I felt no great panic – just a helpless sinking feeling.

'How long have I got?' I asked.

'We can't really say. Perhaps a year. Maybe more, maybe less. I'm asking Dr Harper, a specialist in these things, to come and see you when you are a little stronger.'

I am not sure when the news made its full impact on me. I was totally unprepared for it and frankly stunned by it. I felt numb. Anne, who was sitting in the corridor at the time waiting to visit me, was shattered when she was told. It was a difficult moment for us all, and no one knew quite what to say. It was one of those times when we were silently trying to absorb the information that had shattered us so completely. We were in a state of shock.

'Oh well,' Anne and I said to each other, smiling rather weakly, 'we must learn to live one day at a time, and to thank God for each day as it comes.'

My immediate reaction was to think that I had roughly 365 days more, so that the next day it was only 364, then 363, and so on. This proved to be both depressing and crippling in its negative effect. I had always imagined that for those under sentence of death, the worst experience was probably not the sentence itself but the agonising period of waiting. Every morning you wake up with the same nightmare that does not fade with the day since it is reality. Every night the same dreams haunt you. Imagination loves to feed on fear, and the result can be almost paralysing. Undoubtedly it can hasten the advance of the disease and the moment of death.

Nothing Anne and I could think of encouraged our hope for the future, as far as this life was concerned, although thankfully we knew that our lives were in God's hands and that not even death could separate us from his love.

But death would certainly separate us from one another. When Anne first came in to see me she had composed herself remarkably well, but in the next few days I could see that she was tense. She looked anxious, she spoke in a strained way and her visits were not restful. She was obviously carrying an enormous strain, although several close friends gave us wonderful support and Anne's mother came the next day to look after everything at home.

We felt that we had to be very careful about communicating this unexpected news of the spread of cancer into my liver. It was important for the Christian public to be alerted, because so many people were praying for me, but at the same time I was concerned about how my children and my elderly mother would take it.

We found it more helpful to discuss practical matters about newsletters and press reports than attempting in any way to think through the personal and family implications of dying. We were much too vulnerable for that.

Added to that, the busy hospital routine together with the extraordinary cheerfulness of both nurses and patients gave little time for fears and introspection. I felt too weak to read my Bible, apart from a few verses every now and then, and during the three or four days after my operation when I was in the main ward there was constant activity all around me. In the middle of one night, the patient opposite me seemed to lose all control, shouting loudly and demanding to be sent home by taxi immediately. It took the skill and strength of several hospital staff to control him, and I don't think that any of us got much sleep that night.

The worst times for me were at two or three o'clock in the morning. I had preached the gospel all over the world with ringing conviction. I had told countless thousands of people that I was not afraid of death since through Christ I had already received God's gift of eternal life. For years I had not doubted these truths at all. But now the most fundamental questions were nagging away insistently, especially in those long hours of the night. If I was soon on my way to heaven, how real was heaven? Was it anything more than a beautiful idea? What honestly would happen when I died? Did God himself really exist after all? How could I be sure? Indeed, how could I be certain of anything apart from cancer and death? I literally sweated over those questions, and on many occasions woke up with my pyjamas bathed in cold sweat! Never before had my faith been so ferociously attacked.

I remembered those words of Dostoevsky: 'It is not as a child that I believe and confess Jesus Christ. My "hosanna" is born of a furnace of doubt.'

At this point most hospitals have little or nothing to offer apart from drugs. I once asked a leading physician in this country, 'What hope can you offer a man who is dying?' He replied, 'None whatsoever!' During my short stay in Guy's Hospital I chatted several times to doctors and nurses on this theme of death. Here were men and women facing the hard fact of it every day, yet thoroughly confused by it.

In spite of all the marvellous work that continuously takes place in hospitals, those working there are conscious of 'failures'. Some patients are visibly dying. Others, like me, have a 'death sentence' given to them, however kindly. Increasingly doctors are aware of this, and I was undoubtedly impressed with the sensitivity I was shown in Guy's. I felt throughout that they were treating me as a whole person, not only dealing with the disease, and they obviously cared. I could not imagine being better looked after anywhere, and I was full of praise for the combination of their cheerfulness, compassion and efficiency.

My own doubts and questionings did not last for very long, although in the middle of the night I was not always sufficiently awake to counter the sense of fear and foreboding that at times overcame me. Those were times of seeming abandonment – 'My God, my God, why have you forsaken me?' Yet when Christ uttered those terrible words of dereliction on the cross, he was taking upon himself the sin and guilt of the whole world, so that we might be forgiven. We cannot begin to imagine the horror of Christ's spiritual torment, quite apart from the physical and mental agony of crucifixion. But because of his death, I *knew*, in my heart of hearts, that I belonged to God for ever. Nothing could ever separate me from him.

I also knew that, when it comes to facing death, everyone has 'faith'. As I lay there in the early hours of the morning, I knew that I had to trust someone about the future; and there is no one in the history of the world that I would rather trust than Jesus Christ. But there were questions I had to ask myself.

Did Christ really exist? Yes, I had no doubts about that at all. Even Marghanita Laski, a literary critic and a self-confessed atheist, told me when I debated with her on Radio 4 a few years ago, 'I find the Gospels totally convincing as historical documents.' I knew my Christianity was not built on a dream, a religious idea or a fictional character. It was solidly based on a historical person.

Was Christ really the Son of God? Can he be trusted? He certainly made monstrous and outrageous claims for himself if they were not true. Yet everything about his life, ministry and teaching supported his claims. Here surely was the One Person with the right to speak about all the greatest issues of life and death that puzzle us all. He is the Great Consultant. There is every reason why we should trust him. If, on the other hand, we ignore or reject his words, we put ourselves in a far more daring and dangerous position of faith, especially when facing death. Yes, I told myself, I was absolutely sure I could trust Christ for my future.

Did Christ really rise from the dead? Once again, I had for many years sifted through the evidence for this until I was sure beyond any reasonable doubt. The resurrection of Christ was a plain, historical fact – sometimes described as 'the best attested fact in history'.[1] My confidence about the future was not just a psychological prop because I was frightened of death, nor was it clutching at some slender religious straw. Intellectually, I was as convinced as I possibly could be that Christ had risen from the dead, and this was the solid ground for my own future hopes. Death is not the end. There is life after death. Death is only putting out the lamp at the rise of a new dawn.

I am not saying that I never had any problems after that. It would not be true. But in the middle of those nightmare storms, with waves of doubt and fear lashing all around me, I found that my faith was secure on that immovable rock of Christ.

---

[1] I have examined some of the evidence for the resurrection of Christ in *Is Anyone There?*, Hodder and Stoughton, 1979. See also *Man Alive!* by Michael Green, IVP, 1967, or *The Evidence for the Resurrection* by Prof J. N. D. Anderson, IVP, 1950.

7

Encouraging Faith

In no way am I, as a Christian, sheltered from the pains and tears of this world. Sometimes I am crushed and brokenhearted.

My God is Real[1] is a title of a book I wrote some years ago as I tried to express my basic beliefs in God. Intellectually I have been persuaded for years about the reasonableness of the Christian faith, and I was thankful that this faith stood firm when facing the ultimate crisis of a terminal illness and death. God proved himself to be real in the darkness as well as in the light, and I knew that my knowledge of him was growing through this experience.

At the same time I longed for God to speak to me. Although my mind was now clear, my heart needed to be warmed. On this more devotional level I turned to a constant source of inspiration for my faith: the Psalms. In the 150 psalms recorded in the Bible we find almost every human mood and emotion honestly expressed, with a strong confidence in a reigning, living and loving God piercing through the gloom of sickness, suffering, loneliness, depression, fear and death. So many psalms spoke to me personally and became vehicles of communication with God that it is impossible to give more than a few examples. Psalm 30 pinpointed my feelings perfectly, now that I had come through the operation:

[1] Kingsway Publications Ltd, 1970.

> I cried to you for help, O Lord my God,
>   and you healed me;
>   you kept me from the grave.
> I was on my way to the depths below,
>   but you restored my life . . .
> Tears may flow in the night,
>   but joy comes in the morning . . .

Fears often loom large at night-time, when every negative thought can grow hideously out of proportion; but the daylight casts away the shadows and restores a right perspective.

Psalm 91 was one which I had often preached on, but now I found the familiar words personally reassuring:

> Whoever goes to the Lord for safety,
>   whoever remains under the
>   protection of the Almighty,
> can say to him,
>   'You are my defender and protector.
>   You are my God; in you I trust.'
> He will keep you safe from all hidden dangers
>   and from all deadly diseases.
> He will cover you with his wings;
>   you will be safe in his care;
>   his faithfulness will protect you and
>   defend you.
> You need not fear any dangers at night
>   or sudden attacks during the day
>   or the plagues that strike in the dark
>   or the evils that kill in daylight . . .
> God says, 'I will save those who love
>   me
>   and will protect those who know me
>   as Lord . . .'

I found God's word to be a wonderful protection from all dreadful imaginings. Even on a human level the existence of anxieties and fears can accelerate the disease and hinder the healing process. A number of years ago my local doctor was an agnostic, yet he used to send some of his patients to our church because, he explained to me, he saw that the people who came to him from our church had a quality of peace about them that was a positive influence in healing.

As I read or prayed through those psalms, I was conscious of my tensions unwinding, my fears disappearing, and once again I was aware of the Lord's love surrounding me. I could literally rest in him. In the words of Psalm 139, which is particularly graphic in the *Living Bible*, although not printed as verse, I found an echo for my thoughts:

> You chart the path ahead of me, and tell me where to stop and rest. Every moment you know where I am . . . You both precede and follow me, and place your hand of blessing on my head. This is too glorious, too wonderful to believe! I can *never* be lost to your Spirit! I can *never* get away from my God! If I go up to heaven, you are there; if I go down to the place of the dead, you are there. If I ride the morning winds to the farthest oceans, even there your hand will guide me, your strength will support me. If I try to hide in the darkness, the night becomes light around me. For even darkness cannot hide from God; to you the night shines as bright as day. Darkness and light are both alike to you . . .

Christian evangelists (I am one of them) sometimes speak of the marvellous things that Christ can do for every person. Christ can bring forgiveness, peace, love, freedom, joy, hope, purpose, fulfilment, and so forth. All that is true, as countless people have experienced. But it is not the whole story, as the psalmist discovered, for example in Psalm 73. As I look around it is often the *un*believer who seems to be free and purposeful, confident and assured. In contrast, I often seem to be anxious, unsure, confused, in pain, and sometimes sunk in that dark pit of depression. Although I proclaim that God is real and answers prayer, to be honest he sometimes seems a million miles away and strangely silent to my frightened cries. But I have discovered over the years that although God never promises to save us from suffering, he does promise to be with us in the midst of it and is himself afflicted by it.

The mystics down the centuries have often referred to the 'dark night of the soul'. This describes those periods when God seems strangely silent and absent in spite of personal need. We wonder what he is doing, why he is withholding his presence from us. We pray to him, but the heavens seem as brass and we feel trapped by the prison of our own dark moods. 'The greatest test of a Christian's life is to live with the silence of God,' wrote Bishop Mervyn Stockwood in a letter to me recently. How far can we go on trusting God when we have no experience of his love? Is it enough to take him purely at his word when we feel no reality behind those familiar phrases? It is comforting to see that the psalmist often battled like this:

> How long, O Lord? Wilt thou forget me for ever?
>   How long wilt thou hide thy face from me?
> How long must I bear pain in my soul,
>   and have sorrow in my heart all the day?
> How long shall my enemy be exalted over me?
>
> Psalm 13

Eventually the psalmist knows too much about God and his faithfulness to be crushed for ever:

> But I have trusted in thy steadfast love;
>   my heart shall rejoice in thy salvation.
>
> (verse 5)

Even when all is dark and silent, possibly for months if not years, we can still know that the Lord is there. His word is never broken. His steadfast love never fails.

8

Prayer for Healing

'They are flying over to pray with you and will be here on Wednesday!'

I could hardly believe the news when Anne brought it to me two days after the operation. She was referring to three pastors from California.

Each January, when I am in California as a visiting lecturer at Fuller Theological Seminary, I go whenever possible to a remarkable church called The Vineyard at Yorba Linda, where John Wimber is the main pastor. This church has grown from nothing to 4,000 in four years, and most of those 4,000 have had no links with any church at all before coming to this one. At the time of writing they have no church building of their own.[1] They meet each Sunday in a school gymnasium which looks as unattractively functional as any other big gymnasium. Each Sunday morning a team of men arrive early to roll out some carpets, put up a large number of chairs, erect a small stage and fix some good PA equipment. About half the congregation sit on terraced benches called 'bleachers' (when someone there asked me how I liked the 'bleachers', I thought this must be the name of their music group so I said that they were really great!). Then at the end of each Sunday, everything is put away, ready for school on Monday morning.

What attracts so many to this church? They come in their

---

[1] They have since moved to a location in Anaheim, California, near Disneyland.

jeans and T-shirts, and superficially nothing could look less like a typical church service. John Wimber, a patriarchial figure with a twinkle in his eye, complete with a bushy beard and an open-necked shirt, leads the service sitting behind an electric piano on which he later rests his Bible and sermon notes. The rest of the music group on the small stage usually consists of three guitarists and a drummer. The whole event is wonderfully relaxed and low-key, with nothing of the showbiz performance common in so many of the big American churches. My first impressions there were dominated by the incredible sense of genuine caring love pervading the entire church, together with a gentle spirit of intimate worship. Although all their songs were quite new to me, I found them easy to learn and anyway was soon caught up in the extraordinary atmosphere of heartfelt praise from the 3,000 who were present.

One of the most powerful attractions of the church, however, is to be found in the 'signs and wonders' which happen at every service. After a sustained time of worship, followed by excellent Bible teaching (usually from John Wimber), those who want to find Christ, or who need healing or other help, are invited into a side room. Probably a hundred or more are counselled and prayed for each week. Remarkable healings take place. And it is not just backaches, headaches and toothaches, although those afflictions are no doubt dealt with too. But the blind receive their sight, the deaf hear, the lame walk, those who are crippled with arthritis are straightened up, those who are barren later give birth to babies, those bound by satanic powers through involvement with the occult are set free. It is not true that *all* who are sick are healed, but a good many are, either immediately or over a period of time during which there is persistent prayer and ministry.

I talked with Mike, an architect, who was so diseased by multiple sclerosis that he could no longer hold his pencil. Of course he had lost his job. At a service in that church God began to heal him over a short space of time, so that now he is fully recovered, working as a professional architect once again.

Last time I was there, a man testified to healing from cancer in the mouth. The chemotherapy had not worked and had been stopped about six months previously. Drastic surgery was now necessary when about half his tongue and three-quarters of his jaw would have to be removed. Although he was not a Christian, the man was brought to this church and God immediately began to heal him. After a few weeks he went back to his doctor and all that could be found of the tumour was some scar tissue.

Similar stories are far too numerous to mention, and some are in the process of being carefully documented at the present time. John Wimber also teaches at Fuller Seminary, and his course on 'Signs and Wonders in Church Growth' is the most popular course ever held there. Seminary professors and other Christian leaders have taken part in this course and testify to the quality and credibility of the teaching.

Over the years I have seen a number of faith-healers at work, and most have left me troubled, if not disillusioned. The strong emotionalism of the meeting, the persuasive pleas for money, the unconfirmed claims of healing – all have left me wary and sceptical. Added to that, for one year in York we prayed fervently for four people who had cancer, three of them young parents. All four died. That rocked our faith in God's power to heal for some time, and we thereafter felt able to pray only for peace in the midst of sickness. Over the years I have been confused and cautious about the whole subject. I have not doubted that God *can* heal, and I have sometimes experienced healing myself, but it has very much been the exception rather than the rule.

What first excited me about John Wimber's church, however, was the indisputable evidence of God's power to heal, coupled with a lot of biblical wisdom and human sanity. They do not have all the answers. They do not guarantee healing. Sometimes they are as puzzled and confused as anyone else. They have their 'failures'. In the first year, when they began to believe and teach that God does heal today, they saw no evidence for it. Those they prayed for remained sick or grew worse, and even those who prayed for them became sick! But they stuck to it, and eventually healings began to flow.

In the Gospels we see John the Baptist in prison having severe doubts about Jesus being the Messiah after all. 'Are you he who is to come, or shall we look for another?' he asked through two messengers. Dr Luke records, 'In that hour he (Jesus) cured many of diseases and plagues and evil spirits, and on many that were blind he bestowed sight. And he answered them, "Go and tell John what you have *seen and heard*..." ' (Luke 7:21f). Here were the signs of the kingdom, the proof of his Messiahship. In the early Church it was the bold preaching of the Gospel together with the demonstration of the power of God, seen visually in the healings that took place, that helped people to believe in Jesus. For example, in Acts 8 we read that Philip went to Samaria to preach Christ. 'And the multitudes with one accord gave heed to what was said by Philip, when they heard him and *saw the signs which he did*. For unclean spirits came out of many who were possessed, crying with a loud voice; and many who were paralysed or lame were healed. So there was much joy in that city.' People need not only to hear about Christ, but to see some evidence of the truth of the Gospel by a demonstration of the Spirit's power.

For a long time I had theoretically believed in the truth of all this, and I had seen *some* healings – together with the striking effect of them – in my own ministry. But never before had I found such a wholesome and powerful healing ministry as at Yorba Linda. Therefore when I was told that John Wimber and two others were flying out to pray with me, I could hardly believe it. Anne and my children, who had seen God's power at work through John and his team in York, were of course thrilled with the news that they were coming. Anne was positively glowing when she told me. Her bright

eyes sparkled, and it was the best news she could have
brought me.

'John Wimber, Blaine Cook and John McClure are arriving here on Wednesday.'

'That's fantastic!' I replied, hardly able to believe it. The
two Johns were both pastors of remarkable churches, and
Blaine had a clear, God-given healing ministry. I knew that
they were praying for me. But for all three of them to fly over
from California seemed incredible. I knew the enormous
demands on their time and energy. 'Why bother with me?' I
asked myself. 'Why me?' My eyes became moist.

'What did they say?'

'Simply that they loved you and were coming straight
over! And they will be here for three days!'

'Well, we must pay for their tickets of course,' I said. 'If we
got all our savings together I think we can manage it. Where
are they staying?'

'They're booking rooms in a hotel because they don't want
to be a burden on anyone!'

I was astonished by such an expression of love. Although
their wide experience with healing obviously gave me fresh
encouragement and hope, I think it was this tangible expression of caring love which did more for me than anything
else. How often had I been too busy to see a sick person when
it meant only a couple of hours out of my day! Here were
three extremely busy men flying across the Atlantic and
spending almost a week of their time – to visit me!

When Anne left, I was filled with praise that God loved me
so much – a love wonderfully expressed through his world-
wide family. I opened my Bible and read several psalms of
thanksgiving and praise. However long or short my life might
be, nothing was more profound or important than knowing
that God loved me. I was almost ready to die immediately
that I might know the fulfilment of God's love in heaven. But
I did not think that these friends were flying over just for my
funeral!

On the Tuesday after my operation, the various tubes were

removed out of my body, which I found slightly unpleasant but I was thankful to be less tied down.

'Sister,' I asked, 'is there any chance of my going back into the side room, since the three pastors are arriving tomorrow and want to spend time praying with me?' I had already talked to the Sister and nurses about my friends and their remarkable healing ministry. I knew the ward staff were at least intrigued, and all had been sad about the discovery of cancer in my liver.

'Yes, that should be possible,' she replied.

I hoped there would be no relapse. That evening, when the house doctor was in the ward, I had a persistent attack of hiccups which simply would not go away.

'Put a tube down his throat,' said the doctor. The shock treatment of this had the desired result: my hiccups vanished instantly.

The next day I was wheeled into the side room and tidied up for the normal doctor's round. They had only just left the room when I heard a familiar and welcome voice.

'Hi there, David. How yer doin'?'

'John!' I said, almost jumping out of my bed. 'How wonderful to see you. And Blaine! And John! I can hardly believe it!'

'Well, you don't look as if you're exactly dying!' said John with a twinkle. 'You look great!'

'You sure do,' said Blaine and John McClure.

I thought it was a bit of flattery, since I had lost a lot of weight and was not exactly the picture of health. But my eyes sparkled with joy at their presence. I have seldom met with such genuinely loving and caring people as those three. They had just flown into Heathrow after a sleepless night, and had come straight from the airport to the hospital. I knew that they loved me and that they had flown over because they believed that God wanted to heal me.

We chatted about the events of the last two weeks, and they explained that this was only a preliminary visit. After a good night's sleep they would return tomorrow to pray for me. But as we talked, they sensed the power of God coming upon them, so they began to pray. They praised God for his presence with us, for his authority over life and death, and they prayed against the spirit of unbelief, fear and death that was pervading the room.

After some time of praise and worship, Blaine became aware of the activity of the Holy Spirit, and laid hands on my abdomen. The three of them went on praying, cursing the cancer in the name of Christ, commanding it to wither, and then they claimed God's healing in my body. If this seems a little strange, it is no more so than the incidents in the Gospels where Jesus rebuked a fever (Luke 4:38f) or cursed a fig-tree (Mark 11:12–25). The power of God was certainly with him.

I felt a tremendous surge of heat as well as vibrations in my body, and I knew that God was at work. This went on for half an hour or more, and we all had no doubt that God was with us.

'That was quite a time!' said John Wimber (as indeed it was). 'We had no intention of praying for you until tomorrow, but it seemed that God just stepped in! In fact I sense that the work we came over to do has now been done. Anyway, we'll come again tomorrow to see how you are doing.'

As they left, I was undoubtedly 'doing' very well. I was bursting with praise. It was as though I had been lifted up into the presence of God, bathed in his glory and enveloped in his love. The light of Christ banished any remaining areas of doubt and fear, and I knew that, whatever the future might hold, I was safe in his hands. When a friend came to visit me later that day I said 'I feel five hundred times better.' I gather that even my appearance had changed quite dramatically.

When Anne arrived we were obviously both overjoyed.

'Have you found out how much their tickets cost?' I asked.

'They won't take a penny from us,' she replied. 'In fact they've brought us a generous gift for your recuperation.'

It was hard to take it in, but thankfully we accepted this sign of their love.

The two Johns and Blaine came back on the Thursday and Friday. Mostly we talked and laughed. They were convinced that the main work was now done, and there was no need for further lengthy sessions of prayer. Certainly they did pray again, with great authority in the name of Christ – so loudly at times that I thought that everyone in the ward knew exactly what was being said – and again they laid their hands on me to encourage my faith. None of this had the same unexpected touch of power as on the first occasion, but I was sure that God was, through them, continuing the work that he had begun.

John Wimber warned me that sometimes, in his experience, a tumour will grow after a time of prayer, until it begins to wither and die.

'It might well be that the next scan or two will reveal cancer in your liver, a cancer that is growing. But I believe that the root of it has now been cut. And soon it will begin to die.'

When they eventually departed to fly back to Los Angeles, I was left with an overwhelming sense of God, and my whole being wanted to worship him. So I relaxed on my bed and did just that.

9

Enjoying God

Two friends of mine had lent me their stereo tape-recorder together with headphones, and I found that my faith in God's love and power to heal was stirred not only by the psalms and other Bible passages I was reading but by the songs of praise I was listening to. John Wimber had brought me a cassette of one of their evening services, and its spirit of worship gloriously refreshed me. It was like having a relaxing bath or shower! Anne brought me several other cassettes, and I was also sent the latest one from St Michael-le-Belfrey in York called *Come and Worship*. That opened with my favourite song from Psalm 16 'For You Are My God', and I found that the whole cassette seemed to fill my being with praise.

With headphones over my ears, my eyes closed, a beatific smile on my face, and my hands sometimes raised in worship, I must have looked a strange sight! So it was not surprising when the nurse on night-duty looked through the small glass window into my room, saw this apparition and then rushed in to take my temperature and pulse! All was well. In spite of my recent operation and a bleak prognosis, I was transported with joy. The love of God seemed to fill the whole room and I was profoundly aware of his presence. I knew deep within my spirit that nothing could be more wonderful than being perfectly with him in heaven and seeing him face to face, although we had just prayed for healing in order to be on earth for a little bit longer!

At that moment, however, it was not the length of life that was important but its quality; and in the Bible *eternal life* refers to the quality of life, not simply duration. I am not sure that words like *duration* mean very much in the next world anyway since time is a human limitation. God is outside time; and *eternal life* means life with God and with his Son Jesus Christ. This begins on this earth when we commit our lives to Christ, but comes to completion after death. Often I have experienced a foretaste of heaven during times of worship when, in company with God's people, we have been 'lost in wonder, love and praise'. All worries and fears have paled into insignificance. The consuming impression is that God is in our midst, 'inhabiting the praises of his people'.

Churches throughout the world that have seen God at work in unusual power, often in the area of healing, all stress the absolute importance of worship. All too often our faith is earth-bound and we find it hard to believe that God can do anything that our minds cannot explain. It is only as we spend time worshipping God, concentrating on the nature of his Person, especially his greatness and love, that our faith begins to rise. Like a plane soaring through the dark rain-clouds into the fresh beauty of the sunshine, so our faith rises, stimulated by worship and by the new vision of God that worship brings, until we begin to believe that God can work in ways that may be beyond our present understanding.

It is significant that the Church was born in praise. When the Holy Spirit fell on the disciples on the Day of Pentecost, their immediate response was to worship God for all his wonderful works – and they did this in languages given to them by the Spirit. It is not surprising, therefore, that in the same chapter we read that 'many wonders and signs were done through the apostles', and in the next chapter a well-known cripple is healed through Peter and John. Indeed throughout those early chapters of Acts we find this constant blend of worship and wonders, praise and power. An interesting paraphrase by Strong of Psalm 50:23 reads: 'To him that uses praise over and over again, enough to make a trodden path, will I show the deliverance of God.' There are countless examples in the Bible and in Christian biography where a sustained time of praise prepares the way for the Lord to demonstrate his power.

It is a sad commentary on the life of the Church in this country today that worship is often sterile and dull, and at the same time the level of faith to be found in many congregations is dismally low. The two factors almost inevitably go together. And if in God's goodness there is a resurgence of a vital faith, almost certainly it will be accompanied by – or more likely preceded by – a fresh spirit of praise. John Wesley used to tell his disciples to preach faith until they got it. By this he meant that as we proclaim God's word, so our faith in God will grow. The same is true when we worship God.

For many years I had both known and taught the power of praise. During my seventeen years in York I had sought to develop various expressions of worship in our church, and have always tried to stress the vital relevance of this in Festivals of Praise we have led in many different parts of the world. All too often I have attended dreary services when I have come away spiritually more dead than alive. Any thinking person, searching for a personal faith, might well conclude that surely God was not in that place. This is a travesty of the vibrant worship that should always be there when God's people come together to praise his name. The format or liturgy of the service is not a priority for me (although I happen to like the Anglican services), but I long to be in a place where the worship is *alive*. The Jewish festivals in Old Testament days were full of music, singing and dancing, and we can understand why the psalmist said, 'I was glad when they said to me, "Let us go to the house of the Lord!" ' (Psalm 122:1). Those festivals were such exuberant, colourful and joyful events that the sound of thousands of people praising God could be heard for miles around.

I have been privileged to take part in many hundreds of similar occasions which have been marked, not only by an exultant note of celebration, but by a profound sense of God's presence. On such occasions I have seen agnostics and even atheists becoming aware of God and brought to know him and worship him for themselves – essentially through the praises of his people. Constantly, too, I have seen the faith of true believers rise above their own personal problems in such an atmosphere of praise. I have met many who have been healed of illnesses, even major ones such as multiple sclerosis and cancer, through the power of the Spirit of God released in praise. Lives have been significantly changed, stubborn wills broken, relationships restored, faith and hope renewed – all resulting from joyful and intimate worship.

The most common word for worship in the New Testament comes sixty-six times. It could be translated 'I come towards to kiss'. God is love, and he wants us to respond to him in love. He wants us to enjoy a love-relationship with him, expressed partly through praise. People today need to know that God loves them as individuals, just as they are, with all their faults and failings. Often the common feeling is that God, if he exists at all, is a million miles away, aloof, distant, far removed from our personal needs, seemingly silent to all our cries for help. Those who believe in him are usually afraid of him, unsure of him and only too ready to believe that sickness is some sort of punishment for past sins. Comparatively few know, deep down within their hearts, that God really loves them more than they could ever begin to imagine. However, when we 'come towards to kiss' by opening our hearts to him in worship, we are able to receive his love poured into our hearts by the Holy Spirit (Romans 5:5). Whatever our feelings may be (and feelings are fickle) we become *aware* of God's personal love for us. Interestingly the Christian mystics of the past have often referred to God's Spirit as his kiss, so that being filled with his Spirit is simply allowing ourselves to be kissed by God. Here we have the intimacy of love in our relationship with God that we read about so often in the Bible, notably in the Psalms and in the Song of Solomon.

O God, thou art my God,
 I seek thee,
  my soul thirsts for thee;
 my flesh faints for thee,
  . . .

Because thy steadfast love is
  better than life,
 my lips will praise thee . . .

(Psalm 63:1, 3)

As we 'come towards to kiss' in worship, so God comes afresh to us with the kiss of his Spirit.

It is one thing mentally to believe the statement 'God loves you'; it is quite another to have a deep certainty of that within my heart and spirit. Yet that certainty is so crucial in times of crisis: a quiet, settled conviction and faith. I have found that such faith is encouraged (and it needs daily encouragement) partly by meditating on God's word of love in the scriptures, partly by the expression of God's love through caring Christian friends, but perhaps mostly by the inward experiencing of God's love through sensitive and joyful worship.

Never has the reality of such worship meant so mucn to me as during this time when I have had to realise the basic truth that my life is literally in God's hands. The apostle John once wrote that 'there is no fear in love, but perfect love casts out fear' (1 John 4:18). When we are quite sure that God loves us and have his perfect love within our hearts, all fears about pain, sickness and death must vanish. There is no room for them. As soon as we lose that conscious awareness of his love, even when in our minds we may still know it to be true, those fears may return to haunt and disturb.

Faith is a living thing. It is like a plant that needs constant feeding. If we take daily and active steps to nourish our faith we shall find ourselves kept in God's peace and love, whatever storms may be raging around us. When we are feeling ill, it is often the task of others to pray for us and to bring God's love to us. It is their faith that counts, not ours. But one way or another, we need to find God's love and stay resting in it. Nothing is more important than that.

10

Letters Galore!

'We love you very much and know the tender arms of Jesus will enfold you at all times. Constantly praying and praising God for you both.'

That telegram from Edmonton in Canada, arriving just before my operation, was typical of the deluge of cables, letters, cards and messages that flooded in during the following weeks. Over a thousand arrived in the first month, and another thousand or so after that. They came from people of all walks of life and from all over the world. I literally wept when reading the expressions of love and deep tender concern from such a multitude of people, many of whom I never knew personally.

I was profoundly moved when I heard that thousands of Christians in Zimbabwe were praying for me – and I have never been to Zimbabwe! I was astonished to discover that Catholic and Protestant terrorists who had come to Christ were joining together to pray for me in a prison in Northern Ireland: I had several marvellous letters from a former IRA and INLA leader who was on hunger strike in the Maze Prison for fifty-five days and who, having come to the very threshold of death, had turned to Christ and is now serving the Lord 'with a glowing witness', as a mutual friend describes it. This ex-terrorist wrote long letters to encourage my faith and went on to say, 'It is my hope that we who have been through violent organisations can come together in Jesus to spread the message of love and reconciliation in a hate-filled society.' He spoke of over eighty prisoners who had found Jesus, and ended with these words: 'David, my brother in Jesus . . . May God's love and peace which passes all understanding be with you and all your loved ones. Your brother and friend in Jesus . . .'

I was humbled to receive numerous letters from church leaders from almost all denominations throughout the world, including the Archbishops of Canterbury and York and many other bishops from all over the Anglican Communion. Messages of love, concern and the promise of prayer came from almost everywhere: from Singapore to South Africa, from Israel to Argentina, from the United States to Yugoslavia, from New Zealand to Switzerland, from Sweden to South India, from Australia to Canada, and of course from all over Great Britain. Never before have I felt so much a part of the world-wide Body of Christ. The reality of being 'all one in Christ' came home to me with astonishing force. For years I had declared in the words of the Apostles' Creed, 'I believe in the Holy Spirit, the holy catholic Church, the communion of saints . . .' The deep sense of belonging not only to God but also to his family all over the world and throughout all ages brought to me an incredible sense of security and peace.

I had always heard that Christians in communist prisons, or suffering elsewhere for their faith, had thought much about their solidarity with all those in Christ, regardless of denomination, race or colour. Some of my greatest support and most sensitive expressions of love came from Roman Catholic friends, who probably stirred up my faith in the love of Christ more than anyone. I was also particularly touched by the warmth of God's love expressed by Christians of all races in South Africa. Many letters began in the same way, 'Dear David, you won't know me but . . .' Then would follow a moving account of how that person had found Christ through my preaching or writing, or else had been specifically helped by me although I had never known it until my illness.

I remember once being challenged by the question, 'Have you ever thanked those who have been an encouragement to you in the past? Have you ever written to your teacher, doctor, nurse, social worker, employer, vicar, or whoever, and told them how they had helped you at some important moment in your life?' Often I can be critical. I complain readily enough, and do not easily forget those times when I have been hurt or let down. However I realise that I can encourage people when I take the trouble to thank those who have done something positive for me. Prompted by my illness, and perhaps with the thought that I might not be on this earth for much longer, I wrote several letters to this effect and received many more. I was able to praise God that he had been able to use my feeble and faltering efforts to touch other people's lives.

What I found particularly valuable were fairly brief re-assurances of love and prayer. I could not cope with lengthy letters, with a few special exceptions from those I knew very well; but I found great comfort in short affirmative comments such as this one from a wonderful Christian leader and a close personal friend: 'David, my brother, you are loved, appreciated, much prayed for, greatly needed, and we do not "accept" your illness. "God is greater." ' Such letters take only a minute or two to write and bring inspiration out of all proportion to their length.

An ex-heroin addict promised, 'You can be assured of my constant prayers and of my love for you as a sister in Christ,' and she enclosed a moving poem she had written about the time when Jesus had found her in the midst of her addiction:

> When I gave up and prayed to die,
>   you breathed in me your life;
> When I screamed in the darkness,
>   your light shone down on my heart . . .

A retired university professor wrote about the grief he experienced with the news of my illness: '(It) has hurt and distressed me . . . The stark reality of it wounds me . . . Dear David, I know God has been with you all your life, and he will sustain you now to strengthen and restore you, whom he loves so dearly . . .'

David Pawson, the well-known preacher and a personal friend wrote about the time when his wife was diagnosed as having cancer:

> It was then that we discovered the difference between being *willing* to go to heaven while *wanting* to stay on earth (for the sake of family, friends, etc) – and *wanting* to go to heaven while being *willing* to stay on earth for others' sake (which was Paul's position in Philippians 1). We found there was great release in getting through to Paul's position – and that only then could we approach the question of healing in an objective way. We simply told the Lord that *if* he had more work on earth for my wife to do then he knew what he had to do about it. He had and he did, bless him!

I found that especially helpful. I was certainly willing to go to heaven, but I very much wanted to be around for a little longer, at least until my children were grown-up and able to look after themselves and Anne. Knowing how much I missed my own father when he died (I was ten), I did not want them to go through the same difficulties. However, as I continued to abandon everything, including my family, to the Lord, and as I continued to worship him and reflect on his word in the Bible, so I found myself (at least sometimes, to be honest) genuinely *wanting* to be with him in heaven, but willing to stay on earth in order to serve him and others here. It was an attitude of great security, although I realised it should be the constant position of every Christian. In theory it had been mine and I had always looked forward to heaven. But when the crunch came, I was not too sure!

Some letters, inevitably, were less helpful, most of them coming from complete strangers. It is amazing how many I received which went something like this: 'Dear David (or Canon Watson, or Rev, or Sir), You won't know me. I'm sorry to hear you have cancer. My husband got cancer last year and he died last month . . .' Then followed page after page of almost illegible writing giving details of all the painful therapy the husband had to go through, all the traumas surrounding death and all the problems the family had to suffer.

However, these were vastly more helpful than some letters I received. One person wrote with conviction about the after life urging me to 'find a reliable clairaudient medium, through whom you could converse sometimes with your dear wife'!

I could not but smile at the thought that some well-meaning writers had me effectively dead and buried a little before my time! A few letters read like obituaries, and I remembered Mark Twain's comment when he saw, to his surprise, his own obituary in the national papers: 'The report of my death was an exaggeration.' Shortly after I had left hospital someone rang up a Bible College in this country to ask about my progress. When told I had 'gone home', the rumour of my supposed death caused no little stir in some parts of the country.

A number of letters never reached me at all. My wife and secretary carefully screened all the correspondence before letting me see it, and wisely destroyed all the really unhelpful stuff, however good the intentions were on the part of the senders. One man wrote to Anne saying that his own wife had died, even though she believed to the end that God would heal her. However, he went on happily to say, he had now married again and his second marriage was unbelievably wonderful. They were blissfully happy! The next day poor Anne got another letter from this man's second wife to confirm how glorious it now was. So Anne must not be discouraged. She could look forward to good, if not much better, things to come! (I cannot record the words accurately since both letters were promptly destroyed. No doubt encouragement was intended, but neither letter was the height of sensitivity when I was fighting for my life!) Both Anne and

I were beginning to learn that, at all stages of recovery, and especially just after an operation, the emotions are vulnerable. Negative emotions can hinder the healing process and even encourage disease, so should be avoided as far as possible.

Fears and doubts continued to afflict me from time to time, partly because of the confusion we were in, intensified by the thousands of letters that arrived. I sensed that a friend of mine hit the nail on the head when he wrote that 'the thing that is holding back complete healing is a combination of fears and doubts within David . . . Stop asking for complete healing and ask for complete trust.' I observed for a time that when I talked about certain aspects of my illness or expectation of healing, some nervous symptoms were apparent: I became breathless or went often to the loo. Although outwardly I seemed fairly peaceful about the present and future, there was still a battle between faith and fear raging within. I noted with care, therefore, the advice of a Christian doctor who wrote:

It is easier to prepare for healing than for parting. But to fail to prepare for parting is to leave a bitter legacy for those we love. David, if it should be that your disease progresses, make time for Anne, Fiona and Guy, to say thank you and to ask forgiveness and to say goodbye.

It was not what I wanted to read, but it was realistic. After all, the time comes for each one of us to die. It is our only future certainty. I did not think that God's time had yet come – but one day it will. Nothing is more important than our relationships as that day approaches: first and foremost our relationship with God, but also our relationships with others, especially our family. In our busy western society, we put too much emphasis on work, achievements, money and success, invariably at the expense of relationships. Above all, if God allowed me a peaceful rather than a violent death, I wanted time to say goodbye to my family. For those in Christ it is only *au revoir*. We shall meet each other again.

Visitors also were screened so that only a strictly limited number of helpful people were allowed to come. I heard of someone who was hospitalised after a severe road accident, and who subsequently had such a stream of well-meaning visitors that in the first month he had only half an hour alone with his wife. Michael Griffiths, the wise Christian leader who told me this story, urged me 'to guard your privacy and time with your family'. For a good many weeks after the operation I was physically weak and grew tired very easily, so that a careful rationing of callers was important.

Some people found it hard to accept that I did not want to see them at that time. Hilary had to be extremely firm and yet tactful on the telephone on many occasions. I do not doubt that the individuals concerned desired only to cheer me up and to pray with me, but they seemed unable to understand that I was exhausted and that Anne was under considerable strain. The last thing we wanted was to see one person after another, answering the same questions, talking over the same issues, and listening to much conflicting advice. We had to be ruthless about this for a good many weeks. Obviously in hospital I loved seeing Anne and Fiona (Guy being away at school), and I was greatly helped by *brief* visits from close friends who chatted for a short time, read a verse or two from the Bible and then prayed for me. It is what I had done for hundreds of people in the past, but it was good to be on the receiving end for a change. I found two or three visits from John and Diana Collins especially helpful. They sometimes came on Sunday evenings after their services at Holy Trinity Brompton were over. John read to me a promise from the Bible and both prayed. In one sense it was all very simple, but I was aware of their concern and love, and my faith was always encouraged as a result.

There were also a few surprises. I was quietly dozing on my bed one afternoon when the Sister of the ward came in with a young woman in her early twenties. In my sleepy state

I thought she was an actress who used to be a member of my team, so I said 'How lovely to see you!' and gave her a loving kiss on the cheek. When she sat down on my bed, however, I suddenly realised my mistake. As far as I knew I had never seen this girl before in my life! I was too confused to admit my error, and she looked a little surprised as well. Later I discovered that she was the nurse who had taken me to the theatre for the operation, and she had simply come back to find out how I was getting on.

'Lord Ingleby has just rung up,' said the Sister one day. 'He and Lady Masham are coming to see you tomorrow afternoon.'

I was astonished. It was not so much the privilege of being visited by two members of the House of Lords that amazed me; it was the fact that both Lord Ingleby and Lady Masham were confined to wheel chairs (one through illness, the other through an accident), and it seemed incredible that both should take the considerable trouble of coming to my room in Guy's Hospital. But they made it! They bundled themselves into a taxi outside the House of Lords, struggled out again at the hospital, and then wheeled themselves through seemingly miles of corridors until they sailed into my ward.

'How wonderful of you both to come,' I said. And I was so pleased to see them.

'You fight it! You fight it!' said Sue Masham.

'I have every intention of doing so,' I replied, and went on to describe what had happened so far. I knew that both Martin Ingleby and Sue Masham had been great fighters themselves with indomitable courage, not only as far as their own disabilities were concerned, but in their many battles on behalf of the sick and disabled.

Martin was particularly intrigued by the visit of the American pastors, and I told them all about it.

Eventually they left for their separate engagements that evening. As they propelled themselves down the corridor I felt immensely happy. Here were two lovely people who knew all about suffering and facing uncertain futures, but who were undoubtedly winning the daily battle, and with enormous cheerfulness.

On another day I was both amazed and humbled to learn that, together with numerous gatherings for prayer concerning my healing, a special 'healing eucharist' was being held for me in our old church in York, with Bishop Morris Maddocks taking part. Not only that, but on the same evening thirteen other healing eucharists were being held for the same purpose in different centres throughout the country, and I was overjoyed to hear later on how special the services had been for a great many people. Quite apart from the benefit that I was receiving from all this, I learnt of others being healed, broken relationships being restored, and fresh commitments being made to Christ. If nothing else happened, it seemed that my illness had helped all sorts of people to examine carefully their relationship with God and the priorities in their lives. Almost every day brought unusual and encouraging news like this, and I was astonished by the love and concern of so many people, many of whom were strangers to me yet belonging to God's great family of Christians of all traditions.

I was fortunate to be in an excellent ward, which was run by an attractive, gracious, hard-working and extremely efficient Sister, Jill Purkiss, who won the respect of all the nurses and patients alike. Although I have never enjoyed hospitals, I respect the enormous amount of good work that goes on in them, and I could not imagine being in a better ward anywhere. I was able to relax with confidence, and could accept very gratefully the constant care and attention that they gave me. I am sure that this, together with the huge volume of prayer and love, helped to get me on my feet surprisingly quickly.

To begin with, it was rather a struggle. I had been watching fellow-patients staggering slowly down the corridor and returning a few moments later as though they had just finished the marathon. But with my incision from my navel downwards, I was bent double, and on my first excursion one circuit round my bed was all that I could manage! Steadily this lengthened through the gentle and encouraging persuasion of the physiotherapist, and within a few days I was walking briskly – or rather shuffling determinedly – as often as I could in order to rebuild my strength.

The great day came when the stitches were removed, and I knew that good progress was being made. The only minor setback was when I was given an aperient. It had a devastating effect on me. As soon as I left the loo, I had to rush back as fast as my feeble legs could carry me, desperately hoping that another patient hadn't got there first!

'I simply will *not* take any more of that "crippling gravel" you are giving me,' I said defiantly. The 'gravel' was a form of concentrated bran. Quite lethal!

Then the bliss of my first bath! As I lay there, soaking in the water, I felt like a civilised being once again. However short my life would be – I was going to relish all that I found enjoyable, including a bath.

The day came to leave. As I dressed I was conscious of still being extremely weak and a little unsure as to how I – or my family – would cope with my being at home again. But it was certainly good to be going, even though my time in Guy's had been much happier and less painful than I had anticipated, due to the excellent medical care I had received.

Anne came with Teddy Saunders in his car, and they carried the piles of cards and letters that had been flowing in. I felt a little faint and distinctly cold as we wound our way through the busy London streets. The major battle of my operation had now been fought and largely won. The question facing me now was how far I could trust God for the healing of terminal cancer. Various forms of treatment might possibly prolong my life a little – often with considerable reduction of the quality of life. But would I be healed?

11

What is Reality?

With a clear, reasoned and (I thought) strong belief in God, why was my mind finding it hard at times to accept that God was healing my cancer in the liver? I had argued and debated about the reality of God for nearly thirty years, and was intellectually more convinced than ever, as well as seeing him at work in my own life and in the lives of countless others – sometimes in dramatic ways. If God could change the hearts of violent, hate-filled terrorists, re-making them into loving, caring Christians (as I had several times witnessed), the healing of a physical disease should be comparatively simple. Why then did I fluctuate between faith and doubt?

I knew that my problem was primarily cultural. Together with the vast majority of people living in the West, I was bound by the western scientific world-view.

A *world-view* is the way in which we view or consider the world. It is 'a set of presuppositions (or assumptions) which we hold (consciously or unconsciously) about the basic make-up of our world.'[1] For most people the real world is that which we can see, touch, measure or understand. For us, this is not only reality; it is *total* reality. It is what science can explain and what our rational minds can grasp. We are instinctively suspicious of anything beyond this, and tend to dismiss all unexplainable phenomena as misleading or false. On the whole we do not believe in 'ghosties and ghoulies and things that go bump in the night'. In our sophisticated

[1] *The Universe Next Door*, James Sire, American IVP.

twentieth-century society we are instinctively cautious of the mysterious realm of the spirit.

In the eighteenth century, Immanuel Kant maintained that all knowledge was acquired from a combination of what we can reason with our minds and experience with our senses. God, he said, was therefore unknowable. Kant was not the first to say this, but millions of people in the west today hold roughly this position and are agnostic about God's existence and about spiritual realities.

The widespread assumption is that anything that cannot be proved scientifically is either meaningless and not worthy of serious consideration, or at least suspect and well avoided. Statements about God are increasingly dismissed as unfounded superstition, and attempts to heal the sick through faith are opposed (sometimes fiercely) as medically dangerous. We have given the medical profession authority over life and death, and only through the progress of medical science do we hope to find both the cause and cure of disease. Everything outside the strict boundaries of science is viewed as dangerous and false. This is the western scientific worldview.

It is worth stressing at this point that there are defined limits to the scope of science. Science essentially is descriptive in that it describes what can be seen or measured, but it cannot interpret what it sees or measures. For example, science cannot comment on the statement 'Jane was healed through prayer'; it cannot say whether that is true or false. It can only investigate the statement 'Jane was healed'. It is entirely outside the field of science to determine the significance of the words 'through prayer'. The mistake arises if we assume that such words can have no significance at all. In the same way science cannot comment on the beauty of a sunset or on the love between a man and a woman. Such words as 'beauty' and 'love' are outside the language of science, but that in no way diminishes their reality. I heard of an entry in a communist textbook which defined a *kiss* as 'the approach of two pairs of lips with reciprocal transmission of microbes and carbon dioxide'. Tell that to a couple of lovers! As valuable as science undoubtedly is, there are vast stretches of reality which lie beyond its borders.

In spite of this rather obvious fact, the scientific world-view has thoroughly permeated our western society and, almost inevitably, has influenced much of the Christian Church. Although orthodox Christians fully accept the healings, miracles and resurrection of Jesus, as recorded in the Gospels, many have the greatest difficulty in believing that similar healings can happen today. Some take the position that such signs and wonders were only for the apostolic period in order to establish the truth of the Gospel.

Other Christians accept theoretically that God can heal today, since his essential character never changes, but in practice they assume that, although certain extraordinary happenings occurred when Jesus walked this earth, God's healing ministry has now been transferred to the medical profession. No doubt much of it has. We thank God for this. It is therefore the Church's calling, say some, merely to bring God's comfort and peace to the sick, in order to encourage the normal healing process, but not to expect anything more in answer to the prayer of faith.

A few well-known Christians wrote to me offering no hope of healing in this life, but reassured me that heaven was not such a bad place for me to look forward to! 'This life isn't all there is!' said someone. That is wonderfully true. A Christian can have a gloriously positive hope for the future, come what may, since heaven will literally be *heaven*. Nothing could be more perfect than that, and on numerous occasions I have felt that I can hardly wait to get there! Nevertheless I was not sure that my time to leave this world had yet come.

Science is undoubtedly a wonderful part of God's creation. At the same time God is bigger than science, and we should not reject various aspects of his nature or working that lie outside our present scientific knowledge. Paul, in Romans 1, shows the foolishness of those who suppress the truth of God that can be known and who 'worship and serve what God has created instead of the Creator himself.' This is exactly what we have done with science. Instead of seeing science as an invaluable servant for the benefit of mankind, we have elevated it into an object for awe and worship. It controls our minds. It limits our faith. It dictates our understanding. It is the master of our lives and we have become its slaves. What science says is true. No other truth is permissible.

The fact remains, however, that our total human understanding is both finite and limited. God, if he exists at all, is an infinite God and infinitely greater than the finite circle of our understanding. We would all be incurably agnostic unless God had broken through that circle in ways that we can understand. It is the Christian conviction that God has done precisely that: through *creation*, which shows us the power of God, through *conscience*, which shows us the goodness of God, through the *scriptures*, which show us the wisdom and justice of God, but supremely through *Jesus of Nazareth*, who was the Son of God and the living revelation of God on earth. Here is something our minds can grasp concerning the truth of God. 'He who has seen me has seen the Father,' said Jesus. If we want to know what God is like, we start with Jesus. Even here we cannot know the total truth of an infinite God, for that would be impossible for our finite mind, but we can know truths that are important. We may not understand how he healed the sick, nor how the disciples went out and did the same. Certainly the disciples did not understand for they were frequently amazed by the power of Christ; but they went on healing as Christ had commissioned them, for many years to come.

After all, can an infinite personal God possibly be limited by the logic of science? Science may well be a description of the usually ordered nature of God's creation, but that in no way precludes the possibility of his working in extraordinary ways. Christians believe that he has certainly done so many times in the history of God's people, especially during the three years' ministry of Jesus. Why can he not do it again? Although it is a Christian belief that every good gift comes from God and therefore we should thank God for the wonderful discoveries of medical science (I would not be alive without this), it would be a profound mistake to assume that God today can do no more than this. Christians believe that God forgives all our sins, offers us a new life in Christ and promises us a place in heaven. If such beliefs are true (and I have good reasons for believing that they are) these are staggering achievements of God's grace in our sinful world.

Paul once summarised the heart of the matter like this: 'When someone becomes a Christian he becomes a brand new person inside. He is not the same any more. A new life has begun!' (2 Corinthians 5:17, *Living Bible*). This miracle of 'new birth' is a fact I have constantly witnessed over the last thirty years in countless people. Many Christians maintain that this is the greatest miracle of all, since there is no other power on earth that can change human nature. I agree with them. Why then did I find it so difficult to believe in God's power to heal physically? If I accepted the spiritual and eternal blessings of the Gospel, why were the physical and temporal blessings so much harder to believe? What sort of a God did I really believe in? Is he a God who can work within us only what *cannot* be seen and proved? If I genuinely believe that God intervenes in our lives by guiding us, strengthening us and steadily transforming us, why can he not heal us as well? I could see that there was an inconsistency here in my faith – almost an unconscious 'double-think'. The reason could be only my bondage to the scientific world-view.

Eastern and Third World countries which are not so bound to this view have no such problems with healings, and significantly it is in these underprivileged places that we find signs and wonders occurring today with New Testament profusion. Most of these countries could benefit considerably from the achievements of science that we take for granted in our own culture, but it is an age-old principle that God has 'chosen those who are poor in the world to be rich in faith and heirs of the kingdom' (James 2:5). They have no difficulty in believing that God works today as he did through Jesus and the apostles. Maybe no one has told them anything different. They expect healing to be part of the good news of the Gospel, and so they see God's power at work in ways that would astonish the scepticism of the West. Sometimes their beliefs may be confused with superstition and primitive rites. However, total reality for them includes the activity of both natural and supernatural forces, and with a clear conversion to Christ they expect God to heal the sick in answer to the prayer of faith. Often he does.

In all this, it would be foolish to imagine science as an enemy of faith. The Christian believes that all good things ultimately come from God, and undoubtedly we enjoy a multitude of 'good things' as a result of science, not least medical science. We should thank God for everything which helps to prevent or cure disease.

What is needed is not a rejection of science in favour of faith, but a widening of our world-view. We need an alternative world-view which embraces humbly all that science can offer and yet appreciates that there is more to come. It is like seeing the world with an extra dimension which in no way denies the other dimensions but presents another perspective. This is what Jesus meant by the Kingdom of God.

12

Back at Home

I had been warned that going home after a major operation is not always easy. Outside the routine and facilities of a hospital it takes time to adjust to the more usual environment of home life. But I was not ready for some of the battles we had to face.

I was naturally overjoyed to be home again, but felt extremely cold after the considerable warmth of the hospital. It was January 26th, and doubtless the accumulated shock to my system of the past few weeks also contributed to the feeling of being frozen. I went to a small guest-room at the top of the house since it was nearer to the loo than our own bedroom, and there was also a better chance that Anne would sleep even if my nights were disturbed.

What was particularly frustrating was attempting to get my bowels to function properly again. I had eaten nothing for ten days in hospital, and then only small amounts of food after that. Obviously I had not been to the loo for some time, so I was given some aperient to get me started again. Every aperient had a violent reaction on my insides, and for weeks I would spend roughly two hours a day (or night) in the loo. It was the only unheated room in the house and not exactly the height of comfort, but it was exceedingly necessary! Looking back on it all, I can laugh at the earthy way my whole life seemed to be dominated by my bowels! I felt just like an old car: either *won't go* or *can't stop*. It was hard to think about anything else, and certainly my days and nights focused on my either far-too-successful or totally-unsuccessful trips to the loo.

Eventually I triumphed over the problem. I bought myself a cheap cassette recorder with headphones, and during the day-time I listened to an extremely helpful series of cassettes on healing, given by John Wimber; whilst at night, with concentration at a considerably lower level at two o'clock in the morning, I listened to worship cassettes. In this way, and in this somewhat unusual posture, I listened to more than forty teaching cassettes and numerous hours of praise and worship. I ceased to dread my visits to the loo since they became extraordinarily profitable occasions.

Slowly I tried to exercise my body. It was an exceptionally cold time of the year, but protected with coat, scarf and hat I ventured a few yards along the street, only to hobble straight back for another lengthy session in my customary sitting-down position. Soon I was walking a little further, and every day I tried to extend those walks as far as I possibly could, setting myself specific targets each day.

For two lovely weeks I went to a farm in Sussex at the invitation of great personal friends, Michael and Gillie Warren, and each walk in the wintry Sussex countryside became times of special communion with God. In certain directions the piercing wind stung my face, but on the way home I felt its force almost pushing me up the gentle hill. I prayed that I might know the direction of the wind of the Spirit for my future ministry, and kept on asking, 'Lord what do you want me to do?'

I noticed the first green shoots miraculously pushing their way through the hard, cold soil; and I thanked God that the life of his Spirit could also overcome the toughest barriers, including those cancer cells. Even the bare trees bore the promise of life. 'If Winter comes, can Spring be far behind?' As I walked I worshipped him, talked to him, listened to him, and thoroughly enjoyed his presence in the midst of his creation.

Anne herself, however, was now far from well. In less than

a week after my return from hospital she was in bed all day
with pains in her kidneys, pains from a stomach ulcer and a
palpitating heart. These troubles continued for many weeks,
and although she went to the doctor several times for various
tests, it became increasingly clear that these were purely
symptoms of stress. It was not surprising. Anne had experienced considerable stress during our last year or two in York;
this was followed by a most painful time when we moved to
London, since for months we felt almost bereaved having lost
our church family with whom we had been for seventeen
years; and then of course she suffered substantial strains
through my illness and prognosis. During the immediate
crisis in hospital, Anne was an absolute tower of strength.
Now that I was home again, the tensions began to emerge in
her body. It was not an easy time.

Added to that, various people began to send us endless
books and articles on cures for cancer. Every one of them was
a thoughtful and generous gesture, but together they brought
us (Anne in particular) under colossal pressure. Most of the
publications gave the impression that providing we followed
a certain line of treatment precisely, there was just a possibility that I might be healed. Many of the books suggested
special diets, and these often differed from one another,
which we found most confusing; and together they gave Anne
the gut-feeling that my life was in her hands. If she bought
the right food, and prepared it in the right way, and kept me
on the right treatment, all might be well; but if she failed to do
this, the future was bleak. As I saw her becoming more and
more tense with each new book arriving, I realised that any
marginal benefit emerging from a better diet would be
cancelled out immediately by the marked increase of tensions
in our lives and relationship. Although I do not doubt that
some people can benefit from a strict diet and perhaps even
overcome cancer in this way, we felt that simple adjustments,
such as an increase of fruit and raw vegetables and a general
avoidance of unnecessary toxins, was all that we could
handle peacefully.

Nine days after my return home, I had to go to the hospital as an outpatient for my first ultra-sound scan. Everything seemed to go wrong. To begin with our boiler backfired that morning, emitting nauseating fumes throughout the house, and all the central heating was off for a week. It was February and distinctly cold. I nearly fainted in the shower, partly from the fumes, and partly because I wasn't allowed any food before a scan.

When we arrived at the ultra-sound unit, I was told to remove my clothes and put on a paper gown together with a small, thin, ill-fitting cotton robe. I felt semi-naked, and we had to sit in a freezing corridor (I was chilled to the bone) for no less than an hour and a half. It was only three weeks after my operation, and I was feeling far from well. Perhaps these factors coloured my impressions, but for me the whole setting looked bleak. The corridor in which we sat was totally bare without even colourful posters to relieve the institutional painted walls; other very sick cancer patients were waiting their turn with an air of hopeless resignation; and the scan itself seemed not only an assessment of cancer, but a doom-watch of life itself. It reminded me of Solzhenitsyn's *Cancer Ward*, a brilliant but despairing book. The combination of factors surrounding my visit were utterly depressing, clinical, negative and entirely devoid of hope. My spirits, which had been largely on top until now, sank to a record low, and it was several days before I began to recover. Although I am sure that this was far from the hospital's intention, I *felt* little more than a slab of meat placed before sophisticated scientific instruments for the benefit of measuring disease. I was no longer a person with human emotions, fears and forebodings, struggling to maintain some positive hope.

In contrast to this the attitude of Dr Harper, my specialist in the Medical Oncology Clinic whom I saw five weeks later, was marvellous. His thoroughly positive and personal approach, seeing both Anne and me together and discussing all sorts of details of our life, helped to restore confidence. His small clinic was full of attractive posters and served by a cheerful staff.

Nevertheless I have to say that I found most of my visits as an outpatient undoubtedly depressing. Nearly always there have been long and, even worse, unexplained delays. No one knows why nothing *seems* to be happening. On one occasion I sat for an hour and a half on a tiny chair designed for a very small child (there was no alternative), only to be told at last that I was in the wrong queue for an X-ray, even though I had been expressly sent to that area.

On another occasion I was sent by my specialist to the same X-ray unit to book an appointment for another ultrasound scan. After the usual delays, I was told to go to a certain waiting area for an X-ray. I protested, insisting that I should have a scan, not an X-ray. I was overruled, however, and made to go for an X-ray. After I had waited for the rest of the afternoon, a nurse came to say that I was sitting in the wrong place since I needed a scan! These are only trivial points, but the accumulation of inefficiency, of being pushed here and there, of unexplained delays, combined with the impersonality of the whole procedure, created an entirely negative atmosphere which must surely hinder the healing process. At a later date, and with the full agreement of my own doctor, I signed myself off as an outpatient.

For some time I knew the powerful effect that positive and negative influences could have on our health. John Wimber gave me the details of a fascinating book called *Anatomy Of An Illness*, by Norman Cousins.[1] In this book the author describes his own remarkable healing from ankylosing spondylitis, which means the disintegration of the connective tissues in the spine. One specialist gave him only one chance in five hundred for full recovery, although that specialist admitted that he had personally never seen anyone recover from that condition. Cousins found it increasingly difficult moving his limbs, his jaws were almost locked and nodules appeared on his body.

[1] Published by Bantam Books, 1981.

Years before, Cousins had read Hans Selye's famous book *The Stress of Life*, where the author describes the damaging effects of negative emotions on body chemistry. 'The inevitable question arose in my mind,' commented Cousins, 'what about the positive emotions? If negative emotions produce negative chemical changes in the body, wouldn't the positive emotions produce positive chemical changes? Is it possible that love, hope, faith, laughter, confidence, and the will to live have therapeutic value? Do chemical changes occur only on the downside?'

There was no doubt concerning Cousins' determination to live, despite the medical prognosis, and together with his doctor (who was wholly supportive), he planned a radical treatment for his disease. To begin with, he obtained a lot of comedy films, such as *Candid Camera* and the old Marx Brothers classics. 'We pulled down the blinds and turned on the machine. It worked. I made the joyous discovery that ten minutes of genuine belly laughter had an anaesthetic effect and would give me at least two hours of pain-free sleep.' His blood sedimentation rate readings also dropped consistently after each episode of laughter. He removed himself out of hospital as soon as he could, and went to a hotel room instead which he found much more pleasant and costing only a third of the price (there is no National Health Service in America). With the approval of his doctor, Cousins also prescribed for himself massive doses of vitamin C. Immediately the sedimentation rate dropped significantly further. 'Seldom had I known such elation. The ascorbic acid was working. So was laughter. The combination was cutting heavily into whatever poison was attacking the connective tissue.'

Before long he was completely off drugs and sleeping well. The recovery took many months, and even now is not entirely complete. But for years Cousins has been able to lead a full life, playing tennis and golf, riding horses and playing Bach's *Toccata and Fugue in D Minor* (one of his specific ambitions). The full details of the story are intriguing.

What is particularly important, and this is a point readily

backed by most doctors, is that no medication available is as
potent as the state of mind that a patient brings to his or her
own illness. It seems now incontrovertible that chemical
changes in the body do take place as a result of mental
attitudes or moods. 'The brain produces encephalins and
endorphins, which moderate pain and help set a stage for
recovery. The brain plays a part in the production of gamma
globulin, which is vital for the body's immune system. The
brain produces interferon, which acts as a cancer-blocking
agent. The vast array of substances produced by the brain
are all connected to human development, to the fulfilment of
human potentialities, to the maintenance of health, and to
the war against disease. What is more significant about this
process is that the brain's secretions can be stimulated or
diminished by thought and behaviour and environment.'[2]
Our thoughts, attitudes and reactions to all the many facets
surrounding a serious illness are of paramount importance in
the process of recovery.

[2]*Human Options* by Norman Cousins, Berkley Books, New York, 1983.

13

Strength out of Weakness

Well-meaning visitors can be a problem for anyone who is trying slowly to recuperate. We had endless letters and telephone calls from friends and acquaintances who wanted to see me, talk to me, pray with me and in various ways encourage me. Anne and Hilary were polite but ruthless! At the most they allowed only one visitor a day for the first few weeks, and even those were screened carefully. Some people are always refreshing, but others, with the best of intentions, can be exhausting.

Our first and a very welcome guest was the television personality and cookery expert, Delia Smith, who had written one or two extremely helpful letters when I was in hospital and who had sent a superb arrangement of flowers. Both Anne and I had become very fond of Delia in the comparatively short time since we had known her. Delia invariably brings with her a delightful breath of fresh life and joy, springing from her own deepening relationship with Christ. We loved having her in our home.

'You have been an activist like Simon Peter,' said Delia to me. 'I believe that Jesus now wants you to be more like the apostle John, calling you closer to him and teaching you to listen to him. There will be a new quality in your ministry as a result.'

I listened carefully, willing for God to do whatever he liked in my life. Delia also shared a prophetic word about me given through a close personal friend of hers, Frances Hogan:

The Lord is staking his claim on you. There comes a point in the spiritual life when your apostolate is not more important than your relationship with the Lord. He becomes very jealous of your relationship with him. He has done what the shepherd sometimes does to the sheep. He is not beyond breaking the leg of the sheep in order to save its life. He then heals the leg by binding it up and puts the sheep on his shoulder until it learns a new stage of intimacy with him.

Apparently Frances had also said,

I don't feel the cancer will kill, if you make this deep surrender to the Lord. The Lord wants to bring you to complete identification with Christ's suffering as well as his glory. This is to bring you to the stage of 'I do only what my Father tells me to do, and I say only what my Father tells me to say'. To reach this stage there must be a deeper prayer life – and you must let go some of the apostolate.

As I listened to Delia, I felt that the Lord was speaking directly to me.

My response was to repent of the busyness that had all too often squeezed out any real depth of prayer. Once again I surrendered everything I could think of to the Lord: my work, my travelling, my team, my future, my family and even my life. Every day I sought to renew this surrender, telling God that I was happy with him alone and with whatever he chose to give me. I wanted to take my hands off the reins so that God could do what he wanted in my life. And I would continue to praise him. I thought again of those words from Psalm 16:

You, Lord, are all I have,
and you give me all I need;
my future is in your hands . . .

I found great peace. When we surrender everything to God, we can never lose. It is only when we try to grasp some things for ourselves that one day we shall forfeit them. I remembered those words of Jesus: 'For whoever would save his life will lose it; and whoever loses his life for my sake and the gospel's will save it' (Mark 8:35). I began to discover a new quality of life and my relationship with Jesus seemed to have more depth.

A few days later we were especially glad to welcome Bishop Morris and Anne Maddocks. Morris had been the Bishop of Selby for ten years during our time in York, and we always had the closest relationship with both of them. We loved them, respected them, and often benefited from their wise and gracious healing ministry. This time they came for the express purpose of holding a Communion Service (a 'Eucharist of the Resurrection' as Morris called it) in our home.

There are few more warm and encouraging couples than Morris and Anne. We were thrilled that they could come, and their emphasis on both word and sacrament was one that we appreciated. We covered a table in our drawing-room with a white cloth, and put two candles on it, each ringed with small flowers at their base. It was an unusual but attractive communion table.

Morris put on his bishop's purple cassock and white rochet, and we turned to the collect and readings set for the eighth Sunday before Easter, in the *Alternative Service Book*. They could not have been more appropriate if we had carefully chosen them ourselves:

> Almighty and everliving God
> whose Son Jesus Christ healed the sick
> and restored them to wholeness of life:
> look with compassion on the anguish of the world,
> and by your healing power
> make whole both men and nations . . .

The Old Testament reading was from Zephaniah 3: '. . . The Lord is in your midst; you shall fear evil no more . . . I will remove disaster from you . . .'

Then came a reading from James 5:

> Is any among you sick? Let him call for the elders of the church, and let them pray over him, anointing him with oil in the name of the Lord; and the prayer of faith will save the sick man, and the Lord will raise him up . . .

The Gospel too was about the healing of the paralysed man. In fact the whole emphasis was on God's power to heal and save. We read the passages and spent a few moments meditating on their relevance, with Morris guiding our thoughts.

Guy unfortunately was away at school, but Anne, Fiona and I, together with Morris and Anne, were deeply aware of the Lord's presence in that room. We received the tokens of God's forgiveness and love, and at the appropriate moment Morris anointed me with oil, laying hands upon me and praying for me. It was a time of deep peace and much personal blessing. In many ways it was totally different from the style of John Wimber and his two friends; and yet both forms of ministries, however different, seemed to bring the healing power of God into our lives.

Morris and Anne stayed for a quick tea, as we talked and laughed together. However they had a long journey ahead of them and were already late, so reluctantly we let them go. Our whole house seemed full of God's peace for the rest of that weekend. I knew that my life was safely in God's hands.

The next week, when I was recuperating on their farm in Sussex, Michael and Gillie Warren protected me almost totally from visitors. But I was especially glad to make two exceptions. The first was a visit from the American leaders of my team, Mark and Carol Slomka, who had just returned from their five weeks in California. I knew they had all been praying and fasting for me, and I treasured the letters that I had received from them in the midst of their hectic programme. When I saw Mark and Carol I gave each of them a long hug. It was so wonderful seeing them again. I realised how closely God had brought us together as a team, and how our relationships had deepened through my illness and enforced absence. It was marvellous hearing all the news of how everything had gone in California without me. As usual, I found out that I was quite dispensable! However, I could not wait to see the rest of the team as well.

The next day I had a lightning visit from an outstanding Christian leader in South Africa, Michael Cassidy, and his sister Olave Snelling. Michael and I have been together only for brief meetings over the years, but he once graciously introduced me at a ministers' meeting in Vancouver (where he happened to be at the time) by saying, 'I know of no other Christian leader in the world with whom I identify so completely, and with whom I share my vision so fully.' I was tremendously moved by those words, and Michael and I have always felt 'of one heart and mind' as brothers in Christ.

'We love you deeply,' said Michael, 'and thousands of black Christians and white Christians are praying for your complete healing.'

After a quick lunch, we stood together in a circle and prayed for one another. Then Michael and Olave sped away, trying to reach Heathrow in time to catch Michael's plane to Johannesburg. It was only a short visit, but immensely encouraging. Michael urged me to catch the 'thermal of the Spirit' – to see what God was doing and to go in his direction, strengthened by his power.

Monday, March 7th was my fiftieth birthday! Some of my friends who had reached that milestone before me had enjoyed all sorts of unusual and intriguing celebrations. Mine passed by almost unnoticed, except for some cards and presents mostly from my family. But then I was not up to anything else. However, the doorbell rang in the middle of the morning and there was my team singing on my doorstep and presenting me with a huge birthday card. It was the first time I had seen them all since my operation, and we had a great hour together. It had not been easy for them going to California without me and having to work with two speakers they had never met before. But undoubtedly they had grown spiritually more mature as a result. In particular they had experienced a fresh spiritual renewal with John Wimber and members of his church, which had given them a new vision of God and of the work of his Spirit.

I had promised my Trustees and surgeon that I would do no work until Easter at the earliest. Much of my day was spent in my small book-lined study, reading the Bible and praying, going through the various services in the ASB (the modern Anglican Prayer Book) and listening to numerous cassettes, mostly in the loo. Sometimes I would keep my recorder in the loo all ready! It was a relaxed time, reading, listening, walking, eating and sleeping.

When I was asked, however, by Chris Rees of the BBC if I would do a radio interview with Nick Page, I felt strongly that I ought to agree. It was only two months after my operation and I was still far from strong, tiring easily after any mental or physical exertion, but the BBC team came round to my home for the recording. Nick Page asked some excellent questions, and I answered as best I could about my personal feelings and experiences over the past two months in particular.

I always enjoy such interviews, partly because in a natural and relaxed way I can talk about Christ and about the tremendous quality of life he brings to us, not least a glorious hope for the future – a hope based solidly on his own resurrection.

'But what happens,' asked Nick Page, 'if you find that healing is not coming?'

'If I found it was not coming, I hope I have got to the position of really trusting in Christ that the best is yet to be. You know, actually to be with Christ and free for ever from the pain and suffering, tears and all the problems and injustices of this world, there is nothing more glorious than that. That is why I genuinely am at the place where I really want to be in heaven (sometimes the sooner the better), but I am willing to be on this earth, with all its struggles and battles if he wants me here.'

The interview lasted for an hour, and it stimulated me instead of exhausting me. Chris and Nick seemed pleased, but I had no idea of the interest the edited half-hour programme would cause. It was called *David Watson – A Case for Healing?* and we were deluged with correspondence in response to the broadcast. I have a PO Box, and poor Hilary or Anne would stagger back day after day with bags full of letters. Over a thousand were received within a few weeks. I wrote a general newsletter giving some basic information and expressing my appreciation for the enormous concern.and prayer I was receiving from so many different places, so that Hilary was able to answer nearly all the letters received, mostly with the newsletter. Some letters were cries for help. Hilary did what she could, but obviously we could not say very much.

The programme was so well received that it was repeated on Radio 4 five weeks later, and subsequently on the World Service of the BBC. I heard of several people driving home from work who pulled into the side of the road to listen carefully to it. One gifted young doctor, who described himself as a militant atheist, heard the programme, was deeply moved by it, and that same evening read a book I had written which one of his partners had given him a year before. Totally against his normal self-contained personality, he burst into tears and, feeling rather foolish, knelt down to ask Christ into his life. His conversion was remarkable, and a few weeks later his startled wife also thoughtfully committed her life to Christ.

The BBC had taken the precautionary measure of having the recorded cassette of the broadcast available for sale.[1] Many hundreds were sold, with probably thousands more

---

[1] Cassette available from Anchor Recordings, 72 The Street, Kennington, Ashford, Kent, TN24 9HS.

privately recorded or re-recorded! Careful not to make too many enquiries about this, I was staggered by the number of people in many parts of the world who heard the broadcast, and equally amazed by the impact it was apparently making. It was a reminder to me of the enormous interest in (or anxiety about?) death. It is our one future certainty, and there are no answers to it – apart from Christ.

I was aware of the danger of being given undue publicity because of my open fight against cancer, but I was concerned to talk freely about that 'dreaded disease'. The only way to conquer fears is to face them. Added to that, I wanted to share the wonderful hope that we have as Christians, whatever the future may hold, and to speak honestly about my experiences of God's love and power in the midst of human struggles and anxieties. We had to refuse several journalists wanting interviews, following the broadcast, but I gave my time and energy to as many as I could manage.

Michael Green, the Rector of St Aldate's Church in Oxford and for many years a close personal friend, was kind enough to suggest that the radio interview might emerge as the most powerful and influential talk I had ever given! And yet all I did was to sit in my armchair, still very weak, trying to answer the questions that Nick Page put to me. If God had used that interview to touch the lives of people in many parts of the world, it was (for me) another indication that Christ's power is most effective in our weakness.

14

Planning for a Future

'Where shall we go?' I asked.

Maps and brochures were spread before us, with Anne, Fiona and Guy breaking in with various suggestions.

'How about Polzeath in Cornwall? Or the Lake District?'

'If we want the sun at Easter, why not Florida?' said Guy hopefully.

We had been given by a number of friends generous sums of money for recuperation, and for once in our lifetime we agreed that we would go as a family to a hotel. Always before we had borrowed cottages from our friends. In fact, Anne and I had never stayed in a hotel since our honeymoon nineteen years before (when I was seriously ill with asthma), so that our children had never known such a luxury. It had been far too expensive and out of the question.

This time would be a special occasion. Anne had been far from well over the weeks, and even by Easter she was still suffering from a spastic colon and palpitations in her heart; so I was anxious that she should not have to shop, cook and clean. Fiona and Guy had also suffered from the tensions of the past months. So we were going to spoil ourselves – for a whole week!

After poring over books, hotel guides and maps, we eventually settled on a hotel we had never heard of, in Devon, and found to our delight that they had room for us for the week we had chosen.

Highbullen Hotel, Chittlehamholt in North Devon, was as delightful as its name suggests. Set in a beautiful estate, complete with its own herd of deer, it had about it the atmosphere of a peaceful country club. Anxious to have a quiet week, we had deliberately chosen a hotel where children under thirteen were not allowed, and we were free to enjoy the privacy of our own family life or mingle with a few guests, whichever we preferred. The food was outstanding and the rooms were comfortable. Most important of all, especially for Guy, there were wonderful facilities available. Every morning before breakfast Guy went for a swim in the indoor swimming pool (even I went in once or twice!). Then after breakfast it was a constant round of activities. Each day Guy and I played tennis, squash, golf and snooker (all on the premises) – Anne and Fiona joining in as they wished. I don't think I can remember a holiday when I had been so energetic, and this was only three months after my major operation! Most important of all, it was *quality* time for us together as a family. We knew that we might never have such a holiday again, at least because of the expense, but we enjoyed every minute of it and felt incredibly refreshed by it.

The Devon countryside was magnificent in spring, with myriads of primroses bursting forth everywhere, especially in the banks of the narrow country lanes. It was the time of year when life was rising out of death, fresh beauty peeping round every corner with unexpected glory. Newborn lambs were skipping with joy, and the whole atmosphere breathed hope. It was good to be alive.

Guy and I also had a good long talk about my illness as we walked together one afternoon. 'Gosh!' he said, 'I had no idea that it was so serious. I'm glad you didn't tell me too much when I was away at school last term.' In fact I was amazed by the calm way in which he took it all, asking intelligent questions about the operation, about what a colostomy would have meant, and about the future. He was simply marvellous: free, frank, honest, uninhibited – just Guy. I was proud to be his father.

Naturally I talked to Fiona too from time to time. And in spite of the constant tensions surrounding her at home (with inevitable visits to the hospital, results from scans, etc), she was normally her steady unruffled self and often full of fun. I found her constantly supportive and remarkably caring when she could see I was tired.

We returned home just in time for the children to start their new term at school; and then Anne and I flew out to California to spend ten days with John and Carol Wimber, attending their church services on two Sundays. It was Anne's first visit there, and a few weeks previously she was not at all sure that she wanted to go. Anne always finds it difficult meeting lots of new people (perhaps especially so if I know them already), and she was also anxious about my state of health and about her own pains and palpitations. However we went.

The flight was not too difficult for me at all, although we were glad to arrive at Los Angeles, at about three a.m. by British time. John and Carol were away for a couple of days, but we had a marvellous welcome from Bob and Penny Fulton, whom I had come to love dearly over the last four years. Bob is the assistant-pastor with John Wimber. Thoughtfully and generously they took us to a comfortable motel for two nights, to help us recover from the flight before moving to John and Carol's home. I saw Anne relax as soon as Bob and Penny met us. I knew she would, because I had so often experienced their open, loving and accepting friendship where there is no need to say the right words or do the right things before you are welcomed. I knew that they, and others in their church, loved people unconditionally – and it is a love which quickly drives away all fears and melts down all barriers.

At our first service in that church on Sunday morning I noticed Anne shaking a little before the service had even started. Was she nervous or cold?

'I just *knew* that God was with us,' she explained afterwards. 'I somehow felt the power of God in my body and I couldn't help shaking!'

I never seem to feel anything on these occasions, but I

loved being there: the warmth and love of the congregation, the reality and intimacy of sustained worship, the sense of quiet expectation throughout, and excellent biblical teaching. God was undoubtedly present, whether anyone shook or not!

Before the evening service started, I asked John Wimber if I might say a few words to thank everyone for praying for me.

'Sure,' he replied. 'They'd like that.'

So at an appropriate spot in the service John announced that Anne and I were present and that I wanted to say a few words.

I was totally unprepared for what followed. As soon as I stood up, everyone (over 3,000 of them) clapped and clapped and clapped. They even stood and went on clapping and clapping. It was like a standing ovation. I would have been terribly embarrassed, except for two things. In the first place I knew that this was a spontaneous expression of their love, and I was not embarrassed by their love – just deeply moved by it. I also knew that this was a 'clap-offering' to the Lord – a way of saying 'thank you' to God for visibly answering their prayers for my healing. It suddenly struck me how much they must have prayed and fasted for me, since they exploded with such applause when I stood up. It was an unforgettable experience.

'Those guys really love you,' said John afterwards.

'I don't know why, but I guess they do,' I replied, still not quite able to take it all in.

During that weekend we kept on meeting people who had been healed from all sorts of complaints and diseases, from backaches to cancer. No wonder nearly a hundred streamed through after the evening service for prayer and counselling. Some asked for healing, some wanted to find Christ, some longed to be filled with the Spirit. But in quiet, relaxed and unemotional ways many from the congregation (some quite young) were praying with those who were needing help. God was manifestly at work amongst them all.

Much of our time with John and Carol that week was spent

in laughter! I don't think Anne and I have laughed so much for years, and it was a refreshing change from the unhealthy intensity of some Christian groups we know. Of course that church also knew when to be serious, when to pray, when to praise, and when to be still before God. They were anything but superficial and flippant. But they had discovered some of the abundant quality of life that Jesus comes to bring, and had learnt how to enjoy all that was good.

We also had some excellent discussions and times of prayer together. John called in some of the 'kids' to pray for us – young people mostly between the ages of eighteen and twenty-three – and we were impressed by the quality of their relationships with God and with one another. They were spiritually alive, sensitive to the Holy Spirit, and full of faith. Admittedly they were not yet fully mature in Christ. Most of them had been Christians for only two or three years. But their loving and prayerful ministry towards us was astonishing.

We had one more marvellous Sunday with them all, and then we flew home. There is nothing in the world like being consciously in God's presence, surrounded by the love of his people. It is literally a foretaste of heaven. I have known many happy experiences during my lifetime, but nothing can be compared to the caring love, wholesome joy and prevailing peace that only God can bring. 'Your presence fills me with joy and brings me pleasure for ever' (Psalm 16:11, *Good News Bible*).

As we approached London Anne's pains and palpitations, which had vanished in California, suddenly returned. Also within a few days I had another scan on my liver which revealed that the cancer was still increasing. As I spoke to John Wimber on the phone, I knew he was stunned by the news.

'We really believe that God *is* healing you,' said John. 'With cancer, it sometimes gets worse before it begins to die. We'll go on praying, and if necessary we'll come straight over and pray with you some more.'

'Thanks John. I'll keep in touch.' At least I was feeling fit and ready for work again.

At this stage I was thinking and praying constantly about my future work, especially since it affected my team of eight who were now not as busy as they would have been if I had not been off work. Under the leadership of Bob Roxburgh they were marvellously fulfilling the engagements I had accepted months previously, but what was God saying to us about our long-term future?

I found it confusing. In some ways I find guidance, if anything, gets harder rather than easier the longer I am a Christian. Perhaps God allows this so that we have to go on relying on him and not on ourselves.

To begin with, I thought that we should try to buy a redundant theatre in the centre of London, to try to communicate the Christian Gospel in ways that many have found meaningful, even when they had been disillusioned by the Church. Certainly I could use the creative gifts of the team to full advantage in such a setting. It became obvious, however, that a venture of this nature would prove enormously expensive, and it was too early to expect people to give money for a work that hinged largely upon a man who was supposedly dying of cancer!

Next I considered taking over one or two of the churches in central London that were all but redundant. The Bishop of London was enthusiastic about my proposals, but as Anne and I went round many possible churches our hearts sank. The buildings were all unsuitable: too small, too badly in need of repair or too depressing for our purposes. We were offered one church with considerable potential, but I said to the Bishop, 'If I were forty and fit I would jump at it, but now that I'm fifty and frail I honestly think it is too much.' He agreed.

My team had to be very patient. Now that I was meeting regularly with them, I was coming up with a new suggestion about our future almost every week – only to find it frustrated a little later. If cancer was one problem I battled with, confusion was certainly another. Yet, if it seemed right for me to spend more time in London and less time travelling, I wanted to get my teeth into something that was both challenging and demanding. My Trustees also had to be patient, since at every meeting they had to consider a new proposal from me. Although I kept praying about the future, I still could not see clearly the way ahead. I felt like a tourist in London, standing in the middle of Hyde Park Corner in thick fog. Several voices were calling me in different directions, but I still could not hear the Lord.

Added to that, the Trustees had a responsibility towards the various committees that had invited me (or were thinking of doing so) for certain events in the future. What plans could we realistically make when medically-speaking the prognosis was so poor? How far would committees be willing to plan a festival in eighteen months' time, involving a fair amount of time and money, when there was no guarantee that I would be there to lead it? The Trustees felt it right to send out a letter in June explaining the position as honestly and as accurately as possible:

We invite the persistent prayers of the Church at large for complete healing. David's present vigour and his increasing appetite for work are consistent with the view that healing is taking place and that his specialist's prescription for an active and long-term ministry is right.

We believe that an inevitable change in policy must be accepted after this illness. The gruelling international programme which involved so much travelling must be curtailed to some extent and a more settled ministry in London should be developed. The trustees were coming to this opinion before the illness, which has dramatically confirmed it. David is perhaps one of the most gifted communicators of the Christian faith and widely accepted across all boundaries in this land as well as elsewhere. We are making plans for his gifts to be used in London on a regular basis, with a special emphasis on training Chris-

tians to develop their own gifts of ministry for the benefit of
others. Details of what precisely this will mean are not yet
available, but the general concept reveals our faith in
God's purposes for David in the future.

The travelling ministry of inter-church festivals and
missions, and also training programmes in seminaries and
for ministers, will continue. It is plain, however, that those
responsible for initiating these events at the local level must
be able to share in our faith and join in our prayers for
healing to continue. We do not expect for some time to be
able to offer further medical evidence which would lift the
responsibility off local committees to make their decisions
in the light of the present facts, and therefore we are
content to accept only such invitations for David as are
made with the present medical condition fully understood.
We are convinced that our own 'risk' of faith is both
reasonable and responsible, but we must ask those who
invite David to accept their responsibility to decide in
faith. It is important that they should be at peace about
their decision.

It was a clear letter, but I was not altogether surprised when
one Christian leader, responsible for a major event overseas
involving the whole team, telephoned me to ask if I would be
well in a year's time! How was I to reply to that? James wrote
in his New Testament letter: 'How do you know what is going
to happen tomorrow? For the length of your lives is as
uncertain as the morning fog – now you see it; soon it is gone.
What you ought to say is, "If the Lord wants us to, we shall
live and do this or that" ' (4:13–16, *Living Bible*). In all our
plans about the future we are entirely dependent upon the
Lord who both gives life, and takes it away.

Never before had I been so uncertain about life and work.
At times I was so confused about the future that I wondered if
there could be any future at all for me on this earth. It was a
tense and anxious stage in my life. I was tempted to question
repeatedly the decision to leave York. In some ways every-

thing would have been much easier had we stayed there.

During this period of convalescence I had time to reflect on a number of basic priorities. Both Anne and I had been exhausted after seventeen exciting but demanding years in York, and spiritually, mentally, emotionally and physically we were nearly 'burnt out'. The Archbishop of York had advised us to have a sabbatical leave a few years previously, but with our children at school it seemed impossible. Unexpectedly we were now having our sabbatical rest, not in the way we imagined, but we were more refreshed and more together as a family than we had been for a long time.

15

A Fifth Dimension

'This is a day of decision,' said Dr Harper, my specialist, when I saw him in May. 'I'm afraid that the scan shows a considerable increase of the cancer in the liver.'

I was a little stunned since I hadn't expected that. I was now feeling remarkably well, physically more active than I had been for some time, and it would not have surprised me if the cancer had already disappeared. I said nothing.

'I think we must put you on to some chemotherapy,' said Dr Harper.

'I'm sorry,' I replied, 'but I definitely don't want that.'

'Are you sure?'

'Quite sure.'

'You've thought out your decision carefully?'

'Yes,' I replied, though I was glad that he did not press me for my reasons there and then. The consultation ended rather abruptly, and Anne and I returned home considerably subdued.

Several people had reminded us of the incident in the Gospels about the fig-tree as a parable of what might be happening. The tree did not die when Jesus cursed it; it withered only later. Perhaps this was what the tumour in my liver was doing, suggested Anne.

Perhaps. With a terminal illness I felt as though I were walking on a tight-rope of faith. It required only the smallest knock to make me feel very insecure. Perhaps no healing was happening after all. Perhaps the disease was taking its usual course. I was undoubtedly depressed, and I feared the worst.

During the next week or two my decision to refuse chemotherapy was tested several times, although Anne shared my decision completely. Several doctors, including some close friends, gently urged me to think again. At the same time I was making my own enquiries. When I asked a few doctors and specialists to be totally honest with me, nearly all admitted that chemotherapy did not heal cancer in the liver. At best the patient's life might be extended a little, but the quality of life could suffer considerably through the effects of the treatment. As time went on, a growing number of the medical profession told me that they felt I had made the right decision.

Added to the dubious results of chemotherapy on cancer of the liver (I understand it can be much more successful with other types of cancer), I was determined to avoid as much negative influence as I possibly could, and I did not want to spend my remaining days (however many or few) waiting in the Outpatients Department of Guy's Hospital.

Moreover, as I listened to numerous teaching cassettes on healing – mostly by John Wimber – and as I studied my New Testament more thoroughly, I became fascinated by the 'fifth dimension' that Christ introduced when he both proclaimed and demonstrated the Kingdom of God.

We live today in a hostile and fractured world. Everywhere we find a profound sense of alienation. We are alienated from God, hence the spiritual confusion and unreality that many experience. We are alienated from one another, hence broken marriages, violence on the streets and hostility between nations. We are alienated from the environment, hence the ravages of hunger, poverty, disease and pollution. We are also alienated from ourselves, hence the mental and psychological afflictions which cause distress in our lives.

It was into such an alienation that Jesus came nearly 2,000 years ago. He saw people as 'harassed and helpless' – a poignantly accurate description of our society today. What is the answer to the tangle of human suffering that ensnares us all, one way or another? It is not education, since tragically the staggering technological progress made in the last few decades now threatens to destroy us all. Nor is it politics. New policies may change the structures of a nation, but until the heart of man is renewed nothing will be significantly different.

Jesus came as the Great Restorer, the Healer of broken lives and relationships. He began his brief but astonishing ministry by saying, 'The time is fulfilled, and the kingdom of God is at hand; repent and believe in the Gospel' (Mark 1:15). Frequently he taught about the kingdom: there are one hundred references to the kingdom in the first three Gospels alone. He gave instructions about entering the kingdom, he urged his disciples to pray for the coming of the kingdom, he illustrated the kingdom in parables and spoke about the future blessings of the kingdom. He also demonstrated the power of the kingdom.

What, then, is the kingdom? In the Bible it means specifically the *authority and rule of a king*. So the kingdom of God means the rule or reign of God. When Jesus came preaching the kingdom he was introducing God's New Society: a new age had come. There was now release for those who were captive to the old order of sin, suffering and death. It was not that those enemies of man were now banished. But those who sinned could be forgiven, those who were sick could be healed, and those who died in Christ would be more alive than ever.

One of the most helpful definitions of the kingdom is that given by Hans Küng: 'God's kingdom is creation healed.' Saviour means healer. Salvation is much wider than the forgiveness of sins (all-important as that is); it means *wholeness*, with God's authority and rule affecting every area of our lives. Christ has come to bring peace on earth and so end the alienation which sooner or later destroys us all.

For many years I had been convinced that, through Christ and through his death on the cross, our relationships with God and with one another could be healed. What fascinated me afresh was the space given in the Gospel records to the healing ministry of Christ – a ministry which continued by the power of the Holy Spirit through the disciples in the early Church.

It was clear that Jesus healed *all* who came to him. He never turned anyone away. A leper once came to him and said, 'Lord, if you will, you can make me clean.' At once Jesus stretched out his hand to touch him and said, 'I will; be clean' (Matthew 8:1–3). It is unthinkable that Jesus could have replied, 'Sorry, but this leprosy is for the good of your soul!'

At the same time I noticed that there was a mystery about the healings of Jesus. In the Pool of Bethesda there was 'a multitude' of sick people. Jesus stepped across them and healed only one. Why? I don't know. When the Centurion's servant was sick, Jesus healed him from a distance; he did not have to be there. Why could he not do this with all the sick in Palestine at that time? I don't know.

The difficulty may be all part of the 'now' and 'not yet' of the Kingdom of God. The Kingdom has now come, since Christ has come to be our Saviour and King; but it will not yet be consummated until Christ comes again with power and glory. Even where healings are experienced widely not all sick people are healed. Christ taught us to pray 'Your Kingdom come', and we are still to wait with patience for what we see only in part at present.

Because of the 'not yet' of the Kingdom, I could not accept the more extreme view contained in quite a few letters: 'Once you have claimed God's healing, you've got it!' I knew this was based on the general promise of Jesus: 'Whatever you ask in prayer, believe that you have received it, and it will be yours' (Mark 11:24). But some texts read, '. . . believe that you *are receiving it* . . .' This I could accept. Over the months I have often said publicly, 'I believe that God is in the process of healing me. Every day I thank him that he is healing me. But, logically speaking, it is possible that I am wrong.' God only knows.

I saw too that Jesus healed out of compassion. This was the motivation that prompted Jesus to spend himself for the

poor, the sick and the needy. There is great healing power in
love, especially the love of God. What helped me more than
anything was the expression of that love through numerous
Christians who obviously cared for me, prayed for me,
encouraged me, thus surrounding me with the love of God.

Jesus also healed when there was a prevailing atmosphere
of faith. Four men once brought a paralysed friend to Jesus,
and they were so determined that they broke up the roof of a
house and lowered their friend to the feet of Jesus since there
was no other possible way of getting through the crowds.
That took some initiative. When Jesus saw *their* faith, he
forgave the sick man his sins and healed him of his paralysis.
Clearly this unusual demonstration of faith helped towards
the miracle of healing.

On the other hand, even Jesus was hindered by unbelief.
At his own home town, Nazareth, he could do 'no mighty
work . . . because of their unbelief'. He could heal only a few
sick people (Mark 6:5f). I have found that my own faith in
God's healing is inevitably vulnerable, and influenced to
some extent by the faith or unbelief of those around me.
Constantly I need to encourage my faith by worshipping God
and by reading his word; but on top of that, the supportive-
believing prayer of others, especially my team, has been a
vital factor in the 'fight of faith' over these past months.

Jesus also healed more effectively when the Spirit of God
was moving in power. 'The power of the Lord was with him
to heal' (Luke 5:17). I am not quite sure what this means,
since Jesus was constantly full of the Spirit of God. But I
thought of that first day when John Wimber and the two
others came to see me. They had not expected to spend time
praying with me then, but they became aware of 'the power
of the Lord' coming upon them. I have also known times
when healings *flow*, one after another, without any apparent
effort in terms of prayer, counselling or whatever – simply
because the power of God is unusually present.

Jesus sometimes had to pray more than once. After he
prayed for a blind man, he asked, 'Do you see anything?' The

man replied, 'I see men; but they look like trees, walking.' So Jesus laid hands on his eyes again, and this time sight was fully restored (Mark 8:22–26). Many in the healing ministry today advocate what they call 'soaking prayer'. Ever since the initial ministry from John Wimber and others I have welcomed every opportunity of being prayed for, often with hands laid upon me. Almost every night Anne lays her hands on my liver, curses the cancer in the name of Jesus, and prays for healing. The team has likewise prayed for me frequently, often in very moving ways. I have no doubt about the cumulative effect of this 'soaking prayer'.

Jesus also imparted this healing ministry to others. It was not only to the apostles, although we need to remember that at that time even they were totally inexperienced and often full of unbelief. Jesus also sent out seventy disciples, telling them to heal the sick and to proclaim the Kingdom of God. And those seventy came back thrilled with what they had witnessed: 'Lord, even the demons are subject to us in your name!' (Luke 10:1–20). Moreover it seems from the Great Commission that Christ wanted this ministry to extend to all his disciples: they were to do *all* that he had commanded them, and from his own example this surely would have included healing. Certainly this is how the New Testament Church understood it, and 'many wonders and signs' took place.

In this century there is little doubt that there has been a huge resurgence of spiritual gifts, including healing, in spite of the lack of them for many generations. For too long we have over-intellectualised the Christian faith, reducing much of it to the level of words and propositions. 'Knowing God' has become little more than statements about God – and even here the Church has been cautious and confused.

Others in the Church have been less confused. They fully accept the element of the miraculous in the New Testament, but believe that such expectations for today are foolish in view of the scientific progress that has developed over the years. They rightly reject an unthinking Christianity, and are weary of a simplistic view of healing, which can cause at best disappointed hopes and at worst a total abandonment of faith. Many are struggling honestly with the valid application of biblical teaching to the culture of today, desiring to maintain an intellectual integrity throughout.

So much is valid, providing that once again we do not reduce God to the level of our own understanding. God's thoughts are not our thoughts, and his ways are not our ways. He is infinitely greater than all that we can conceive by human logic or scientific research. We need the Spirit of God to lift our faith until we believe in God who through Jesus forgave sin, cared for the oppressed, healed the sick and cast out demons. *That* is the God in whom we are to believe, and only as we trust him for his power to work today, even when our minds cannot comprehend it, will we see God's kingdom come.

If we really want to see the Kingdom of God amongst us, we must let it begin in our own hearts. We need to bow our wills to Christ's authority and bend our minds to his word. He calls us to love God with all our heart, mind, soul and strength, and to love our neighbours as ourselves. The rule of the kingdom is love, and love learns to trust whether it understands or not. Children do this all the time. They have no difficulty in trusting when their minds are not yet able to comprehend. Although we should become mature in our thinking as Christians, we need a child-like simplicity in our faith in God. It is through this faith, said Jesus, that we enter and enjoy the Kingdom.

16

Is Suffering Punishment?

'How could this happen to you?' Many people have asked me this question. The implication is that there seems to be something unfair about the fact of my cancer. Not only am I a Christian and a clergyman, but I have spent most of my life trying to help people find the love of God – and look at the way I have been rewarded for all my work! To be honest I have never thought in terms of unfairness at all, but others on my behalf have been puzzled, some depressed, and a few even angry.

This raises the greatest and most common objection to belief in God: *the problem of suffering*. I am well aware that in countless other cases the apparent injustices are far more horrific than in my own. Why are tens of thousands of babies born deformed every year? How could God allow millions of innocent and helpless people to die of starvation? For what divine purpose are young parents struck down by fatal diseases, children killed in road accidents, good people swept away by flood or destroyed by fire? How can senseless tragedies cut young people down in their prime of life?

It is worth noting that suffering becomes a problem only when we accept the existence of a good God. The common exclamation 'Good God' is often used when faced suddenly with bad news that is hard to understand. If there is no God, or if God is not good, there is no problem. The universe is nothing more than random choices and meaningless events. There is no fairness, no vindication of right over wrong, no ultimate purposes, no absolute values. 'Man now realises

that he is an accident,' said the modern painter Francis
Bacon. 'He is a completely futile being (and) has to play out
the game without reason.' If there is no 'good God', that is
the logical consequence, and to protest about suffering is as
foolish as to protest about a number thrown by a dice.

> Life has no reason,
> A struggling through the gloom;
> And the senseless end of it
> Is the insult of the tomb.

If we accept, however, the Judaeo-Christian belief that
God is a just God who is all-powerful, all-wise and all-good,
we are immediately faced with enormous questions about the
vast catalogue of human suffering. Why does God allow it?
How could there be any conceivable purpose to it? Even if we
could find theoretical answers, these seem to vanish quickly
when faced with personal pain, tears and anguish. 'Man is
absurd,' wrote Jean-Paul Sartre, 'but he must grimly act as if
he were not.' Life becomes little more than gritting one's
teeth in the midst of purposeless pain.

Often in the Bible the question of suffering is raised, but
nowhere is it so thoroughly developed as in the Book of Job,
which Tennyson called 'the greatest poem of ancient or
modern times'. We are told at the start of this story that Job is
a good and upright man, yet in spite of that he is overwhelmed with appalling tragedies. At first all his animals
and servants are either stolen or destroyed. Then his seven
sons and three daughters are killed by a devastating tornado.
Finally Job himself is smitten with 'loathsome sores from the
sole of his foot to the crown of his head'. His appearance
becomes so gruesome that his friends scarcely recognise him,
and in every way he is tormented with grief and pain.

Understandably Job goes through a wide range of human
responses. He loathes himself, is angry with God and finally
lapses into self-pity: 'Have pity on me, have pity on me, O
you my friends, for the hand of God has touched me!' (19:21).

The burning question posed by the whole book is Why? Why has it happened, if God is still God? Why should a righteous man suffer? Why is there such injustice in the world? *Why?* The rest of the story of Job looks at possible answers to this baffling question. We shall look at some of the less satisfactory explanations in this chapter and the next, and then see if there is anything more helpful to say in the following two. Throughout I shall refer back to my own situation as a reminder that we are considering real people with serious problems, and not merely a philosophical inquiry. These are some of the questions that I have considered carefully, especially over the last few months.

The story unfolds with Job's three comforters who point the finger, not at Job's misfortunes, but at Job himself. Their understanding of the situation is simple but severe: suffering is always due to personal sin. For Job to suffer so acutely, he must surely be guilty of serious sin. Eliphaz the Temanite asks, 'Think now, who that was innocent ever perished? Or where were the upright cut off?' Bildad the Shuhite goes even further by declaring that the calamity falling on Job's family is clear proof of their transgressions, since all godless people will perish. Zophar the Naamathite then puts the final nail in Job's coffin by saying, 'Know then that God exacts of you less than your guilt deserves' (11:6). We see here the origin of the expression 'Job's comforter' which has come to describe someone who only aggravates the distress of the person he is supposed to comfort.

The direct equation of suffering and sin is clearly inadequate and in most cases disastrous. It is seldom as simple as that. In a few cases it may be true of course. Sexual promiscuity may result in venereal disease; over-work may lead to heart attacks; lack of forgiveness, it is thought, may cause or intensify arthritis. Sometimes we have only ourselves to blame for the painful consequences of our sinful actions. Although in the Gospels the implication is rare, on one or two occasions Jesus suggests that sin could have been the basic problem behind a sick person's condition. When a paralysed man was brought before him, the first words that Jesus said to him were, 'My son, your sins are forgiven' (Mark 2:5). Since this man's forgiveness was linked with his healing it is at least possible that his sin was connected with his disease. At another time Jesus healed a man who had been sick for thirty-eight years, and then he said, 'See, you are well! Sin no more, *that nothing worse befall you*' (John 5:14). Here was a serious warning of the solemn consequences of deliberate sin.

In this liberal age we tend naturally to avoid any thought of God's judgment. Yet if we look carefully at the Gospel records we see strong warnings given frequently by Jesus. It is significant that the one person who has shown us more than anyone of the love of God has also told us more than anyone (in the Bible) of the judgment of God. Love risks being rejected. Love will never force. If we don't want God, we won't have God; if we want to be on our own, on our own we shall be, with all its tragic outcome. In Romans 1, Paul talks about those who suppress the truth of God that can be known and who turn their backs on him. Three times Paul writes, 'God gave them up.' If they are determined to live a sinful life, with all its disastrous consequences, God with infinite sadness lets them get on with it. He lets them go or gives them up. It is therefore possible to experience something of God's holy displeasure here and now, if only as a loving warning of the final awesome judgment to come. 'It is a fearful thing to fall into the hands of the living God' (Hebrews 10:31).

Having said all this, in the vast majority of cases it would be quite wrong to link personal suffering with personal sin. When meeting a man born blind, the disciples asked Jesus if this man or his parents had sinned. Jesus replied that neither had been responsible for his blindness: 'He is blind so that God's power might be seen at work in him' (John 9:3, *Good News Bible*). The man was promptly healed.

The danger about coupling suffering with sin is that the sick person may often feel guilty anyway. Many times I have talked with those who are seriously ill, and I have found them anxiously wondering what they had done to bring about their condition. They blame themselves; or if they cannot live with that, they project their guilt on to others or God. It's someone's fault! The trouble is that either feelings of guilt, which are often imaginary, or direct accusations, which are often unfair, only encourage the sickness. Both hinder healing.

Yet I know how easy this is. Sometimes I have thought of my asthma or cancer as being punishment for sin. I remember with shame many foolish things I have done in the past, and with a fairly sensitive conscience it is not hard to feel both guilty and condemned. The positive side is that every affliction has caused me to search deeply within my heart and to repent of every sinful action or attitude that I could discover. I have known many people who have been dramatically healed following such repentance together with the experience of God's forgiveness. It is no bad thing, therefore, to consider carefully our life in the sight of God in order to know the joy and freedom of his love.

At the same time, the negative side of all this comes when such heart-searching leads to nagging and unhealthy feelings of guilt, and perhaps to a very poor image of God. Is it conceivable, when we see Jesus healing the sick and forgiving the sinful, that God should say, 'Ah, there's David Watson. He slipped up rather badly last month so I'll afflict him with asthma for the next twenty years.' Or later, 'He's upset me again, so this time I'll destroy him with cancer.' Such thoughts are not only ridiculous; they are almost blasphemous, and utterly alien to a God of infinite love and mercy as we see him so clearly in Jesus. However, ever since I have had cancer I have often needed the confirmation of God's personal love towards me. In this, the attitude and actions of others have been more important than their words. I am thoroughly aware of my failings and only too willing to believe that my sickness is what I deserve – indeed much less than I deserve. As far as straight justice is concerned that is true. But when I reflect on God's love and mercy in the scriptures I am comforted, especially when that love is *shown* by other Christians around me.

Once when I was deeply depressed, possibly due to a sense of personal failure, a friend wrote to share what he thought God was saying to me, although he knew nothing about my depression at the time.

My child, I want you to know and feel that I know and love you. I love you because I first knew you. I know you at depths that are even hidden from you. My Spirit searches every corner of your being. I love you, not because I don't know and understand you, but because I do know and understand you. I want you to know and feel that I love you as you are, not because of what you have already achieved for me in my power, not because of what you hope to achieve, but because of who you are, my child. Enjoy who you are, my child; my child who has nothing to prove but the depths of your Father's everlasting and unchanging love.

I took that as a prophetic word, a word from God, and it completely unlocked my depression. I had been blaming myself about some quite trivial matter (I was exhausted at the time), and although I was constantly telling others how much God loved them, I needed to hear and know that for myself.

We assume there must be some cause and effect in suffering, and the sensitive person will quickly suppose that he is to blame for any sickness or tragedy that may come. More than ever, then, others need to reassure that person repeatedly that God loves him just as he is. In the last few months I have received some highly insensitive letters from people I have never met, urging me to repent if I want to be healed. Different sins are specified. Apparently I need to repent for my double-mindedness, for my pride, for my unbelief, and even for being a member of the Anglican Church! No Christian is perfect, of course, and no doubt there is much in my life that still needs purifying. But at a time when my conscience is *over*-sensitive through my illness, more than anything I need to be reminded of God's love. 'Job's comforters', for me, have proved little more than the accusations of Satan. What Job needed (and so did I) was not theology but sympathy, not condemnation but affirmation, not cold moralising but warm compassion. Painful wounds call for love, understanding and healing.

17

Is Suffering a Test?

'What have I done to deserve this?' No question is more persistent in time of sickness or pain.

Job's comforters eventually retire from the scene (after thirty-one chapters linking suffering with sin!), their accusations having been vigorously refuted by Job. Then comes a much younger man, Elihu, who is diffident about speaking, but is angry with the condemnation of the other three and disappointed with the self-righteousness of Job. He offers a second explanation to suffering.

God is not a judge and executioner, but a teacher. There is a disciplinary and chastening process behind Job's affliction.

> . . . He opens the ears of men,
>   and terrifies them with warnings,
> that he may turn man aside from his deed,
>   and cut off pride from man . . .
> Man is also chastened with pain upon his bed . . .
> Then man prays to God, and he accepts him . . .
>
> (33:16–19, 26)

Repeatedly Elihu expounds the same theme:

> If they are bound in fetters
>   and caught in the cords of affliction,
> then he declares to them their work
>   and their transgressions, that they are
>   behaving arrogantly.

He opens their ears to instruction,
 and commands that they return from iniquity.
If they hearken and serve him,
 they complete their days in prosperity,
 and their years in pleasantness.
But if they do not hearken, they perish by the sword,
 and die without knowledge.

(36:8–12)

Constantly God is trying to train and fashion us into his will, and the process may be painful at times. We must humbly accept that he knows what he is doing, and later we will see the value of it.

There is much in the rest of scripture, including the New Testament, to show that Elihu was certainly nearer the mark than the other comforters. In the parable of the vineyard, Jesus said that the gardener *prunes* the fruit-bearing branch 'that it may bear more fruit' (John 15:2). All pruning hurts. 'The Lord disciplines him whom he loves, and chastises every son whom he receives' (Hebrews 12:6). Our faith, said the apostle Peter, may be tested by fire so that one day it may redound to the glory of God (1 Peter 1:7). Paul also referred to a godly grief producing repentance that leads to salvation, and he showed the Corinthian Christians how their suffering led to renewed earnestness and zeal, love and justice (2 Corinthians 7).

There is no doubt that millions of Christians all down the centuries have become more Christ-like through suffering. I know of many who have an almost ethereal beauty about them, refined through pain. In fact those who have experienced more of the love of God than anyone I have ever met have also endured more suffering. When you crush lavender, you find its full fragrance; when you squeeze an orange, you extract its sweet juice. In the same way it is often through pains and hurts that we develop the fragrance and sweetness of Jesus in our lives. An agnostic Professor of Philosophy at Princeton University became a Christian when he studied carefully the lives of some of the great saints of God throughout the history of the Church. What struck him especially was their radiance in the midst of pain. Often they suffered intensely, far more than most other people, yet through all their agony their spirits shone with a glorious lustre that defied extinction. This philosopher became convinced that some power was at work within them, and this discovery eventually brought him to Christ.

In the words of Rabbi Joseph B. Soloveitchik, 'Suffering comes to ennoble man, to purge his thoughts of pride and superficiality, to expand his horizons. In sum, the purpose of suffering is to repair that which is faulty in a man's personality.'[1] Much of that is true, and the examples of courage, faith, patience and compassion that have grown out of suffering are legion. A man who spent over twenty years in Communist prisons in Czechoslovakia where they broke his bones but not his spirit, later referred to those years as the richest of his life. His character was marked by serenity and joy. It is sometimes said that the most distant object we can see in the bright light of day is the sun; but in the dark of night we can see stars which are millions of times further away. Christians down the ages have discovered the 'treasures of darkness' and have gained a richness of maturity and spirituality that would have been impossible when the sun was shining.

It is worth noting, however, that the suffering mentioned in the New Testament that can produce great qualities of spirituality is nearly always that of adversity and persecution. Although the precise interpretation of some passages is debatable, such as Paul's thorn in the flesh, there is little or no reference to sickness as being part of God's chastening process. Too easily we apply the expression of 'taking up our cross' to sickness when originally Jesus meant something

---

[1]Quoted in *When Bad Things Happen to Good People*, Harold S. Kushner, Pan, page 28. (An intriguing book, born out of personal suffering and much counselling, but to my mind extremely unsatisfactory and at times far from the teaching of scripture.)

entirely different. Disease cannot be taken as 'sharing Christ's sufferings'. However, those of us who often visit the sick have surely come away on many occasions with our own faith stimulated by the reality of Christ's love and peace in those who suffer.

Young though he was, Elihu was wise in his comments to Job, but suffering cannot always be explained in its educational and disciplinary effect. What can we say to the mother of a child who has just been killed on the roads? If it was a lesson to be more careful on the roads, the instruction came too late for the child, and it was hardly comforting for the mother. It might have crippled her with guilt. The lesson was altogether too expensive. Rabbi Harold S. Kushner makes a fair point when he says, 'I am offended by those who suggest that God creates retarded children so that those around them will learn compassion and gratitude. Why should God distort someone else's life to such a degree in order to enhance my spiritual sensitivity?' Elihu's theory of discipline is right in some cases, but it becomes bizarre in others. Could the God who revealed himself so perfectly in Jesus conceivably invent such a callous system of moral education? And if the Lord genuinely loves those whom he chastens, could he inflict such appalling suffering on innocent children for the purpose of loving correction?

A refinement of Elihu's teaching is that God allows suffering for a test. The classic illustration of this is in the story of Abraham and Isaac (Genesis 22). Abraham was told by God to sacrifice his only son Isaac, and he obeyed right up to the point of raising his knife to plunge it into the body of his son. Isaac's life was spared by God at the last moment, but this was the ultimate test of Abraham's faith, and therefore God was able to trust him with much blessing. It is significant that those whom God has unusually blessed down the ages have also endured unusual pain, often some form of persecution but other afflictions as well. The twentieth century prophet, A. W. Tozer, once wrote: 'It is doubtful if God can bless a man greatly without hurting him deeply.' The apostle Peter also told his readers not to be surprised by the 'fiery ordeal' which would soon come upon them. He told them to rejoice in sharing Christ's sufferings 'because the Spirit of glory and of God rests upon you' (1 Peter 4:12–14). Blessings and buffetings usually go hand in hand.

The whole story of Job, too, could be seen as a test. In the prologue (chapters 1 and 2), Satan comes before God and is given permission to afflict Job in any way he wants, up to a certain point. After the first catastrophe concerning his possessions and family, Job is still able to declare, 'The Lord gave, and the Lord has taken away; blessed be the name of the Lord.' Satan comes back again, and this time God gives him permission to smite Job's body, but not to take away his life. Job initially stands up to the test once again, and says submissively, 'Shall we receive good at the hand of God, and shall we not receive evil?' Later, however, the wretched discomfort of his disease undermines his peace and he begins to curse the day of his birth. The rest of the book effectively asks the question, 'If suffering is allowed by God as a test of our faith, why does he do it? What is to be gained by it? Is it really necessary?'

One or two people have said to me that God must love and trust me very much to test me with an inoperable cancer. I have never replied to them, partly because I question the theology on which they base their remarks and partly because, if they were right, I frankly wish that God did not trust me so much! I would be quite content with less trust on his part and less suffering on mine. It would be a curious way of showing his love to me, and I cannot imagine that I could even think of inflicting such a thing on my children, had I the power to do so.

A more serious objection to this viewpoint is that numerous people suffer far more acutely than I have ever done, and many of them have clearly been crushed by the test. As a result of their pain they have suffered nervous breakdowns, their marriages have broken up or they have become bitter atheists. If suffering is to be regarded purely as a test of our faith, God at times seems to have miscalculated wildly.

The attempted answers to suffering that we have seen so far are therefore inadequate, even if they hold important elements of truth. In the next chapters we shall see if there is anything more to be said and if we are even asking the right questions.

18

What is God saying to me?

During the last few months I have felt extremely vulnerable. Unexplained aches and pains all too easily appear sinister. For the last three months, for example, I have had increasing backache – a common complaint but something I have never known in my life. Has the cancer gone round to my spine? What exactly is going on? Both my doctor and specialist say that in their opinion it is purely muscular and postural. But the pain continues, especially when I am standing (as I often am), and I wonder why? Why *now*? It is an easy temptation to fear the worst.

Then the tumour in my liver, which for the first time I could feel a few weeks ago, began to harden and became sore – so sore, in fact, that I could sleep only in one position. Again, what was going on? In one difficult week recently, my specialist thought that the tumour in the liver was definitely growing, but three days later my surgeon was sure that it was *not* growing – if anything slightly smaller and softer.

During this period we had special times of prayer for my healing. They were always extremely helpful. The sore, hard lump is no longer sore (and much softer), but the pains in my back seem to get worse – for whatever reason.

Walking by faith is rather like walking on a tight-rope: at times it is exhilarating, but it requires only the slightest knock to make me feel insecure and anxious. In the last week or so I have been bothered more by asthma, which probably indicates an increased level of stress. I have also not been sleeping so well as before.

I mention all this, not to wallow in self-pity (I *still* believe that God is healing me) but to emphasise that the question 'why suffering?' is far from theoretical. I am profoundly aware that many millions in the world are suffering much more acutely than I am, yet the pains and vulnerability are still there.

For those who believe in a good God, the dilemma is so acute, that Rabbi Kushner concludes that God cannot be all powerful after all. Using the analogy of quantum physics where it seems that certain events happen in the universe at random, Kushner believes that there is 'randomness in the universe . . . Why do we have to insist on everything being reasonable? Why can't we let the universe have a few rough edges?'[1] According to Kushner, God is not in control of everything, although he is on our side whenever bad luck dominates. Evil sometimes finally prevails and is not always overcome by good. Kushner claims that God does not have the whole world in his hands, and therefore is not responsible for malformed children, for natural disasters, or fatal diseases. These simply lie outside his jurisdiction.

It is a neat theory, and it saves us from the unacceptable conclusion of blaming God for all the evil in the world. However, if God is not in ultimate control, he cannot truly be God. If there is no final justice, no eventual triumph of good over evil, God is not the God who has revealed himself in the Bible and in the person of Jesus Christ. If there is some whimsical evil force greater than God, making God finite and limited, we live a futile existence in a meaningless world – as the atheist maintains. If God is not God of all, he is not God at all. There is little hope for any of us, apart from resigning ourselves to a fortuitous mortality in a universe ruled by chance. We cannot ultimately be sure of anything except being at the mercy of unleashed and unpredictable evil.

However, the ringing conviction of the scriptures is that *the*

---

[1] *When Bad Things Happen to Good People*

Lord reigns! Even in the one supreme case of truly innocent suffering, the crucifixion of Jesus, God knew what he was doing. He had not lost control. As Simon Peter declared, all the rulers put together could do only what God had planned to take place (Acts 4:27f.). At the time no one could see why such excruciating suffering should destroy the only sinless man that had ever lived, the Son of God himself. Later the disciples saw it as clearly as could be. 'Christ died for our sins once for all,' wrote Peter. 'He the just suffered for the unjust, to bring us to God' (1 Peter 3:18, *New English Bible*). There on the cross Christ bore the penalty for our sin once for all, so that we might be reconciled to God.

Nevertheless, although Christians down the ages have seen in Christ's sufferings the salvation of the world, what can we say about the myriads of others whose sufferings and death have never had any special significance, or none that we could discern?

James Mitchell in *The god I want* once wrote angrily: 'The value of a god must be open to test. No god is worth preserving unless he is of some practical use in curing all the ills which plague humanity – all the disease and pain and starvation, the little children born crippled or spastic or mentally defective: a creator god would be answerable to *us* for these things at the day of judgment – if he dared to turn up.' Here is the bitter anger that many feel towards God when faced with senseless and hopeless suffering.

Interestingly enough we find many expressions of anger against God in the Psalms. The psalmist often reveals the deepest hurts of his heart, whether they are godly or not.

> Why dost thou stand far off, O Lord?
> Why dost thou hide thyself in times of trouble?
>
> (Psalm 10:1)
>
> My God, my God, why hast thou forsaken me?
> Why art thou so far from helping me, from the words of
>   my groaning?

O my God, I cry by day, but thou dost not answer;
and by night, but find no rest.

(Psalm 22:1f)

My tears have been my food day and night,
While men say to me continually, 'Where is your God?'

(Psalm 42:3)

Here are some cries taken almost at random from the Psalms. Similar quotations are numerous. It is worth mentioning that when we feel angry, bitter, helpless or in despair, it is good to be honest with God about our feelings. In fact, it is much better expressing our anguish *to* God than talking resentfully *about* God to others. God can take on anger. Indeed he did take our anger and all our other sins when his Son died on the cross for us. He wants us to be honest with him and not to put on a pious mask when we approach him.

At the same time, the psalmist in Psalm 73, having complained bitterly about his continuous suffering, comes humbly to realise that his attitude to God was all wrong:

When my thoughts were bitter
and my feelings were hurt,
I was as stupid as an animal;
I did not understand you . . .
What else have I in heaven but you?
Since I have you, what else could I
want on earth?
My mind and my body may grow weak,
but God is my strength;
he is all I ever need . . .

(vv 21–26, *Good News Bible*)

Behind much anger about suffering is our human arrogance which assumes that God must somehow justify his existence and explain his actions before we are prepared to consider the possibility of believing in him.

Sometimes I am asked, 'Is God relevant to me?' But that is

not the crucial question at all. A much more vital issue is this:
'Am I relevant to God?' The astonishing answer is that each
of us is incredibly relevant to an infinite God of love who is
with us in all our afflictions and wants to deliver us from
negative reactions to those afflictions. In our natural self-
centredness we tend to think that we are at the centre of the
universe, and that God (if he exists at all) is there simply to
meet our needs. We regard him as a servant whom we call in
from time to time to clear up the mess we are in – a mess often
of our own doing. But we are not at the centre of the universe.
God is. And God is not our servant. He is our Lord. The
question is not 'Why should I bother with God?' but 'Why
should God bother with me?' That is a much harder question
to answer. There is no reason why God should bother with
me at all, since I have so often turned my back on him. But he
does. For God is love. Sometimes it is only through suffering
that our self-importance is broken. We need humbly to
realise our own smallness and sinfulness in contrast to God's
greatness and holiness.

Franklin D. Roosevelt, when President of the United
States of America, used to have a little ritual with the
naturalist William Beebe. After dinner together, the two men
would go outside and look up into the night-sky. They would
find the lower left-hand corner of the great square of Pegasus.
One of them would then recite these words: 'That is the spiral
galaxy of Andromeda. It is as large as our Milky Way. It is
one of a hundred million galaxies. It is 750,000 light years
away. It consists of a hundred billion suns, each one larger
than our sun.' They would then pause for a few moments,
and Roosevelt would finally say, 'Now I think we feel small
enough! Let's go to bed!' Although man has great dignity,
being made in the image of God, he must also appreciate his
smallness and his natural inability to grasp more than a tiny
fraction of total reality.

This was the substance of God's answer to Job. In four
great chapters God gently challenged Job as to how much he
understood about God and his ways of working. Humbly at

the end of it all, Job realised that he knew virtually nothing, and his demand to fathom all the answers to his suffering was both foolish and unreasonable. 'I have uttered what I did not understand,' he said. 'I despise myself, and repent in dust and ashes.' Then God began to bless him once again.

Some will not find this satisfactory. Together with our suffering, they will say, do we also have to be browbeaten by God into submission? Is that the moral of the story? We should not think of it like that. If we have any conception of the greatness of God we should refrain from pressing the question *Why?* however understandable that might be. On many thousands of issues we simply do not and cannot know. Why does God allow the birth of severely handicapped children? I don't know. Why are some individuals plagued with tragedies for much of their lives, whilst others suffer hardly at all? I don't know. Why is there seeming injustice on every side? I don't know. The questions are endless if we ask why? Instead we should ask the question *What?* 'What are you saying to me, God? What are you doing in my life? What response do you want me to make?' With that question we can expect an answer.

It is my conviction that God is always trying to speak to us in his love, even when his word is hard to accept. 'Man shall not live by bread alone,' said Jesus, 'but by every word that proceeds from the mouth of God.' This was a quotation from the Old Testament which Jesus used when being tempted by his adversary in the wilderness. More important than anything is knowing God's will and doing it. It is far more important than having intellectual answers to all our philosophical questions about God and man, suffering and pain. Life anyway is short and uncertain, but God's word endures for ever. However, our lives are often so full of other things that we find it impossible to hear or discern what God is saying to us. Our ears are deaf, our minds dull and our wills stubborn. We do not hear God speak, or if we do, we fail to respond.

It is sometimes only through suffering that we begin to listen to God. Our natural pride and self-confidence have been stripped painfully away, and we become aware, perhaps for the first time, of our own personal needs. We may even begin to ask God for help instead of protesting about our condition or insisting on explanations. I have met several people who do not profess any commitment to Christ who still pray when facing suffering.

During the ministry of Jesus on earth, a tower fell in Siloam and killed eighteen innocent people. 'Why did God allow it?' was the immediate question pressed by those around him. We may have exactly the same question when we hear of accidents, earthquakes and disasters every day in the news. Jesus replied, not by answering the vexed question of suffering nor by giving a satisfactory solution to this particular tragedy. As perfect Man, accepting our human limitations, Jesus may not even have known the reason why. Instead he came back to the practical challenge of God's word: 'I tell you . . . unless you repent you will all likewise perish' (Luke 13:1–5). It may sound a little bleak, but Jesus was far more concerned with a person's eternal well-being than merely satisfying an intellectual curiosity. Here he was dealing not with the question of Why? but with the question What? What is God saying in this calamity? It is a reminder that life in this world is frail and uncertain. We cannot boast of tomorrow. It is therefore vital that we sort out our relationship with God here and now. Then we are ready for anything. 'Teach us to number our days,' prayed the psalmist 'that we may get a heart of wisdom' (Psalm 90:12).

Through the unexpected diagnosis of cancer I was forced to consider carefully my priorities in life and to make some necessary adjustments. I still do not know why God allowed it, nor does it bother me. But I am beginning to hear what God is saying, and this has been enormously helpful to me. As I turn to the Bible, I find passages coming alive for me, perhaps more than ever before. As I praise God or listen to worship cassettes, my vision of the greatness and love of God is being continually reinforced. I am content to trust myself to a loving God whose control is ultimate and whose wisdom transcends my own feeble understanding.

C. S. Lewis once put it graphically like this: 'God is the only comfort, he is also the supreme terror: the thing we most need and the thing we most want to hide from. He is our only ally, and we have made ourselves his enemies. Some people talk as if meeting the gaze of Absolute Goodness would be fun. They need to think again!' God is so concerned that we should know his love that he will sometimes speak to us in severe terms if we will not listen to him in any other way. The suffering may be ours or that of someone else whom we know and love. Whatever it is, we should think carefully about what God is trying to say to us. C. S. Lewis elsewhere emphasises that it is a poor thing if we turn to God *only* in suffering, *only* because there is nothing better to be had. 'It is hardly complimentary to God that we should choose him as an alternative to hell; yet even this he accepts. The creature's illusions of self-sufficiency must, for the creature's sake, be shattered.'[2] Humbly we need to learn that because God is love, there is the awful possibility of neglecting and forfeiting his love, and at the same time he offers us the unspeakable joy of knowing that love in our own experience, perhaps especially in the midst of suffering.

Joni (pronounced Johnny) Eareckson, as an athletic young girl of seventeen broke her neck when diving into the sea and has been totally paralysed from the neck down ever since. She suffered considerably during her lengthy periods in hospital, and even as a deeply committed Christian found herself asking, often with anger and frustration, the question Why? A wise friend said this to her: 'You don't have to know why God let you be hurt. The fact is, God knows – and that's all that counts. Just trust him to work things out for good, eventually, if not right away.'

'What do you mean?' asked Joni.

[2] *The Problem of Pain*, Bles.

'Would you be any happier if you did know why God wants you paralysed? I doubt it. So don't get worked up trying to find meaning to the accident.'[3]

If we insist on pursuing the question Why? we shall only increase our sense of frustration and perhaps bitterness. We only add to our injury and block the way for God's love to reach us.

Michel Quoist has expressed it well in one of his *Prayers of Life*.[4] He imagined God speaking to him:

> Son I am here.
> I haven't left you,
> How weak is your faith!
> You are too proud.
> You still rely on yourself . . .
> You must surrender yourself to me.
> You must realise that you are neither
>   big enough or strong enough.
> You must let yourself be guided like a child.
> My little child.
> Come, give me your hand, and do not fear.
> If there is mud, I will carry you in my arms.
> But you must be very very little,
> For the Father carries only little children.

It is this quiet, restful, child-like trust in the Father of love that will enable us to experience his peace, even in the very worst of storms.

---

[3] *Joni* by Joni Eareckson, Pickering and Inglis, 1976.
[4] Published by Gill and Macmillan Limited, 1963.

19

Overcoming Suffering

Two fathers came to see me within a space of a few months. Each had lost a young child tragically. One child, aged four, had died of leukaemia; the other, aged five, had been drowned in a swimming pool in their own back garden. One father had been a professing Christian before the disaster but became a bitter and militant atheist as a result; the other had been a professing humanist but became a committed Christian as a result. They both had roughly the same suffering to contend with, but their reactions were widely different. One had his bitterness to endure as well as his suffering, which in the long run might well have been worse – it was certainly worse for other people; the other found the peace and love of Christ, which transformed his suffering. In all our afflictions, it is not so much our situation that counts but the way in which we react to it. And our reactions can affect, to a remarkable degree, the outcome of our lives.

I remember meeting a woman who had been a severe and chronic schizophrenic living permanently in a mental hospital. As a young girl she had been sexually assaulted, and each counselling session returned to this nightmare in her past. A Christian minister visited her and surprisingly challenged her about her attitudes, 'You are full of self-pity; self-pity is a form of pride. Unless you repent of your pride you will never be healed.' The woman was understandably furious. However, although she was clearly not responsible for her tragic suffering as a young girl, she *was* responsible for her present responses to that suffering. Slowly she began to repent.

Within a year she was healed and out of hospital. Later she went as a Christian missionary to the Arctic.

Pat Seed, a woman in her fifties, was told a few years ago that she had cancer and only six months to live. Instead of resigning herself to her situation (which would almost certainly have resulted in an early death), she immediately embarked on a fund-raising campaign in order to buy a sophisticated scanner for the early detection of cancer, for the Christie Hospital in Manchester. She worked so hard at this that she scarcely had time to think about anything else, including her own terminal illness. She not only outlived her six months; today, six years later, she has raised more than three million pounds for life-saving equipment. She has been presented with an MBE by the Queen at Buckingham Palace, and she has now been declared entirely free from cancer. Moreover, over 5,000 patients have now been scanned by the equipment bought through her fund-raising, and probably many lives saved. Because she reacted positively to her situation she was able to change it radically. Pat Seed made this interesting comment in a newspaper interview: 'I heard about two cancer patients, both men, who like me were given six months to live. One went home, made arrangements for his funeral, and died a fortnight later. The other went home, looked at his seven children and thought: "How on earth will this lot cope if I go?" Now twenty years later, those children have grown up and he's still alive.'[1] Repeatedly it comes back to our attitudes, which are often more important than the affliction itself.

I too have felt it right to plunge myself into my work, although making a few adjustments where necessary. Although I tire more easily than before, I have been preaching, writing, broadcasting and travelling to a considerable extent. At times my programme has been too full and I have occasionally been trapped by the demands and expectations of others. More firmly than ever I am learning

[1]Quoted in the *Daily Mail*, May 26th, 1983.

to say 'No'. However, I am far from inactive and my diary is full for the best part of a year ahead. I certainly have as much work as most people could manage.

'David, you're crazy! You're doing too much!' say some of my friends.

'I agree. I have been pushing it too hard recently. But often I spend a quiet evening with my family and I firmly keep one day off a week!' Then I look through my diary to see if I could cancel one or two engagements. Both Hilary and Anne have been invaluable in trying to protect me from unnecessary work, however 'fruitful' it might be.

It is not always easy working hard when in the back of my mind I am conscious of the continuing battle against cancer, backache and asthma. Yet I have not the slightest doubt that a positive attitude to the present and active planning for the future can both aid the healing process. I have also been aware of a greater knowledge of God over these months, and people tell me that there is a new authority in my ministry.

Suffering can often produce great depths of character, mature understanding, warm compassion and rich spirituality. Of course we should always strive to heal the sick and relieve the oppressed; and we should rejoice that in heaven we shall finally be set free from all pains and tears. But suffering can make us more like Christ. The sparkling radiance of a diamond is caused by a lump of coal subjected to extreme pressure and heat over a long period of time. Again, a beautiful pearl emerges when an oyster has to cover an irritating object with layer upon layer of smooth mother-of-pearl lining excreted from its own body. When we suffer in various ways, God is able to use all the pressures and irritations to reveal something of his radiance and beauty in our lives.

God never promises to save us from adversity, only to be with us in the midst of it. Richard Wurmbrand is a Rumanian pastor who endured fourteen years in various Communist prisons, where he was repeatedly tortured for his faith in Christ. 'They broke four vertebrae in my back and many other bones. They carved me in a dozen places. They burned me and cut eighteen holes in my body.' For three years he was in solitary confinement thirty feet below ground level, during which time the only persons he saw were his torturers. In despair he asked God to speak to him, to say something to him. At that moment he heard a terrible piercing cry. It was from another unfortunate victim who was being tortured. But Wurmbrand heard it as a cry from God's heart. God was revealing what he felt like when he saw his children in pain. 'In all their affliction he was afflicted' (Isaiah 63:9). God shares in our suffering. In that filthy underground prison Wurmbrand discovered a beauty in Christ that he had not known before. He literally danced for joy.

God can do anything, and theoretically could have programmed us as robots, impervious to pain and unable to inflict it on others. Had he done so, life might have been simpler, but there would also have been no feeling, no freedom, no relationships, no love – nothing of those human qualities which make life worth living. Instead, God has made us with a genuine freedom of choice to go his way or ours; and because we have all naturally gone our way instead of his, we live in a fallen world which is still often staggeringly beautiful but which is sadly marred by sin, suffering and death. God has therefore entered our world in Christ and suffers with us.

William Temple once put it like this: ' "There cannot be a God of love," men say, "because if there was, and he looked upon the world, his heart would break." The Church points to the Cross and says, "It did break," "It is God who made the world," men say. "It is he who should bear the load." The Church points to the Cross and says, "He did bear it." ' Although Christ has suffered once-for-all on the cross for our sins, he still today weeps with those who weep, he feels our pain and enters into our sorrows with his compassionate love.

This raises a very important point. I have been acutely aware of the unusual privileges I have received – perhaps because of my writing and preaching around the world. Not every cancer-sufferer will have pastors flying over from California to see him. Not everyone afflicted will have the benefit of many thousands praying. Why should I be a special case?

The flat answer, of course, is that I am not. God is no respecter of persons, and loves each person equally with his immeasurable, steadfast love. In human terms, that love will naturally vary in expression. But God's unfailing love is the one constancy that everyone of us can trust.

We need also to realise that God's love was most perfectly portrayed *through* the supreme suffering of Jesus on the cross. That intensity of suffering is, almost paradoxically, the measure of God's love. God, in his love, may not spare us from severe suffering (there is no guarantee that he will spare me or anyone else reading this book). But even when everything seems dark, painful, desperate and hopeless, God still loves, is still there, and will never fail us. The cross is the ultimate proof of that.

The prayer for the sick in the Alternative Service Book for the Church of England puts it well:

> Heavenly Father,
> giver of life and health:
> comfort and restore those who are sick,
> that they may be strengthened in their weakness
> *and have confidence in your unfailing love*;
> through Jesus Christ our Lord.

More often than not we cannot find answers to suffering, if by answers we mean explanations. Why did the plane crash? Why did a loved one die of cancer? Why was that child killed on the roads? We may never find a satisfying explanation, and the danger is that we may end up blaming someone, either ourselves or God. There are seldom good *reasons* for suffering, but there can be good *responses*. I am not suggesting that such good responses are easy. Far from it. For me it has often been an act of the will to listen to worship cassettes, to read the scriptures, to receive communion, to join in with other Christians, to pray and praise and to meditate on the sufferings of Christ. However the more I make myself aware of God's love (whether I *feel* his love or not – usually I don't), the more God can change my negatives into positives. It is a battle, especially at night, but it is certainly important. Unless I eat physically, I waste away; and unless I 'feed spiritually' in ways I have described, I submerge in the seductive sea of self-pity.

As we learn to respond positively, however, we shall be able, one way or another, to overcome suffering so that the explanation becomes no longer of major importance. Those who learn that lesson often achieve a remarkable quality of life that may be far in excess of the trouble-free existence of others. It is not what we *do*, but who we *are* that matters most in life; and it is not *what* we endure, but the *way* we endure it that counts. We can overcome evil with good.

Jesus clearly warned us not to build all our hopes and happiness on this life. Inevitably we live in a fallen, evil world, and one day we stand to lose everything except those qualities that have eternal value. He urged us again and again to lay up for ourselves treasures in heaven, 'where neither moth nor rust consumes and where thieves do not break in and steal' (Matthew 6:20). There is no immunity promised to anyone from the pains and sorrows of this world, but we are to be confident in our hope that the best is yet to be.

The author of Lamentations in the Old Testament once felt utterly crushed by his sufferings: 'My soul is bereft of peace, I have forgotten what happiness is,' he said. He was 'bowed down' within himself – until he deliberately, as an act of the will, called this truth to mind and so stimulated his hope:

> The steadfast love of the Lord never ceases,
>   his mercies never come to an end;
> they are new every morning;
>   great is thy faithfulness.
> 'The Lord is my portion,' says my soul,
>   'therefore I will hope in him.'
>
> (3:22–24)

Looking positively towards the future has helped me in my present need. Since my life is in the hands of God, I am able to trust that God's love is always there and God's plan is always good.

Throughout the centuries, a strong hope for the future has kept God's people firm in their faith in the midst of appalling anguish. The apostle Paul wrote, 'I consider that the sufferings of this present time are not worth comparing with the glory that is to be revealed to us' (Romans 8:18). Elsewhere he talked about being 'afflicted . . . perplexed . . . persecuted . . . struck down', and yet he could write, 'For this slight momentary affliction is preparing for us an eternal weight of glory beyond all comparison' (2 Corinthians 4:17). If we look at the eleventh chapter of that letter we see what 'slight momentary affliction' Paul was referring to:

> Five times I have received at the hands of the Jews the forty lashes less one. Three times I have been beaten with rods; once I was stoned. Three times I have been shipwrecked; a night and a day I have been adrift at sea; on frequent journeys, in danger from rivers, danger from robbers, danger from my own people, danger from Gentiles, danger in the city, danger in the wilderness, danger at sea, danger from false brethren; in toil and hardship, through many a sleepless night, in hunger and thirst, often without food, in cold and exposure . . .
>
> (2 Corinthians 11:24–27)

Yet compared with the 'eternal weight' of God's glory, all this catalogue of suffering was as nothing. The secret was that Paul kept his eyes on the eternal perspective, and this put all his personal agonies and anxieties into proportion. 'We look not to the things that are seen but to the things that are unseen; for the things that are seen are transient, but the things that are unseen are eternal.' Without this dimension of eternity and without a strong hope in heaven, the problems of our human existence might fill us all with despair. But once we know the love of God for ourselves and believe in life after death – or life *through* death – our outlook on this life, with all its pains and sorrows, can be transformed.

Not everyone, however, shares that confidence. Rabbi Kushner writes, 'Because we so desperately want to believe that God will be fair to us, we fasten our hopes on the idea that life in this world is not the only reality . . . (But) neither I nor any other living person can know anything about the reality of that hope.'[2] If left to our own wisdom, that would be true. But the coming of Christ to this world, his clear teaching about the future, his death for our sins and his resurrection from the dead (with all the massive evidence for that), alters the whole situation. We are not left without hope. We *can* know something about life after death. We have good reasons for our faith, solid historical reasons. We can know the risen Christ here and now. For the Christian, the future will be glorious, and that changes our whole attitude to present suffering. If we think of this world only, we have difficulties. But if we see that neither distress nor death can separate us from the love of God, we have a living hope which transcends all the trials of our present existence.

When I was recently in Montreal I met a wonderful black Christian from Uganda called Henry. Henry was one day travelling with his friends on a bus in Uganda when they were ambushed by guerrillas. Shots were fired and Henry had half his face blown away, from the nose downwards. It

[2]*When Bad Things Happen To Good People.*

was a miracle that he survived at all. A Christian organisation called World Vision paid for him to go to Montreal, a city famous for its outstanding medical school, and covered the fees necessary to rebuild Henry's face. When I first saw him he had many more operations to come, and I could not help flinching when I saw the mask that had once been a face. His eyes, however, still sparkled. Since Henry was quite unable to speak he wrote these words: 'God never promises us an easy time. Just a safe arrival.' That is the hope that has kept Henry in God's peace throughout his terrible experience.

It is the hope that all those in Christ can enjoy.

20

Getting Going Again

As I stood up to preach it was an astonishing sight. It was my first sermon since my illness, and I was more than usually nervous. Holy Trinity Brompton, a lively Anglican church in central London with a large and youthful congregation, was packed out. Normally the church seats about 1,000, but extra chairs were out and many were standing at the back and round the side aisles. For good reasons, no publicity had been given about my preaching, so I did not presume that the crowds were there because of me! At the last minute I agreed to preach on May 15th instead of a member of their staff, and I was given the theme: 'The Health of the Kingdom'.

'I confess that I'm a little nervous standing here,' I began. 'But first of all I want to thank you all, more than I can possibly say, for all your prayers over the past months. I wish I could thank you all personally, but I am profoundly grateful – and, thank God, I am feeling very fit.'

I went on to give the precise situation, medically speaking, and encouraged them to continue praying if they wished to do so. I then spoke on the healing ministry of Jesus and the New Testament Church, when the Kingdom of God was both demonstrated and proclaimed with power. At the end I offered some suggestions as to why we did not see more healings in the western Church today, concluding with an exhortation to trust God's word and Spirit, and to get cracking! I knew that many in that church, like me, had been inspired by the teaching and ministry of John Wimber (as well as others), and were already actively praying for people after almost every evening service. I went forward myself that night for further prayer.

I loved being back at work again, and I made it my determination to go on preaching Christ, unfolding as many of his 'unsearchable riches' as I had yet discovered, for as long as God gave me health and strength. I was also deeply moved when John Collins, the Vicar of that church, once again called the congregation to prayer and fasting on my behalf.

In those summer months I began to travel again, although only in short bursts. I went to a Sales Conference in the Lake District organised by Hodder and Stoughton for their staff. I went to a dinner at my College in Cambridge, St John's, meeting friends whom I had not seen for over twenty-five years. On the way there, I visited a clergyman who was dying of cancer and prayed with him. I heard only this week that he has been getting steadily better ever since, even though no one expected him to live beyond May (five months ago now). Repeatedly I found, wherever I went, that my illness gave me immediate opportunities to talk about Christ, my experience of his love, my belief in his healing and my hopes for the future. Now when people ask me 'How are you?' I answer frankly: 'I'm feeling pretty well, thanks. But in fact I've got cancer.'

This unexpected reply to a conventional greeting has led to many excellent conversations about basic issues concerning life and death, God and faith, and I have been thankful not to be trapped in the usual irrelevant chit-chat which dominates so many social functions.

A further milestone was reached when I started working with the team again. Anne and I had missed enormously our daily meetings with them, although these had recently begun again whenever they were in London. However, in July, I returned with the team to Dartford, where we had led an excellent Christian festival in the Orchard Theatre the previous September – each night throughout the week the theatre having been completely full. On this occasion we were there for two nights, and were told that the theatre could have been filled three times over. I knew once again that many of those present had been praying for me throughout the year, so the sense of thanksgiving and praise was excellent. It was marvellous being back there again and even more so being with the team. When talking with each member of the team privately I was amazed – and delighted – to discover that all were willing to commit themselves to this work for another year, although they knew that a risk of faith was involved in this.

The next week I recorded seven late-night programmes for TV South, called *Company*. I liked the format of these, with three people sitting round a kitchen table having a cup of tea or coffee, chatting about various topics, with the camera 'eavesdropping' on the conversation. Since I was the guest for the week, much of the discussion centred round my illness and reactions to it, and the relevance of Christ in every situation. Everyone seemed pleased with the resulting programmes.

Within a few days I was off again, this time with both my family and my team, to lead a Families' Christian Houseparty, with about 130 people of all ages coming from different parts of the country. None of us wanted to go! Fiona and Guy feared that it might be a week of solid and intense religion, Anne disliked houseparties that were not part of the life of our own local church, and I shared the misgivings of the team that this was not the same style as our usual work.

In fact we all had a marvellous week, even if we were exhausted at the end of it. These houseparties had been well established by the organisers for a number of years, so we were thankfully not responsible for the administration. But the team excelled with the teenagers; and, as usual, they illustrated my talks in a delightful way with their worship, drama, mime and dance. 'Can we go again next year?' was the first question Guy and Fiona asked when we drove away.

I was also thankful that my health had sustained my first full and fairly intensive week. I had to teach at least twice a day, counselling individuals in between. Apart from the beginnings of backache and the danger of getting overtired, I felt remarkably well.

Four days later we were off to York for the start of our family holiday. Emotionally neither Anne nor I could have gone to York any earlier. Having lived and worked there for seventeen years, our roots had gone very deep and the tender transplant into London had been in constant danger of 'rejection' over the past year. Although we were not yet settled in London, we felt that we could at least meet those whom we had known and loved so much without being emotionally overwhelmed by it all.

It was wonderful being there, however. I knew how much they had suffered and prayed because of my illness, and just to be there to say 'thank you' was a marvellous experience for us. We loved the gentle and sensitive worship in the church services – a quality of worship that has melted many hearts in the past because it conveys the gentle, healing love of God. Conversations were inevitably brief, but even a minute or two with those who had been especially close to us, were full of silent eloquence. When you love someone deeply, you don't have to *say* very much. Even trivial comments convey a depth of feeling that is mutually understood.

On the Sunday night I preached. I must have preached many hundreds of sermons in that church, St Michael-le-Belfrey, next to York Minster. But this time it was a special, never-to-be-forgotten occasion. In spite of a cloudburst and torrential rain for over an hour before the service, the church was bulging at the seams with people. The seating capacity of the church is approximately 700, but it was estimated that well over 1,000 were present that evening. It was tremendous looking round to see so many with whom I had shared my life deeply in the past. When people have experienced many joys and pains together over the years, there is a depth of fellowship between them that nothing can destroy.

I preached, and Anne prophesied, giving clear directions for the church which confirmed the growing convictions of

the leaders. And the service ended. Not quite. I stood at the
door for about an hour and a half saying goodbye to each of
the 1,000 or more present, shaking hands, hugging or kissing,
whatever seemed appropriate. I thought of the farewell given
to the apostle Paul by the Ephesian elders: 'They all wept
and embraced Paul and kissed him.' To experience the godly
love of God's family is one of the most treasured riches for
those in Christ. If heaven is like this, only much more so, why
are we so reluctant to go there?

It was not yet heaven, however, since my back was almost
killing me after all that standing!

The next day we drove up to Scotland (my back still very
sore) leaving the morning mists in York, and tasting the
unspoilt beauty of the Western Highlands, from the long
sweep of Loch Lomond through the threatening crags of
Glencoe into the towering majesty of Ben Nevis. Our destina-
tion was Glenfinnan, where Bonnie Prince Charlie once
summoned his supporters before marching south to claim the
throne.

Good friends of ours had lent us their lodge in Glenfinnan,
and we joined forces with the Saunders family for ten days in
one of the most beautiful settings imaginable. My back was
causing persistent trouble, which considerably curtailed my
movements apart from a geriatric stroll once a day. But Anne
was in her element, rising at the crack of dawn (almost) to
exercise her puppy in the fresh Scottish air, with the early
mists lifting up the mountains as the sun began to shine
through. Guy spent successful hours by a small loch, pulling
out one rainbow trout after another, which we all enjoyed for
breakfast. Fiona did nothing very energetic, spending most of
her time reading or playing cards with members of the
Saunders family. It was altogether a very good holiday,
rounded off with a few days visiting the great castles of
Northumberland and another brief visit to York, before
returning to London.

For a couple of days John and Carol Wimber came to see
us again, on their return from Sweden to the States, to find

out what progress I was making. All the outward signs of the cancer were good. My blood tests were normal. I was working hard, eating well and sleeping soundly (most of the time).

'My back however is hurting quite a bit,' I said. 'I would be glad if you would pray for it.'

'Sure, we often pray for backs and we never have any problems!' replied John with a twinkle in his eye.

John, Carol and Anne prayed. We all believed that God had heard our prayer. But nothing happened! My back continued to be just as painful as before. Why? I don't know. I do know that countless backs and many more serious problems have been healed by Christ through the ministry of John and others. Sometimes the cause of the pain is healed instantly. Sometimes it is a much more drawn-out battle. Once again, we may not understand the reasons for this, but we can make the right responses. I continued to thank God that he was at work, healing my back and releasing me from cancer.

This time John asked another pastor to see us, Kenn Gullickson and his wife Joni. We had met Kenn and Joni before, and knew that God had given them a special ministry of healing life's hurts. All of us have inner and often deep-seated hurts due to our past experiences. What we may not always consciously realise is that these wounds can leave behind equally deep-seated areas of resentment or bitterness. On the surface we may not be aware of anything wrong, but hidden from our conscious mind may be numerous painful incidents where we have suppressed anger and frustration. Until these areas are recalled and specifically dealt with, God's healing process in our lives can be thwarted.

Certainly I could think of countless occasions when I had been hurt by others.

'But as far as I know I have forgiven everyone everything,' I said to Kenn. 'I don't think I'm harbouring any grudges.'

Kenn explained the importance of thinking of one person at a time, writing down every occasion when I had been hurt by that person. Then I should go through that list one by one, specifically forgiving the individual concerned for each hurt caused, asking God to do the same, praying that God would forgive me for my wrong reactions to those situations, calling on the love of the Spirit to heal those wounds, and finally inviting God to bless the person who hurt me. In this way I could remove any blockages that were still there to God's healing power.

'With some people I can think of, this is going to take ages!' I said.

Kenn led me in prayer as I tried to deal with the hurts in the past from one person, and then left me to continue the process.

It is not always wise to investigate the causes of an illness, but sometimes it may help. Canon Jim Glennon, who has held powerful healing services in St Andrew's Cathedral, Sydney for twenty-three years, wrote in a letter to me: 'Not infrequently physical problems have emotional causes that are linked to an event or events anything from six months to two years before the onset of the physical consequence.' Many doctors engaged in cancer research are of the same opinion. Dr Carl Simonton, Director of Cancer Counselling and Research Centre in Fort Worth writes: 'We believe that cancer is often an indication of problems elsewhere in an individual's life – problems aggravated and compounded by a series of stresses, six to eighteen months prior to the onset of cancer. The cancer patient has typically responded to these problems and stresses with a deep sense of hopelessness or "giving-up". This emotional response, we believe, in turn triggers a set of physiological responses that suppress the body's natural defences and make it susceptible to producing abnormal cells.'[1] This may not be the only cause of cancer but it is certainly worthy of serious consideration.

I thought back to one or two incidents in the past few years

---

[1] Quoted by Jim Glennon in *How Can I Find Healing?*, Hodder and Stoughton, 1984.

that had wounded me very deeply, as well as many other conflicts and hurts in the past. It is impossible to say what the root cause of the cancer might be, but at least those hurts might have contributed to the breakdown of the immunity system. Another Christian friend remarked in a letter, 'One night as we were praying for you . . . I had the oddest feeling that you were suffering from a deep wound caused by the strife of tongues.' I immediately underlined that sentence when I read it. Certainly this is no time for recriminations, since these may only increase internal tensions and so aggravate the disease. When I am angry, in most cases I do not harm the person who has hurt me, but I rob myself of peace – and peace is integral to all healing.

Kenneth McCall once said that '*Fore-give-ness* is love given *before* another has either given it, earned it, accepted it, or even understood it.'[2] That is the nature of God's love, who sent his Son to bear our sins long before we ever thought of loving him. Love takes the initiative. When we have been hurt badly, we may not have the capacity to love the person who has distressed us. But God's love, which knows no such limitations, can be continuously poured into our hearts by the Holy Spirit.

I have described the inner healing that Kenn taught me only briefly, and if possible it is important to pray with a wise Christian counsellor who understands this process and has some experience. Although there could be a danger of introspection, it is much more like trying to get a splinter out of a finger. We have to probe a little, painful though it may be, until the foreign matter is removed. Bitterness is entirely foreign to God's purpose of wholeness for our lives. In the context of healing, the writer to Hebrews says 'Strive for peace with all men . . . that no "root of bitterness" spring up and cause trouble . . .' (12:14f). Unless we are willing to deal with any remaining bitterness in our hearts, we cannot rightly expect God to bring his healing and peace.

[2] *Healing the Family Tree.*

Someone wrote to me about a time when she had become aware of an unforgiving spirit in her heart. She repented of this, and asked for God's forgiveness and healing. 'But it was not until I got home that I realised that I was able to make movements easily and painlessly, that I had hitherto been either unable to make at all or had done so with pain!' She had been completely healed from arthritis in her lower back, and this came as soon as she had found peace in terms of her personal relationships.

I am still working through this area of inner healing, and I know that the sheer busyness of the last two months has so far prevented me from finishing the healing process that Kenn began. However I see the value of removing every hindrance to the work of God's Spirit in my life.

Recently I have had the most severe attack of asthma that I have known for many years. No medication seems to have affected it. Every night I wake up after about two hours of sleep, scarcely able to breathe. What is going on now? Is the cancer spreading to my lungs? Is it the result of a year of obvious stress, coupled with too many speaking engagements? I don't know.

Two nights ago, since I could not lie down to attempt to sleep, I prayed about every painful event and negative reaction from the past that I could think of (at least I made a start: two hours was far from sufficient). I confessed to God the times when I had both hurt and been hurt. I confessed that my rush back into normal work had begun to squeeze out my prayer routine. I confessed one or two relationships in which I still found it difficult to find peace. There was much more besides. It was a good time – like having a spiritual bath! Then I went to sleep, but woke breathless two hours later. This time I surrendered my life again to him, and listened to a worship cassette until I eventually fell back to sleep.

Why it all happened, I don't know. I record it simply as an indication that the battles do not seem to be over.

What is important – and what I gained from that rather

sleepless night – is that when we walk in love, our hearts, minds and bodies can be renewed daily by the Holy Spirit of love. The sooner we experience the healing of our emotions and relationships, the better we shall be able to attack the physical disease within us. At the very least we shall be at peace.

21

The Present Moment

Eleven months have passed since the cancer in my body was first detected – eleven months of the limited life I am expected to have left, the original sentence being about one year. The medical prognosis is still the same, and the latest scan showed a further increase in the tumour. The future officially is bleak, and I am getting used to people looking at me as a dying man under sentence of death. Nothing is certain. I'm not out of the wood yet. Everything is a matter of faith.

That is why I have written the book at this stage. I am not looking back at a painful episode in the past; the difficulties are still with me. I am not writing from a position of comparative safety; I am at present in the thick of it, with humanly speaking no answers, no certainties, no proof of healing – nothing except a somewhat daunting unknown. And yet in reality, my position is not fundamentally different from that of anyone else. No one knows what the future holds. Our lives are full of ifs and buts and supposings. Nothing is sure apart from death. Whether we like it or not, everyone has to live by faith. The *object* of faith is naturally of absolute importance, and may vary considerably. Some will trust in God, others in money, luck, prosperity, health, medicine, philosophy or wishful thinking. But no one can escape the risk of faith when it comes to the greatest issues of life and death.

The opposite to faith is fear, and I have found that there is a constant running battle between the two. In one sense, fear is faith in what you do not want to happen. Job once said, 'The thing I fear comes upon me, and what I dread befalls me' (3:25). There is a powerful truth in that statement. When we are afraid of something, we almost pre-condition it to happen. Our fears, however unfounded and irrational they may be, can trigger the fulfilment of those fears.

Fear has been described as the greatest threat to health in our generation, simply because fear is so widespread. Fear is a great deceiver and destroyer. It robs our minds of peace; it distorts our understanding; it magnifies our problems; it breaks our relationships; it ruins our health; it goads us into foolish, impulsive and sometimes violent action; it paralyses our thinking, trusting and loving.

Repeatedly Jesus had to rebuke his disciples for their fears and lack of faith: 'Why are you afraid? Have you no faith?' (Mark 4:40). The context of that particular challenge is interesting. The disciples were in a boat, caught in a violent storm on the Sea of Galilee; and even though some of them were tough and experienced fishermen, they were scared stiff. So they woke Jesus, who was asleep in the boat: 'Teacher, do you not care if we perish?' It seemed to them that he did not care, since he was sleeping peacefully in the tempest. At once Jesus rebuked the wind and the waves, and there was a great calm. But Jesus was clearly disappointed that his disciples had not yet learned to trust God in the midst of their difficulties. '*Why* are you afraid?'

God never promises to protect us from problems, only to help us in them. If we leave God out of the picture, those difficulties might so strip away our sense of security that we feel vulnerable, anxious and afraid. On the other hand, those same difficulties could drive us back to God and so strengthen our faith. We might feel just as vulnerable, but we *have* to trust God because there is really no alternative; and then we discover that God is with us in the dark as in the light, in pain as in joy. When I was going through a traumatic time in my life, a friend of mine said, 'You cannot trust God too much.'

What we may not realise is how much we are trapped by

our own thoughts and words. If we fill our minds with negative ideas, we may plunge into self-pity, despondency or fear. Even our bodies may react negatively with disease. The more we reflect on our hurts, the more we shall be bound by bitterness and prone to physical afflictions, such as arthritis. If we fail in some task and dwell upon that failure, we may get angry with ourselves (and no doubt angry with others also), and this could precipitate deep depression – depression is often a matter of suppressed anger. The more we think about our fears, or express them to others, the more gripped by anxiety we shall become, to the point of crippling phobias.

I have had to watch all this carefully over the last eleven months. When I've had a difficult day or week, I sometimes find myself saying, especially in the middle of the night, 'I've got cancer, it's spreading and I'm dying. How am I going to tell the children?' At times like these I sweat a bit. But when I am more awake I realise that negative thoughts only acceler-ate the disease and could lead to an early death. How then should I control my thoughts? Should I say instead, 'I'm fit and well and there's nothing wrong with me at all?' That would be a positive remark and possibly beneficial; but it is not an honest statement and has no substance apart from wishful thinking. It might be called 'faith', but it's a danger-ous faith without any solid foundation. That is the weakness of those who teach 'the power of positive thinking'. Without any doubt positive thinking is far better than negative, but the question remains: what are the grounds for such definite thoughts? What is the basis of such faith?

As a Christian I am called to rest my faith firmly on God and on the promises of God's word. Jesus said that this was the solid rock on which the house of my life would stand firm against even the fiercest storms. Constantly Jesus endorsed the authority of God's word: he knew it, taught it, lived by it, and corrected his opponents by bringing them back to the truth of it: 'You are wrong, because you know neither the scriptures nor the power of God' (Matthew 22:29). Here too was the basis of faith for the apostles and the early Church:

they knew that God was faithful and that his word could not be broken. Convinced of the ultimate reality of this, they went through fire and water, torture and martyrdom, because they knew that nothing at all could ever separate them from the love of God in Christ Jesus (see Romans 8:28–39 and Hebrews 11).

This has also been the faith that has sustained countless Christians down the centuries, many of whom have suffered acutely for their commitment to Christ. Martin Niemöller was incarcerated in a Nazi concentration camp for many years, but was allowed the Bible as his one possession. He wrote: 'The Bible: what did this book mean to me during the long and weary years of solitary confinement and then for the last four years at Dachau cell-building? The word of God was simply everything to me – comfort and strength, guidance and hope, master of my days and companion of my nights, the bread which kept me from starvation, and the water of life which refreshed my soul. And even more, "solitary confinement" ceased to be solitary.' This is the constant experience of those who have dared to take God at his word, despite all the odds against them.

In order to maintain a positive faith and not give way to negative fears, I have found it important to go on thanking God for the truth of his word and for the power of his Spirit at work within me. When I am asked (as I often am), 'How are you?' I reply truthfully, 'I'm feeling fine, and I believe that God is continuing to heal me. But I should be grateful for your prayers.' That is where my faith stands. From God's word I do not doubt that he wants to heal me, and there have also been personal assurances of this healing through the remarks of many Christians from all over the world. Of course I realise that logically speaking we may all be wrong. But my faith is neither groundless nor mindless. I have good reason for believing that God *is* healing me, and I shall go on trusting him and praising him whatever I may be feeling like. I cannot honestly say 'I *have* been healed' because there is no medical evidence to support that at present. A few Christians have written (rather unhelpfully) rebuking me for my lack of faith in not accepting that healing is now an accomplished fact. However, I can only be honest with where I am; and since my faith is in a God who is not limited by the scientific world-view I believe that God *is* healing me, and I am accepting many engagements for the next year or two without thinking too much about the 'risk' entailed. From a Christian perspective, that seems to be both a reasonable and a responsible position of faith.

Nevertheless, I am aware of the spiritual battle involved. I was temporarily thrown when a close Christian friend of mine asked if I was booking a reserve speaker for my various engagements. I knew he was deeply concerned to remove all extra pressures from me, but his question still disturbed me. There is admittedly a fine dividing line between faith and foolishness, but how could I genuinely believe in God's healing if I were at the same time booking an alternative speaker in case I were ill?

At the end of September I went with my team to the beautiful Bernese Oberland in Switzerland to lead a week's conference for Christian pastors and workers. It proved a wonderful week. In spite of everything having to be translated into German (which none of our team spoke), the sense of God's presence and the joy of Christian fellowship was almost breathtaking. There were pastors from Eastern Germany and Poland too, which added to the quality of the week. As a special bonus we had an afternoon cruising down Lake Thun, a day in Bern (surely the most beautiful capital in the world), and another day up the mountains overlooking the Eiger and Jungfrau. Ironically, all previous English speakers invited to this annual conference had cancelled, sometimes at the last moment. I was the only one who actually made it, even though no one was entirely certain about this until we arrived! I am glad to say that no alternative speaker had been booked on this occasion!

In October I found myself speaking at a number of special lunches, dinners, services and festivals where there were excellent numbers and an unusual degree of interest, no doubt partly due to my illness. My autobiography *You Are My God*, published on October 3rd, had record sales, running into its fifth printing by the end of that month! Also I had more interviews on radio and for the press than I had known during several years put together. I thought again of that prophetic word given before my operation that my future ministry would increase rather than decrease.

'What if you are not healed?' I am sometimes asked. Although it does not help to dwell on that question too much, I realise that it is a perfectly fair one; and that is where the Christian hope for the future is so enormously important. Of course I cannot *know* that I shall have ten to twenty years more to live. I cannot *know* that I have even one. But that is also true of every one of us. With all our planning for the future, we need to live a day at a time and enjoy each day as a gift from God. 'This is the day which the Lord has made; let us rejoice and be glad in it' (Psalm 118:24). Some Christians speak of the *sacrament of the present moment*: we need to live, not just a day at a time, but moment by moment, seeking to do God's will for each moment of our life. That alone is the way in which we can know the fullness of God's joy and peace.

'What about those who are praying for you, if you are not healed? Will not their faith be severely shaken, if they are so convinced that you will be well?' Once again, that is a reasonable question. My answer is that it's God's responsibility! God is so much bigger than our mistakes. Indeed our relationship with him deepens only when we work through disappointments, confusion, bewilderment and, at times, despair. I cannot let the thought of 'disappointing those who are praying for me' become a negative pressure in my life. I am delighted that so many *are* praying for me, and I believe that their prayers are being answered. If I am wrong, God is well able to handle that one. He has had plenty of experience!

In the Bible, one shining example of faith is Abraham who left his homeland in obedience to God, and who trusted God's promise of a son even when he was 100 years old and his wife ninety. The apostle Paul made this comment about Abraham: 'No distrust made him waver concerning the promise of God, but he grew strong in his faith as he gave glory to God, fully convinced that God was able to do what he had promised' (Romans 4:20f). The tense of the Greek verb suggests that as Abraham *went on* giving glory to God (i.e. praising God), his faith became strong and the miracle happened.

This is the way in which we encourage our faith. Basing our trust on the assurance of God's word and faithfulness, we continue to praise God for the truth of his word until it is fulfilled. In Hebrews 11, the great chapter on faith, the writer acknowledges that sometimes faith is not rewarded this side of heaven. But whatever the size of the problem, the length of the battle, or the outcome of our faith, we are called to trust in God and to keep our eyes on Jesus.

That, after all, is the ultimate purpose of our life. 'Eternal life', said Jesus when praying, 'means knowing you, the only true God, and knowing Jesus Christ whom you sent' (John 17:3, *Good News Bible*). Nothing is more important than our relationship with God, both for this life and for the next.

A doctor complained recently, 'Our patients expect us to make them immortal!' Many cling tenaciously to this life because they fear there is nothing more to come. Today's preoccupation with youth and youthfulness demonstrates the same deep-seated anxiety about the future, especially that last enemy death, of which cancer seems the most frightening symbol.

One day we stand to lose everything of this world, and no one knows when that day will come. Once we have lost our lives to God, however, we belong eternally to him; and in Christ we have all that is ultimately important. If we spend our time worrying about ourselves, we have missed the whole point of our existence. C. S. Lewis expressed it like this: 'Look for yourself, and in that long run you will find only hatred, loneliness, despair, rage, ruin and decay. But look for Christ and you will find him, and with him everything else thrown in.'[1] That is the only security that ultimately makes sense.

God offers no promise to shield us from the evil of this fallen world. There is no immunity guaranteed from sickness, pain, sorrow or death. What he does pledge is his never-failing presence for those who have found him in Christ. Nothing can destroy that. Always he is with us. And, in the long run, that is all we need to know.

[1] *Mere Christianity*, Fountain Books, 1952.

22

What Happens at Death?

Faced with terminal cancer and with the medical prognosis of an early death, I thought carefully about the perpetually puzzling question, what happens at death? When the moment comes – as it will for every one of us sooner or later, whether we think about it or not – what will be the experience of death and what, if anything, lies beyond it?

Philosophers, writers and poets down the centuries have always been intrigued by this question. Job asked, 'If a man dies shall he live again?' John Betjeman, in one of his poems imagines himself waiting for an operation, and wonders, 'is it extinction when I die?'

Some state dogmatically that extinction is all that we can expect. Bertrand Russell talked about the 'night of nothingness': 'There is darkness without and when I die there will be darkness within. There is no splendour, no vastness, anywhere; only triviality for a moment, and then nothing.'[1]

All this, of course, is pure theory. By our own wisdom we do not *know* what happens at death. We cannot, since it lies beyond our present experience and outside the limits of human knowledge. Indeed, the mystery surrounding death has no doubt been partly responsible for such a growing interest in spiritualism and in occult practices in general. In the absence of a living Christian hope, the vacuum has to be filled with some alternative, however unsatisfactory. After the death of my father I dabbled in a few séances myself, to

[1] *Autobiography*, vol. 2, George Allen and Unwin, London, 1968.

see if I could get in touch with him. I have since become aware of the considerable dangers of such practices, and the Bible gives wise and clear warnings about them.

The cruel and inescapable fact of death, however, causes many people to consider carefully the meaning of their lives. When I was in New Zealand in 1973 I read this fascinating comment in a newspaper article by the Director of radiotherapy and radiology in that country:

> Cancer makes people start thinking about the quality of their lives. Everything they do has a keener edge on it and they get more out of life. In fact some people never become completely human beings and really start living until they get cancer. We all know we are going to die some time, but cancer makes people face up to it . . . They are going to go on living with a lot of extra enjoyment, just because they have faced the fear of death. Cancer patients aren't dying. They're living. I h ve never seen a suicide because of cancer.[2]

That has certainly been my own experience, and I am much more aware of the value of each day, and the importance of making good use of it. The quality of my life has far from diminished. Philosophers have always maintained that the key to life is coming to terms with death. No one can live well until they can die well. In the famous words of Samuel Johnson, 'When a man knows he is to be hanged in a fortnight, it concentrates his mind wonderfully!' Certainly all the great issues of life and death come into sharp focus when the future is known to be precarious.

What is the nature of death? There is much confusion about this, understandably, and the Bible significantly talks about 'the shadow of death'. We do not see clearly what it is, nor what lies ahead of us. Sometimes death is referred to as a horizon. A horizon marks the limit of what I can see now, but

[2]Quoted in the *Palmerston North Evening Standard*, June 7th, 1973.

does not mark the limit of where I can go later. There is something beyond a horizon.

The essence of death is *separation*, and the Bible distinguishes three forms of death.

First there is *spiritual death*, when we find ourselves, naturally through our sin, separated from God. If I go my way and not God's, it stands to reason that I shall separate myself from him. That is why God often seems so remote and so unreal. God's answer to spiritual death, as we have already seen in this book, is the offer of spiritual life through the cross of Jesus Christ. Christ died to bring us to God, so that we might know God and enjoy his love for ever. Nothing can ever separate us from that love, once we have come to him through Jesus Christ.

Secondly, there is *physical death*, when the soul is separated from the body, and the person is separated from family and friends. When two people get married it is 'till death us do part'. Death ruthlessly breaks the deepest bonds of love. God's answer to physical death is that, instead of a physical body which is subject to pain and sickness, weariness and decay, he gives us a spiritual or resurrection body. In Paul's great chapter on this theme (1 Corinthians 15), he takes the analogy of a seed sown in the ground and dying before it can bear fruit, and he writes: 'What is sown is perishable, what is raised is imperishable. It is sown in dishonour, it is raised in glory. It is sown in weakness, it is raised in power. It is sown a physical body, it is raised a spiritual body.' There is scarcely any resemblance between a small seed sown in the ground and the lovely flower developing from it. Had we no previous experience, it would be impossible to imagine the transformed beauty of the flower by looking carefully at the small and unimpressive seed. Yet there is a continuity between the two. Out of death springs a much more glorious life. So it is with our spiritual body.

It is obviously impossible to describe precisely what this resurrection body will be like, since we do not yet have any first-hand experience of it. Perhaps our nearest hint is the resurrection body of Jesus which was clearly recognisable to his friends, and yet different. He could pass through locked doors; he could both appear and vanish at will. Professor Donald Mackay of Keele University, one of Britain's foremost experts on the communication system of the human brain, has made this interesting comment:

> It is not as disembodied spirits that God promises us eternal life, but as personalities expressed in a new kind of body – what the apostle Paul calls a 'spiritual body'. Just as a message is still the same message, whether it is spoken in words or flashed in morse code, so, according to the Bible, we shall be the same persons, whatever the material form in which our personalities may be expressed. Nothing in the scientific picture of man, however complete it may one day become, could affect the truth of this doctrine one way or another.[3]

Thirdly, there is *eternal death*, which means total separation from God and from all good. When the sun shines with strength, the plants with their roots in the soil grow and flourish, but the plants without their roots in the soil wither and die. It is a natural law; it is also a spiritual law. If we are not rooted and grounded in the love of God, we cannot escape his righteous judgment. The essence of God's judgment is that, with infinite sadness, he underlines the decision that *we* make about him. If we rule God out of our lives, we are ruled out of his life. That is our decision, not his. In his great love for us, he has sent his only Son so that we might never have to face the appalling consequences of his judgment; but if we do not want his forgiveness, we shall not have it. If I do not want God in my life I will not know him.

However, God's answer to eternal death is the free offer of eternal life through Jesus Christ, based on the solid assurance of Christ's resurrection. The apostle Peter put it like

---

[3]From an essay in *Inter-Varsity*, 1970.

this: 'Blessed be the God and Father of our Lord Jesus Christ!
By his great mercy we have been born anew to a living hope
through the resurrection of Jesus Christ from the dead, and
to an inheritance which is imperishable, undefiled, and
unfading, kept in heaven for you' (1 Peter 1:3f). Paul too had
a longing to depart this life and to be with Christ, which he
knew would be 'far better' than anything that he could
experience on this earth.

For those who have put their trust in Christ now, death
means that we shall be perfectly with him, more alive than
ever, and free from pain, sickness, anxiety, depression and
sin. On the memorial of Martin Luther King are these simple
words:

Rev Martin Luther King Jr
1929–1968
'Free at last, free at last,
Thank God A'mighty I'm free at last'

The Church is the only society on earth that never loses a
member through death! As a Christian I believe, not just in
life *after* death, but in life *through* death. In the words of a
Russian Christian, 'The moment of death will be the inrush
of timelessness.'

What happens at death? It is of course impossible to
answer this with any precision, since we cannot draw from
past experience. The Bible speaks in general terms, necessarily using metaphors and pictures, although the under-
lying truth of these is clear.

From the teaching of Jesus, it seems that at the moment of
death there will be a *great divide* between those who know and
love God, and those who do not. An amazing number of
parables alone indicate this division: the wheat and the tares,
the sheep and the goats, the great banquet, the rich fool, the
wise and foolish bridesmaids, those with or without wedding
garments, the drag net of good and bad fish, the house on the
rock and the house on the sand. 'The message of Jesus is not

only the proclamation of salvation, but the announcement of judgment, a cry of warning and a call to repentance in view of the terrible urgency of the crisis. The number of parables in this category is nothing less than awe-inspiring.'[4] It is impossible to escape this basic truth which rings repeatedly throughout the Gospel records.

In one of his most telling parables (Luke 16:19–31) Jesus spoke of two men who died. One was comfortably rich, deaf to God and blind to the needy; the other was wretchedly poor, trusting only in the mercy of God. At death a great chasm was fixed between them, the rich man in hell and the poor man in heaven. It was impossible to cross from one side to the other – there is no suggestion anywhere in the Bible of a second chance after death. The rich man in torment becomes concerned about the spiritual state of his five brothers. He was told that they, like all of us, had the clear warnings of scripture. If we ignore these, nothing will persuade us, not even someone returning from the dead. With all the metaphorical language taken into account, the teaching about God's judgment after death is so unmistakably clear, especially in the teaching of Jesus, that we have only ourselves to blame if we ignore it.

C. S. Lewis once saw this epitaph on a tombstone:

> Here lies an atheist
> all dressed up but
> with nowhere to go.

Lewis added his own comment, 'I bet he wishes that were so.'

It is important to add, however, that Jesus also indicated that God's judgment depends on the opportunity we have had to respond to his love and mercy (Luke 12:47f). Since God has revealed himself in some measure to everyone in this world, at least through creation and conscience (see Romans 1:18–32 and 2:1–16), no one is without excuse. However,

[4]J. Jeremias.

without attempting to be dogmatic, it is my personal belief that those who put their trust in God's love and mercy *insofar as they understand him*, will be accepted by him. As a motorist may cross a bridge on a motorway without realising that the bridge is even there (let alone any details about it), so it may be possible for a person to come to God 'over the bridge' of Christ without knowing anything about him. That person's understanding, joy, assurance, faith and hope will all naturally be limited, until he does discover the truth about Christ. But personally I do not believe from the scriptures that there is no hope at all for those who do not, or cannot, call themselves Christians. If in their hearts they have truly responded to God, however little they know about his Son or his gift of salvation, God may well accept them on that Day of Judgment. What *is* clear, however, is that those of us who do know, or can know, have no excuse whatsoever if we 'neglect so great a salvation' (Hebrews 2:3). At least we can rest assured that God, who is Judge over all the earth, will do what is right.

Certainly, for those who die in Christ the future will be unimaginably wonderful. The expression used several times is 'falling asleep' (see 1 Thessalonians 4:13–18; 1 Corinthians 15:20). When we fall asleep after a tiring day, the next thing we know is waking refreshed the following morning. So it will be for the Christian. We fall asleep in Christ, and then wake up on the resurrection morning with our new spiritual bodies.

From a human perspective, hundreds of years may have elapsed between death and resurrection. But time is a human limitation. God is essentially outside time. 'With the Lord one day is as a thousand years, and a thousand years as one day' (2 Peter 3:8). When Jesus was hanging on the cross, he promised the dying thief who cried to him for help, 'Truly, I say to you, *today* you will be with me in Paradise' (Luke 23:43). Time is relative to motion, as Einstein has shown us. For example, at the speed of light the passage of time vanishes. Everything happens now! Subject as we are to the dimensions of time during this life, the concept of a timeless eternity is hard, if not impossible, to grasp. We can therefore only grope for metaphors and pictures about heaven.

We cannot know exactly what we shall be like after death. The apostle John put it like this: 'It is not yet clear what we shall become. But we know that when Christ appears, we shall be like him, because we shall see him as he really is' (1 John 3:2, *Good News Bible*). That should be sufficient for us. Heaven is being 'with Christ' when we shall be 'like him'. There will be a wonderful sense of being fully in God's presence, in an unspoilt and unbroken atmosphere of love, joy and praise.

If we think of all the best and most glorious moments in our lives, the perfection of what we experience always seems just beyond our reach. As with striking a succession of matches to light a dark room, those moments invariably seem to flicker and fade. Heaven will be like turning on the full light. The perfection will be there for us to enjoy, undefiled, unflickering and unfading. 'And the city had no need of sun or moon to shine upon it, for the glory of God is its light . . .' (Revelation 21:23). Here is the summit of all our highest hopes and dreams.

In one sense, the Christian is not preparing for death. Essentially he is preparing for *life*, abundant life in all its fullness. The world, with its fleeting pleasures, is not the final reality, with heaven as a shadowy and suspect unknown. The best and purest joys on earth are only a shadow of the reality that God has prepared for us in Christ. Eternal life begins as soon as we receive Christ as our Saviour. We can start enjoying it now, in increasing measure, and should be preparing, not for death, but for the consummation of that perfect quality of life when we are completely in God's presence for ever. Quantity of life is not nearly so important as quality, even for 'terminally ill' patients. By the way, I don't like that word 'terminal', which means the end of something. In reality, when the body of the Christian dies, the really wonderful journey has only just begun. Even my secular dictionary defines heaven as 'a place or state of supreme bliss.' So it is.

Death for the Christian, it is sometimes said, is like the old family servant who opens the door to welcome the children home. Although it would be a mistake to base our beliefs on the experience of those who have clinically died but later have been restored to life, it is worth noting that of those who were Christians nearly all speak of walking peacefully into a garden full of staggeringly beautiful colours and exquisite music (or some similar description), so that it was with great reluctance that they came back to earth again.

It never worries me that we are not able to grasp more clearly the true nature of heaven. We can understand something of which we have no first-hand experience only by describing something with which we are familiar. We are limited by language. But for those who know God and who are trusting in Christ as their Saviour and Lord, there is nothing to fear, and it is sufficient to know that we shall be like him and perfectly with him. Nothing could be more wonderful than that. Never fear the worst. *The best is yet to be*.

When I die, it is my firm conviction that I shall be more alive than ever, experiencing the full reality of all that God has prepared for us in Christ. Sometimes I have foretastes of that reality, when the sense of God's presence is especially vivid. Although such moments are comparatively rare they whet my appetite for much more. The actual moment of dying is still shrouded in mystery, but as I keep my eyes on Jesus I am not afraid. Jesus has already been through death for us, and will be with us when we walk through it ourselves. In those great words of the Twenty-Third Psalm:

> Even though I walk through the valley
>   of the shadow of death,
>   I fear no evil;
>   for thou art with me . . .

January 1984

Any struggle with cancer and death is likely to have unexpected twists and turns. A sudden burst of joy when dark clouds that threaten a raging storm give way to sunshine and springtime hopefulness. Or just the reverse when our faith and hope are plunged into that ugly pit of depression.

When I sent the manuscript of this book to the publishers I was feeling remarkably fit, apart from the puzzling backache that had bothered me for three or four months. 'How well you look!' everyone said to me. And I felt it. My waist was trim, my appetite good – I felt thoroughly *alive*!

Abruptly everything changed.

With the enjoyment of being back at work again, especially with my team, I threw my new energies into all that I could. After the Pastors' Conference in Switzerland, we had exciting visits to Manchester, the Isle of Wight, Belfast and Dublin, plenty of preaching engagements in London, as well as some broadcasting and writing. I knew it was too much, but everywhere we went the crowds and enthusiasm exceeded all expectations. At a Diocesan Service of Renewal in Southwark Cathedral (which seats 800) an estimated crowd of 2000 turned up. Autumn '83 was a time when God seemed to be working with unusual power.

Then my body protested against all this activity by the most severe attack of asthma I have had for many years. In the past, such attacks had been controlled quickly by a certain course of steroids. I took this again, but my asthma continued unchecked, giving me broken nights and much discomfort. One side-effect was a thoroughly unpleasant development of thrush in my mouth during our Irish tour.

Still my asthma got worse. So I was given the highest dose
of steroids I have ever had, which again aggravated the
thrush. So with the generosity of some close friends and with
the encouragement of many (including Anne) I flew over to
California for special prayer at John Wimber's church, since
I felt I was losing the battle.

I was there for only eight days, and they were marvellous
in their love, concern and prayer support. Each day different
teams of Christians, experienced in the healing ministry,
prayed for me, for periods ranging from two to five hours a
day. Yet, for whatever reason, everything seemed to get
worse. The asthma persisted, so that I slept badly each night;
my legs, ankles and feet blew up like balloons; and my
abdomen grew at an astonishing rate until I looked like a
pregnant woman in about her seventh month! My arms and
shoulders withered into mere skin and bones, and instead of
returning from California bursting with new health (as I had
expected), I looked more dead than alive.

Drastic changes had to be made. Virtually all speaking
engagements for the future were cancelled immediately,
including major events in California, Norway, Sweden and
Vancouver – which had been carefully planned for anything
up to two years previously. My team would have to be
disbanded by the end of April at the latest. I was now literally
fighting for my life.

'God hasn't done anything for David,' people are now
beginning to say. 'We've prayed and prayed, and nothing
has happened at all.' Medically speaking, that seems to be
true. I am a fairly typical cancer patient with secondaries in
the liver. Temporary remissions may occur, but then everything may suddenly 'explode'. At the moment there is still
some uncertainty as to which symptoms are due to the
steroids, having been on these for almost two months (I took
my last one, I hope, this morning and the asthma is better).
But there is no doubt that my liver has considerably enlarged
due to sudden activity of the cancer cells.

However God has been far from inactive in my life. At

about one a.m. on Advent Sunday morning, I had a bad asthmatic attack. In my helplessness, I cried out to God to speak to me. I'm not very good at listening to God, but between one and three a.m. God spoke to me so powerfully and painfully that I have never felt so broken before him (and still do).

He showed me that all my preaching, writing and other ministry was absolutely *nothing* compared to my love-relationship with him. In fact, my sheer busyness had squeezed out the close intimacy I had known with him during the first few months of the year after my operation.

God also showed me that any 'love' for him meant *nothing* unless I was truly able to love from my heart my brother or sister in Christ. As the Lord put various names into my mind I began to write letters to about twelve people asking for forgiveness for hurting them, for still being inwardly angry against them – or whatever. It was the most painful pruning and purging I can remember in my entire Christian life. But fruitful! Already some replies to my letters have reduced me to tears.

Whatever else is happening to me physically, God is working deeply in my life. His challenge to me can be summed up in three words: 'Seek my face.' I am not now clinging to physical life (though I still believe that God can heal and wants to heal); but I am clinging to the Lord. I am ready to go and to be with Christ for ever. That would be literally heaven. But I'm equally ready to stay, if that is what God wants.

'Father, not my will but yours be done.' In that position of security I have experienced once again his perfect love, a love that casts out all fear.

David wrote the last pages of this book during the first week of January 1984.

On January 8th he preached at St Michael's, Chester Square, from Jude verses 20–5. He said:

> The last couple of months have seen some pretty sweeping changes in my own life. I have had to cancel all my engagements outside London and after travelling for many years I would have found that very difficult if it had not been for God so clearly calling me back to this love relationship with him. Even death itself is not a threat.

On January 15th he preached again at St Michael's, this time on Psalm 91, which he found 'highy relevant'.

> He who dwells in the shelter of the Most High,
>   Who abides in the shadow of the Almighty,
> Will say to the Lord, 'My refuge and my fortress;
>   My God in whom I trust.'

From January 16th David's condition deteriorated rapidly. He continued to see close friends from time to time and on Monday 30th he said to David MacInnes: 'I am completely at peace – there is nothing that I want more than to go to heaven. I know how good it is.'

David remained at home nursed by Anne and her mother. He saw members of his team when they returned from five weeks in California, and especially enjoyed times with his children. Late on the evening of Friday, 17th February he said to Anne: 'I'm very tired; let's go home.'

*   *   *

David Watson died peacefully very early next morning, February 18th.

'The Lord Reigns'